The Struggle against Imperialism

The Struggle against Imperialism

Anticolonialism and the Cold War

Edward H. Judge
and
John W. Langdon

ROWMAN & LITTLEFIELD
Lanham • Boulder • New York • London

Published by Rowman & Littlefield
An imprint of The Rowman & Littlefield Publishing Group, Inc.
4501 Forbes Boulevard, Suite 200, Lanham, Maryland 20706
www.rowman.com

Unit A, Whitacre Mews, 26-34 Stannary Street, London SE11 4AB, United Kingdom

British Library Cataloguing in Publication Information Available

Library of Congress Cataloging-in-Publication Data Available

ISBN 978-1-4422-6583-7 (cloth : alk. paper)
ISBN 978-1-4422-6585-1 (electronic)

♾™ The paper used in this publication meets the minimum requirements of American National Standard for Information Sciences—Permanence of Paper for Printed Library Materials, ANSI/NISO Z39.48-1992.

Printed in the United States of America

Contents

List of Maps   vii

Preface   ix

1   Introduction: The Struggle against Imperialism, and Its Cold War Connections   1

2   Empires, Ideologies, and Nations: Imperialism, Anti-Imperialism, and the Cold War   5

3   "Long Live the Victory of People's War": Anti-Imperialism and the Cold War in Asia   37

4   "We Are Today Free and Independent": Anti-Imperialism and the Cold War in the Middle East   71

5   "Scram from Africa!": Anti-Imperialism and the Cold War in Africa   99

6   "So Far from God . . . So Close to the United States": Anti-Imperialism and the Cold War in Latin America   121

7   "Every Country Decides Which Road to Take": The End of the Soviet Russian Empire   145

8   "Empires Wax and Wane": Overview and Conclusions   173

Notes   197

Glossary   203

Suggestions for Further Reading   211

Index   221

About the Authors   231

Maps

Map 2.1. European Boundary Changes and Occupation
Zones, 1945   25

Map 2.2. Divided Germany and Divided Europe, 1945–1955   28

Map 2.3. Divided Europe: NATO versus Warsaw Pact,
1955–1991   31

Map 3.1. The Chinese Civil War, 1946–1949   41

Map 3.2. The Korean War, 1950–1953   44

Map 3.3. Vietnam, Laos, and Cambodia, 1954–1975   57

Map 4.1. Arab-Israeli Conflicts, 1945–1960   76

Map 4.2. Arab-Israeli Conflicts, 1960s–1980s   91

Map 5.1. Postcolonial Africa   103

Map 6.1. Cold War Clashes in Central America and
the Caribbean   123

Map 6.2. Cold War Clashes in Latin America   134

Map 7.1. European Boundary Changes and Soviet Satellites,
1945–1948   154

Map 7.2. Divided Europe: NATO versus Warsaw Pact,
1955–1991   156

Map 7.3. The Disintegration of the Soviet Bloc, 1989–1992   170

Map 8.1. Decolonization and Cold War Clashes in Africa and
          the Middle East, 1945–1990   180

Map 8.2. Conflicts and Crises in the Middle East, 1960s–1980s   186

Map 8.3. The Disintegration of the Soviet Bloc, 1989–1992   191

Preface

For more than two decades, at our typical liberal arts college, we have team-taught a variety of courses on the history of the Cold War era. During that period, we also developed and published a Cold War history text (*A Hard and Bitter Peace: A Global History of the Cold War*) and a Cold War documents reader (*The Cold War through Documents: A Global History*), and both are currently in their third edition. We have increasingly sought to make both our courses and our texts more global, incorporating not just the Cold War conflicts between the Communist East and capitalist West, but also the concurrent struggles against imperialism by peoples and nations in Asia, the Middle East, Africa, and Latin America. On the whole, we have been very pleased and satisfied with these courses and texts, and with their highly favorable reception by our students and colleagues.

In recent years, however, we have become increasingly convinced that the Cold War and the struggle against imperialism can and should quite profitably be studied and taught together, not as distinct developments but as interwoven aspects of a complex global conflict involving old colonial powers, anti-imperialist movements, emerging national states, and the Cold War superpowers. Inspired by this conviction, we decided to devise and develop a new text that focuses on the Cold War era from the perspective of the struggle against imperialism and the complex interactions between imperialism and anti-imperialism, rather than mainly on the superpower conflict.

We do not, however, intend for this approach to replace the old one, nor do we intend for this new text to supplant or replace our more traditional offerings. We intend it instead as a supplement to those offerings and as a concise and engaging approach that will provide fresh insights and perceptions to colleagues, students, general readers, and anyone else who is interested in this era. We see it as a potential text for use in such college courses as Modern World History, The Cold War, Twentieth-Century Global History, and The World since 1945—either on its own or in conjunction with other treatments of this era (including our own Cold War texts).

However it is used, we believe it will provide a cogent and concise description of the post–World War II era and reveal connective dimensions of that era that remain hidden in books that focus solely or primarily on the Cold War. Much as Marxists provided new insights into history by focusing on socioeconomic class and feminists did likewise by focusing on gender, we believe that we can gain new insights by approaching the Cold War era mainly from the perspective of the struggle against imperialism.

In our several works on the history of this era, we have been aided not only by the wealth of scholarship and the numerous documents and memoirs that have emerged since the end of the Cold War, but also by the input and insights of students, educators, and others who have used our books and provided helpful suggestions. We are deeply grateful to them, as well as to our colleagues and editors—including Douglas Egerton, Bruce Erickson, Mark Kulikowski, Larry Eugene Jones, Mark T. Clark, Lawrence H. Madaras, Eleanor McCluskey, Sally Constable, Charles Cavaliere, Rob DeGeorge, Jeff Lasser, Susan McEachern, Jehanne Schweitzer, and Rebeccah Shumaker—who have assisted us in various ways in producing our various editions. We are also especially grateful to Al Andrea, who shepherded and guided us through an earlier version of this work that went unpublished. And we are indebted above all to our wives, Susan Judge and Janice Langdon, whose patience, devotion, and loving support have sustained us in all our scholarly and educational endeavors.

1

❧

Introduction

The Struggle against Imperialism, and Its Cold War Connections

In the decades that followed the Second World War, global affairs were dominated by two concurrent but seemingly distinct developments. One was the global **Cold War**: an intense international conflict between the Communist East, led by the Union of Soviet Socialist Republics (USSR), and the capitalist West, led by the United States of America, waged by all means short of direct, all-out combat between those two assertive superpowers. The other was the **struggle against imperialism**: a complex series of movements, endeavors, campaigns, and conflicts by which oppressed peoples and colonized nations sought to gain freedom from imperial subjugation and other forms of foreign domination.

As that era recedes into history, however, it becomes increasingly apparent that these two dominant developments were not really distinct but, instead, were so inextricably interconnected that neither can properly be understood without the other. It is thus the thesis and the theme of this book that **anti-imperialism** and the Cold War were not just separate developments that occurred at the same time and occasionally intersected, as often perceived in that era, but rather that they were intertwined elements of a complex global struggle involving old colonial powers, anti-imperialist movements, emerging national states, and the two Cold War superpowers, both of which publicly opposed imperialism but practiced forms of it nonetheless.

The areas of interconnection between the Cold War and the struggle against imperialism included especially the following:

1. They both developed out of situations arising from the two world wars, which pitted coalitions of the main imperial powers against one

1

another. The First World War destroyed the old Russian, German, Austrian, and Ottoman Empires; it helped bring to power in Russia a Communist regime committed to a global struggle against capitalism and imperialism; and it advanced the principle of national self-determination: the right of each nationality to freely decide its own political status. The Second World War shattered whatever remained of the myth of Western European superiority, weakened the old colonial powers, and discredited racist imperialism, which was practiced by the Germans and Japanese before and during World War II. Many people hence came to view racism and imperialism as immoral, so even as the Soviets and Americans each practiced a form of imperialism, they both extolled anti-imperialism and national self-determination, making it awkward for Western Europeans to maintain their colonial empires.

2. They were connected by Communist ideology, which depicted Western imperialism as a natural outgrowth of industrial capitalism, supplying the USSR with a compelling rationale that linked the Cold War conflict between capitalism and **communism** with the simultaneous conflicts between colonized peoples and their European overlords. Based on the earlier analyses of Karl Marx, the nineteenth-century revolutionary socialist who called upon workers in industrialized nations to overthrow the capitalist order, and Russian Marxist leader V. I. Lenin, who had argued that imperialism was merely an advanced stage of capitalism, the identification of capitalism with imperialism became a key component of Marxism-Leninism, an ideology that (among other things) sought to unite the anti-imperialist struggles of non-Western peoples with the anticapitalist struggles of Western industrial workers. The Soviets thus were able to link capitalism with imperialism and communism with anti-imperialism, effectively combining the Cold War and anti-imperialism into a single global struggle.

3. They were connected by the leaders of the anti-imperialist movements who, in working to secure and maintain their independence, sought in various ways to exploit the ideals, resources, and rivalries of the Cold War superpowers. Many such leaders were Western-educated members of colonial elites, and thus deeply familiar with the ideals of both Western liberal democracy and Marxist-Leninist Soviet-style socialism. Some claimed to see the American Revolution as a model for their own movements, not only because it promoted the ideals of freedom, human rights, and self-government, but also because it provided an example of how to gain independence by exploiting a rivalry between imperialist powers, in that case Britain and France. At the same time, however, the sense that the Marxist-Leninist identification of capitalism with imperialism seemed to fit their historical experience and that Soviet-style socialism seemed to suit their ideals and needs, combined with the fact that the main Euro-

pean imperial powers were America's Cold War allies, led many of the nations emerging from **colonialism** to look to the USSR for support. Some newly emerging national leaders sought to practice nonalignment, thus hoping to avoid becoming entangled in the Cold War, while at the same time playing off the superpowers against each other in order to get badly needed economic, military, and technological aid. But in order to obtain such aid, they often found that Cold War dynamics compelled them to get it mainly from one side or the other, and thus effectively to become clients of one superpower or the other, thereby emerging as Cold War participants whether they liked it or not.

4. They were connected by the behavior of the two Cold War superpowers, the United States and the USSR, which despite their anti-imperialist ideals functioned in many ways as imperialist powers. Rooted in revolutions against the British and Russian Empires and outwardly committed to anti-imperialism and national self-determination, they each nonetheless pursued imperialistic policies based on their desire to globalize their ideals and protect nations in their orbit from the imperialist machinations of the opposing superpower. Each thus practiced imperialism in the name of anti-imperialism, using the other's imperialist behaviors as a rationalization for its own. In so doing they effectively limited the sovereignty of their allies and clients, granting them some leeway to run their own internal affairs as long as they did nothing that might harm the perceived global interests of their allies and overlords in Washington or Moscow. The struggle against imperialism thus came to be directed not only against the old colonial powers but also against one or both of the Cold War superpowers.

In exploring these connections and developing these themes in the chapters that follow, we have adopted an approach designed to supplement, but not necessarily supplant, the more traditional accounts of the Cold War era that focus mainly on the superpowers and opposing Cold War camps.[1] Our approach here is to focus instead on this era largely from the perspective of the struggle against imperialism, highlighting the actions and outlooks of colonized peoples and emerging nations while also examining their interactions with the dominant powers of both East and West. And since the timing and form of the struggle against imperialism differed from one region to the next, we have opted to approach this era both globally and regionally, with global overviews in chapters 2 and 8 and regional coverage in chapters 3 through 7. This approach enables us to provide both the overall context of the Cold War era and the distinctive attributes of the anti-imperialist struggles in Asia, the Middle East, Africa, Latin America, Eastern Europe, and the USSR. It also allows us to consider the Cold War and the struggle against imperialism not just as concurrent developments that sometimes intersected but instead as intertwined elements of the same global phenomenon: the transformation away from a world order based on large colonial empires to one encompassing a vast array of large and small independent nations—including several powerful realms that publicly rejected imperialism yet nonetheless sought dominance through less formal political, cultural, and economic means.

2

❧

Empires, Ideologies, and Nations

Imperialism, Anti-Imperialism, and the Cold War

On September 2, 1945, the day that World War II officially ended with a formal Japanese surrender, a small Asian man spoke to a large crowd in the Vietnamese city of Hanoi. "All men are created equal," he proclaimed in his native tongue. "They are endowed by their creator with certain inalienable rights; among these are life, liberty, and the pursuit of happiness."[1]

After citing these words as an "immortal statement" from the US Declaration of Independence, he went on to paraphrase the French Declaration of the Rights of Man, proclaiming that "All men are born free and with equal rights, and must always remain free and have equal rights."[2] The speaker, who called himself Ho Chi Minh ("he who brings enlightenment") went on to declare independence for Vietnam, which he considered his nation but which France still regarded as part of its colonial empire.

In retrospect, Ho's declaration was far more than just an assertion of independence by a small Southeast Asian nation. It also marked the onset of the postwar wave of nationalistic anti-imperialist struggles, rooted in prewar and wartime events, that lasted for decades, destroyed the global colonial empires forged by the great powers of Western Europe in the preceding centuries, created numerous new national states, and inspired them and others to work to free themselves from imperialist domination. Indeed, Ho himself made it clear that his declaration had global implications, boldly asserting that the principles he cited applied to "all the peoples of the earth."[3]

Ho's declaration might further be seen as a foreshadowing of the Cold War between the Communist East, led by the Soviet Union, and the capitalist West, led by the United States, that engulfed the world during the same decades as the struggle against imperialism. For Ho Chi Minh was a Communist, wedded to the Marxist-Leninist views that Western imperialism was a natural outgrowth of industrial capitalism, that capitalism and imperialism were therefore one and the same, and thus that colonized nations fighting for independence were natural allies of the global Communist movement. Although Ho's declaration cited the ideals of the American and French Revolutions, and made no mention of world Communism or the Soviet Union, the declaration was directed primarily against Western imperialism as practiced by the French in Southeast Asia and by implication against anyone anywhere who might support the reassertion or continuation of Western colonial rule. And France, which in 1949 would become a founding member of NATO, the Western anticommunist alliance led by the United States, was determined to restore its colonial rule in Southeast Asia. So the logic of Ho's situation and ideals would soon compel him to lead his small nation into long and devastating wars, first against the French and later against the Americans. And Vietnam's anti-imperialist quest for national independence would thus become part of the global Cold War, bringing Southeast Asia decades of almost constant conflict.

Vietnam's experience was tragic but not unique. Its struggle against imperialism, like others that got entangled and entwined with the Cold War, had roots in earlier centuries, when France and other European powers had engaged in global expansion, created vast overseas empires, and subjected much of the non-Western world to Western imperial rule. In time the endurance of these empires was challenged by resistance from the colonized and subjugated peoples, by conflicts among the Western imperial powers, and by new ideologies that promoted liberty, equality, and national independence, setting the stage for the global Cold War and the anti-imperialist movements of the twentieth century.

THE RISE OF EUROPEAN COLONIAL EMPIRES

In the centuries preceding the twentieth, each of Europe's major powers had created and maintained a **colonial empire**, a term historically used to describe a diverse group of dependent societies, or **colonies**, controlled by a centralized state power, sometimes called the **metropole**, or "mother country." In the process, these powers practiced **imperialism**, meaning that they sought and exercised **hegemony**—that is, economic, cultural, and political dominance—over other societies, which included mainly, but not exclusively, their colonies.* Almost from the very outset, Western imperialism combined economic exploitation and political domination with the imposition and inculcation of Western culture and beliefs.[4]

The story of how Europe's colonial empires were formed is a familiar one. In the fifteenth century, seeking to circumvent established Eurasian trade routes and thus gain wealth by directly conducting commerce with Asians for goods (such as silks and spices) highly prized in Europe, the Portuguese and Spanish embarked on a series of great oceanic voyages. In the process they not only created new connections with Africans and Asians but also accidentally "discovered" the Americas, eventually bringing immense wealth and power to their small Iberian kingdoms.

In the sixteenth century, eager to enhance their wealth and power, they each formed an extensive empire. Spain's from its origins was essentially colonial, consisting mainly of colonies—lands that were settled and controlled by Spanish subjects under the rule of Spain—in the West Indies, southern North America, Central America, much of South America, and the Philippine Islands. Portugal's at first was primarily commercial, made up mainly of trading posts along the coasts of Africa and Asia, but it eventually came to also include a very large colony in Brazil and some smaller but still sizable African colonial possessions.

The Spanish initially gained great wealth by exploiting their colonies' resources, mainly by mining precious metals such as gold and silver; the Portuguese did so by buying Asian products, especially spices, and selling them back in Europe at a profit. In Brazil, however, the Portuguese found that they could make a fortune by setting up sugar plantations, as they had done on islands off the African coast, and then selling the sugar back in Europe—a practice also implemented by the Spanish in the West Indies. As the native people of the Americas, known to Europeans as American Indians, were largely destroyed by diseases from Europe such as smallpox and measles, both the Portuguese and Spanish increasingly used slaves brought from Africa as labor to exploit their colonies' riches. And through coercion and conversion they imposed and instilled their cultures—including their languages and Catholic Christianity—in their colonies.

In the seventeenth century other European powers, seeing the success of Spain and Portugal, created and expanded their own colonial empires. Initially, these empires were mainly commercial, run by enterprises such as the English and Dutch East India Companies, which owned large merchant fleets, established trading settlements, and eventually took over much of the trade between Europe and Asia. But increasingly, especially

---

*A power that exercises economic, cultural, and/or military dominance over other regions without making them formal colonies is often said to practice **informal imperialism**. The regions thus dominated by this power are said to be within its **sphere of influence**.

in North America, the French and English also created vast colonial empires, settled by French and English subjects who moved there on a permanent basis and produced descendants who stayed there. In the Caribbean, the French and English also added colonies that prospered from slave-grown sugar, while in northern Asia the Russians formed a vast land empire by expanding eastward across Siberia (and for a time into northwestern North America). As European settlers exploited these regions' resources, they also implanted their languages and religions while connecting and conflicting with the native peoples.

By the eighteenth century, then, European empires encircled the globe. Small European nations, mainly Portugal, Spain, the Netherlands, France, and Great Britain (formed in 1707 by the union of England and Scotland), ruled vast far-flung colonial realms and dominated global trade. And as the center of maritime commerce shifted from the Indian Ocean to the Atlantic basin, global wealth and power likewise shifted from Asian empires and African commercial centers to the imperial powers of Western Europe.

Then, between 1750 and 1825, a combination of conflicts among European powers and rebellions in their American colonies seemed to spell the end of European rule in the Western hemisphere. The Seven Years War (1756–1763), a complex global conflict fought in Europe, North America, India, and on the high seas, resulted in a sweeping victory for Britain, which thereby acquired most of France's North American empire. But it also led to conflicts between the British and their own original American colonies, led by English settlers who had gotten used to running their own affairs with little interference from Britain. Now, as the British government forbade the colonists from moving west into lands it had taken from France (to minimize clashes between colonists and the American Indians living there) and began to impose taxes on the colonists (to help pay for the war debt and their own defense), the colonists grew increasingly resentful. Claiming that such policies should not be implemented without their consent, they eventually rebelled and declared independence, asserting that Britain had violated their "unalienable rights," and that governments must be based on the "consent of the governed."[5] Improbably, they defeated the British in the ensuing American Revolution (1775–1783), thanks partly to their own resolute efforts and partly to aid from France, which allied with the colonists to avenge its earlier defeat by Britain. In creating a new republic, the United States of America, the former colonists showed that it was possible for colonial peoples to gain independence by exploiting conflicts between imperial powers and by wearing down their oppressors in a lengthy liberation war. But they also showed that the formerly oppressed can become imperial oppressors, as they relentlessly moved west and subjugated the American Indians and others who stood in the way of US expansion, effectively creating a large land empire.

France, meanwhile, gained little but the joy of retribution by aiding the American rebels against the British. Indeed, the war effort added to the French regime's massive debts, provoking it to attempt to tax France's nobility, which in turn helped to spark the momentous French Revolution of 1789. Not only did this revolution declare a new government based on "the natural, unalienable, and sacred rights of man"[6] but it also wound up seeking to destroy both the monarchy and nobility. And by creating conditions that helped to spark a slave revolt in Saint-Domingue, a French Caribbean colony that prospered from slave-grown sugar, it cost France its most lucrative remaining American possession, which in 1804 became the independent nation of Haiti.

By this time France was under the rule of Napoleon Bonaparte, who, after conquering much of the rest of Europe, invaded Portugal in 1807 and Spain in 1808, setting the stage for the dissolution of their American empires. The Portuguese crown prince escaped with his court to Brazil, where he continued to reside and rule for the next thirteen years, meanwhile becoming king of Portugal in 1816. On returning to Portugal in 1821 he left behind his son, who would go on to rule Brazil as an independent empire. The Spanish king was deposed by Napoleon in 1808, providing both an occasion and a pretext for Spain's American colonies to rebel, supposedly in support of the unseated monarch. But the revolts continued even after he returned to the throne in 1814, and by 1825 Spain's once great American empire was for the most part gone, replaced by a number of newly independent Spanish-speaking nations.

Most of Europe's former American colonies thus gained independence, profiting not only from revolutionary valor and ideals but also from conflicts among the imperial powers. Yet the influence of Europe, exercised through cultural and economic ties, remained very strong in the Americas, which continued to be ruled by the descendants of Europeans, who conducted commerce with Europe, spoke European languages, followed European faiths, and oppressed non-Europeans, including American Indians and African slaves. And European trading settlements—some with sizable territories, governments, and military forces—still rimmed the coastal regions of Africa and southern Asia. The age of European empires was by no means over.

INDUSTRY AND IDEOLOGIES

In the eighteenth and nineteenth centuries, even as political revolutions helped Europe's American colonies gain independence, a different kind of revolution was further propelling Western Europe and North America—collectively called the West—to global supremacy. The **Industrial Revolution**—a historic transition from an agrarian economy (in which most people lived in rural villages and produced their own food and goods through manual labor) to an urban system of mechanized production (in which people lived in cities and used machines in factories to make goods to be sold in a commercial economy)—provided the nations of the West with unprecedented wealth and power. By 1860 little Britain, the first nation to industrialize, had surpassed enormous China as the world's largest economy, while Belgium and France were also emerging as industrial powers. By the early 1900s Germany, unified as a nation in 1871, had surpassed Britain as Europe's industrial leader, while Italy, Austria, Russia, and Japan had also begun to industrialize. And across the Atlantic the United States had become an industrial giant, with assets and wealth far exceeding those of any other country.

Industrialization dramatically affected how people in Western countries *lived*. Millions whose families had for centuries resided in rural villages, surrounded by lands on which they raised their own food, were now compelled by economic forces to move to cities and take jobs in factories, where they worked for wages. Hours were long, pay was very low, and conditions were often appalling, especially in the early years of industry. Dwelling in crowded and squalid slums around the factories, the workers and their families formed a new class that was later labeled the urban **proletariat**: landless laborers living in cities and working in industry for wages. In the same cities also dwelt a much smaller assortment of wealthier people—such as merchants and bankers, doctors and lawyers, factory managers and factory owners—who lived comfortable lives in nice homes and apartments and were sometimes called the **bourgeoisie**.

Industry also affected the way that people *thought*. Faced with the transformative effects of the Industrial Revolution, combined with the ideals reflected in the revolutions of France and the Americas, Europeans developed new **ideologies**—secular systems of ideas and beliefs that sought both to explain and to transform modern societies. The most consequential of the new ideologies were liberalism, socialism, and nationalism.

Liberalism, as its name suggests, was based on the principle of liberty. In politics it advocated constitutional governments with limited powers, representatives elected by the people, and protection of individual rights, while generally reflecting the values and attitudes of the bourgeoisie. In economics it promoted **capitalism**, a system based on free market competition with little or no government interference.

Socialism was in many ways the antithesis of liberalism. While liberals extolled liberty, individualism, and competition, socialists valued equality, community, and cooperation. Distressed by the gulf between the "haves" and "have-nots" and dismayed by the poverty and suffering of the working classes, socialists called for more equal distribution of the wealth, with sharing of resources, collectivized labor, and welfare programs to assist the poor.

Some socialists, called **communists**, advocated a working-class revolution. In 1848 Karl Marx and Friedrich Engels, two prominent German socialists, published *The Communist Manifesto*, a radical document that urged workers to unite and topple the existing order. According to communists, who as followers of Marx were often also called **Marxists**, societies pitted rich against poor in ongoing class struggles. The powerful and rich—like the landowning nobles of preindustrial Europe and the urban capitalists of the industrial era—controlled the economy and exploited the masses of poor working people. But **Marxism** held out hope for the exploited masses, asserting that industrial capitalism was unwittingly contributing to its own downfall. By bringing together vast numbers of workers in industrial cities and towns, it was inadvertently creating a revolutionary class, the urban proletariat, that would eventually rise up in revolt to overthrow capitalism and establish a classless socialist society. And this would be an international revolution, since Marxists believed that the working class transcended national boundaries and that working-class connections and concerns were far more important than ethnic, cultural, and linguistic ties.

This Marxist internationalism, however, ran counter to the growing appeal of **nationalism**, a fervent devotion to one's own ethnic group and to its embodiment in a unified, strong, and independent country. In ousting monarchies and replacing them with republics, the revolutions in France and the Americas helped to transfer people's allegiance from the person of the ruler to the abstract concept of the nation. By relocating people from small villages to cities that had newspapers and public schools, the Industrial Revolution also fostered national awareness, identifying people with their nation instead of just their village or clan. In idealizing the national state—a political realm embracing those who shared a common culture, heritage, and language—nationalists also stressed patriotic pride, strong military forces, and forceful foreign policies designed to show that their country was superior to others.

THE NEW WAVE OF WESTERN IMPERIALISM

Beginning in the nineteenth century, industry and new ideologies helped provide the impetus for a new wave of Western imperial expansion. As Western countries industrialized, they looked more and more to non-Western regions for resources needed to run their industries, as well as for potential markets and investment opportunities. As they competed for power and wealth, they sought to establish or expand their presence in many of these regions. As people in these regions responded, and sought either to resist or take advantage of the Western intrusions, European agents on the spot took measures to assert their control, often with the support of their governments back home. And as European empires grew, people back home in the metropole countries (especially Britain and France) employed old ideals and new ideologies to both motivate and justify imperial behavior, imposing and implanting their cultures and beliefs while taking control of more and more parts of Asia and Africa.

Industry and new technologies also helped provide the means for imperial expansion. Steamships, which did not have to rely on the seasonal winds that had long governed sailing ship travel, helped Westerners readily move people and resources to and from distant places. Steam-powered vessels, which could travel up rivers into African and Asian interiors, helped Westerners gain access to resources and impose military control. Steam-driven dredgers helped them build canals, while steam-powered excavators and dynamite helped them dig mines to extract resources and cut roads and railways to transport goods and materials through harsh terrain. The use of quinine to both prevent and treat malaria helped Western settlers and soldiers survive in tropical climes, while telegraph lines and undersea cables allowed them to keep in contact with company and government officials in their homelands. And deadly new rapid-fire weapons, such as breech-loading rifles and machine guns, helped relatively small European forces destroy Asians and Africans who dared to resist, and often massacre much larger armies with appalling efficiency.

In Europe's former American colonies, the new wave of economic expansion operated largely by noncolonial means. As long as they could get the resources and markets they wanted, the British and other early industrial nations were content to do so through purchases and pressures without asserting formal colonial control. In North America, plantation owners in the US South were only too happy to sell their slave-grown cotton for use in Britain's booming textile mills. And Canada, which had remained under British rule during and after the American Revolution, in 1867 became a British **dominion**—a self-governing nation that maintained close ties with Britain and shared its constitutional monarch. In Latin America, once the Spanish were largely gone, the British were content to dominate markets and extract or purchase resources, using their superior technologies and wealth to own or control many banks, docks, railways, and other such enterprises. And as the United States grew into an industrial power, it similarly dominated the economies of nations to its south.

Culturally, too, the Western Hemisphere remained under European dominance. History's largest mass migrations, in which perhaps sixty million Europeans moved to the Americas between 1815 and 1930, ensured that these continents would maintain close ties with Europe and would continue to be dominated by European cultures, languages, and creeds. American Indian and African cultures also had important impacts, but people of such heritage largely remained impoverished and oppressed, even after they were formally granted legal rights and freedoms. Hence, although the new nations of the Americas were no longer considered colonies, and thus were no longer formally under European rule, economically and culturally they were still part of the European world.

In the Eastern Hemisphere in the same century, this dynamic was reversed, as numerous non-European cultures came under European control. In some parts of Asia and Africa, the Europeans exerted dominance through forceful but informal noncolonial mechanisms. The British and French, for example, gave extensive military aid and loans to the ailing Ottoman Empire, which sat astride vital east-west trade routes in the Middle East, but then forbade it to erect tariffs to protect its producers from European competition and effectively took control of its finances. When Egypt, which was nominally under Ottoman rule, fell deeply in debt after borrowing heavily to help finance a French company's construction of the Suez Canal, the British used their wealth to buy Egypt's canal shares and then occupied Egypt in 1882 to keep the canal secure. When the Chinese sought to crack down on British merchants who were smuggling opium (an addictive narcotic) into China, Britain used its superior ships and weapons to defeat Chinese forces in the First Opium War (1839–1842) and then joined with France to do so again in the Second Opium War (1856–1860). These wars resulted in "unequal" (one-sided) treaties, forcing China to open more ports to Western merchants and missionaries and to grant them exemption from prosecution under Chinese laws. Although the Chinese Empire, like the Ottoman, remained nominally independent, by the century's end the European powers had further imposed vast "concessions" to exploit its resources.

Elsewhere in the Eastern Hemisphere, the Europeans resorted to imposing direct colonial rule. In southern Asia, the Dutch and British governments took over the trading settlements established earlier by their East India companies, resulting in the formation of a formal Dutch colonial empire in resource-rich Indonesia (the "Dutch East Indies") and a massive British colonial empire (the "British Raj") in India. The French, largely shut out of India in the previous century by Britain's victory in the Seven Years War, took over the Southeast Asian countries of Vietnam, Cambodia, and Laos, creating a large new colony they called French Indochina. The

British also set up colonial control over Burma, Singapore, and the Malay Peninsula. As a result—especially after the United States took the Philippine Islands in the Spanish-American War of 1898—by 1900 almost all of South and Southeast Asia were ruled by industrial powers from the West.

In Africa, Europe's colonization was even more extensive. A Dutch settler colony in South Africa, founded in 1652, was taken over by the British in the early 1800s, and the French took advantage of Ottoman weakness in North Africa to conquer Algeria in the 1830s. But it was Britain's 1882 occupation of Egypt, and the king of Belgium's acquisition of the Congo River region through treaties with Central African rulers between 1878 and 1884, that set the stage for a European "scramble for Africa" over the next three decades. Other European powers, hitherto content with assorted settlements along the African coast, now began to scramble for colonies, fearful that all of Africa might be divided up before they secured their share. Germany, emerging as a major industrial power with its political unification in 1871, hosted a conference at Berlin (1884–1885) to set some ground rules. There the major powers agreed that, in order to claim an area, it was not enough for them to simply negotiate treaties with African rulers; they must also establish "effective occupation," ban slavery in the region, and keep it open to trade with other countries.

Promising to honor these agreements, King Leopold II of Belgium expanded his rule over the Congo region, establishing a "Congo Free State" under his personal dominion. Obsessed, moreover, with exploiting the region's rubber resources to produce a handsome profit, Leopold and his agents employed African forced labor, torturing, murdering, or mutilating Africans who failed to fulfill their relentless rubber quotas. Reports of these atrocities eventually sparked international outrage, prompting Belgium's parliament in 1908 to take over the region from King Leopold, ending some (but not all) of the abuses and forming a large and resource-rich colony known as the Belgian Congo.

Meanwhile, other European powers divided up the rest of Africa. Britain and France split up most of the continent's northern half between them, while Britain also added vast new colonial domains in the south. Germany took some lands on the Gulf of Guinea coast and established large colonies in East and Southwest Africa. Italy took territories in North Africa, East Africa, and on the Red Sea, while Portugal expanded earlier holdings dating from the sixteenth century. By 1914 more than 90 percent of the African continent was under European rule.

Whatever doubts there may have been about the wisdom and morality of these ventures, their very success seemed to many in the West to confirm the superiority of their institutions and values. As Western powers vied for colonies, their peoples came to see imperial expansion as a matter of nationalist pride, reflecting the preeminence of their cultures, societies, and armies. As more and more people in the West gained voting rights and acquired some education, and as newspapers raised their awareness of world affairs, many of them took warlike pride in their countries' colonial conquests.

European ideals and beliefs also helped to idealize imperial activity. In many parts of Africa and Asia, missionaries, doctors, and teachers from the West sought to spread Christianity, dispense Western medicine, and "civilize" the people by teaching them Western ways. The French called this their "civilizing mission" (*mission civilisatrice*), and British poet Rudyard Kipling, welcoming the US rule of the Philippine Islands, labeled this Western endeavor "The White Man's Burden."

As Kipling's title indicates, this blend of idealism and arrogance also had racial connotations. Celebrating Western science and "progress," some European thinkers took the notion of natural selection, used by British naturalist Charles Darwin to explain his evolutionary theories, and applied it to human societies, portraying human progress as a product of a struggle for "survival of the fittest" between the strong and weak—and rationalizing imperial expansion as part of that global struggle. Others went so far as to classify humans into distinct racial categories, ranking white Europeans at the top, and using such ideas to both explain and justify Europe's global domination.

But Western technology and ideology could also prove to be a two-edged sword. As Europeans sought to develop and administer their colonies, they often found it useful to train some of their subjects to use Western weapons and ways, educating them in Western ideals and even sending some to prestigious Western schools. And as Asians and Africans sought to respond to Western domination, they learned to use these weapons, ways, and ideals to their own advantage.

RESPONSES TO WESTERN DOMINATION

Responses to Western domination varied. Some societies sought forcibly to resist Western incursions. The Chinese, for example, fought the British and French in the Opium Wars and the French in Southeast Asia, and the Zulu peoples of southeastern Africa fought British expansion there. In 1857 British-trained Indian soldiers called sepoys revolted against the British, and in 1900 a Chinese martial arts society, known in the West as the Boxers, led a violent anti-Western rebellion in northern China. In these instances and others, however, Western technology and weaponry made resistance and rebellion futile.

Other societies, including Egypt, parts of India, and Latin American nations rich in raw materials required by Western industry, sought wealth by selling their resources to Western nations. But this practice gave them little real autonomy, since the lands and mines supplying these resources typically were owned and exploited by Westerners, who paid local workers miserable wages, used the profits to boost Western industry, and undermined local artisans and markets by inundating them with inexpensive Western machine-made goods. Thus although these countries remained independent in nominal political terms, in economic terms they were mainly suppliers and subordinates of Western industrial powers.

A few societies retained some independence by playing Western nations against each other and emulating Western ways. In Southeast Asia, for example, the kings of Siam (now called Thailand) astutely exploited the French-British rivalry to keep their country independent, further reinforcing their realm with a centralized administration, an educational system, and Western technologies such as railways, telegraphs, and printing presses. And in eastern Africa the Ethiopians, faced with efforts by Italy to take over their ancient Christian kingdom, raised a large army that was fueled by nationalist pride, armed it with modern rifles supplied by Italy's French foes, and then soundly defeated the badly outnumbered Italians at Adowa in northern Ethiopia in 1896. This stunning triumph showed that Africans and Asians, inspired by nationalist zeal and armed with modern weapons, could ably resist European intrusions and defeat European armies.

Some colonized countries sought to gain autonomy by taking advantage of the practices and ideals of their Western imperial rulers. In India, for example, British efforts to create a uniform civil service and a network of railways and telegraphs, thus to better rule and exploit the subcontinent's diverse states, inadvertently fostered a sense of Indian national unity. Members of a British-educated, English-speaking Indian elite, trained by the British to play leading roles in Indian society, soon began adopting and adapting Western liberal and nationalist ideals. If freedom, self-governance, and national pride were such essential values in Britain, they reasoned, why should these values not also apply in India? In 1885, with the help of a retired British official, a group of them formed an organization that became known as the Indian National Congress. Somewhat modeled on British political parties, it pushed for more Indian self-governance and later developed into a full-fledged national independence movement. It also served as a model for the African National Congress, founded in southern Africa in 1912 to advance the rights of African peoples.

Of all the countries to resist Western dominance, the most successful was Japan. Forced by Americans and Europeans to open ports to Western commerce in the 1850s, the Japanese reacted by adopting Western-style industries, technologies, and ways. As a result, Japan emerged by the early 1900s as a burgeoning industrial country and expanding regional power with imperialist ambitions. In the Russo-Japanese War of 1904–1905, Japan stunned the world by defeating mighty Russia, one of Europe's great powers—shattering myths of European racial superiority and giving hope to other Asians that they too could use Western weapons and ways to combat Western oppression. But Japan's emergence also posed a peril to other Asians: a new imperialist power, eager to expand to gain access to industrial resources, now existed on the edge of Asia.

By this time another response to imperialism was emerging in the West. In 1902 British economist John A. Hobson published *Imperialism: A Study*, a groundbreaking work that tied imperial expansion directly to industrial capitalism. According to Hobson, Western imperialism was a logical outcome of industrial growth: in their insatiable quest for raw materials, markets, and outlets for capital investment, he maintained, Westerners had asserted economic hegemony and often colonial control over vast areas of the non-Western world. This theme was picked up in 1916 by Russian Marxist V. I. Lenin, who argued in *Imperialism: The Highest Stage of Capitalism* that empire-building was merely an advanced phase of capitalism and thus that imperialism and capitalism were practically one and the same. As Lenin soon emerged as the head of a revolutionary Communist regime in Russia, his ideals became an essential ingredient of **Marxism-Leninism**, a revised ideology that sought to combine the anti-imperialist struggles of non-Western peoples with the anticapitalist struggles of Western industrial workers into a global anticapitalist, anti-imperialist crusade.

By forming their own nationalist movements, adopting Western technologies and weapons, and adapting revolutionary ideologies to meet their needs, non-Western people could perhaps begin to work toward eventual liberation. But Western power and wealth were overwhelming, and non-Western peoples were typically powerless and poor. In the eighteenth and early nineteenth centuries Europe's American colonies had gained their independence, not just through ideals and weapons, but also through a series of prolonged, destructive conflicts among their imperial rulers. In the twentieth century, to gain their independence, Asians and Africans would likewise need their imperial rulers to engage in destructive conflicts among themselves. By 1916, when Lenin's work was published, the first such conflict was already under way.

THE WORLD WARS AND THEIR IMPACTS

In 1914 there broke out in Europe a war of unprecedented scope, known at the time as the Great War and later as World War I. On one side was

Germany—a new imperial power that, since its unification in 1871, had also emerged as Europe's mightiest military and industrial power—along with the Ottoman and Austro-Hungarian Empires (declining states that had once ranked among the world's largest imperial realms) and Bulgaria. On the other were the world's current largest imperial powers—Russia, Britain, and France—joined by Belgium, Japan, Italy, and a number of other countries, including eventually the United States. All of the world's greatest empires and all the great industrial nations were thus involved in a catastrophic conflict that, although centered in Europe, also involved colonial peoples and others from around the globe.

World War I was in many ways an imperialist conflict. It was rooted in Russian, French, and British fears of Germany's military and imperial ambitions, and in a complex Balkan conflict involving Austrian and Russian imperial aims and the nationalistic hopes of Balkan states that had recently emerged from Ottoman imperial rule. It began when nationalists with ties to Serbia, one of those emerging nations, murdered the man next in line to become the Austrian emperor, and the Austrians responded with a series of demands that, when not totally accepted, led to their invasion of Serbia. The Russians sided with their Serbian friends, and the Germans, alarmed by Russia's decision to embark on a massive military buildup, backed their Austrian allies to the hilt. When Russia's French allies refused to pledge neutrality, the Germans, by preconceived plan, invaded France through neutral Belgium, prompting Britain to join the war on the side of the Belgians, French, and Russians. Almost all of Europe was soon at war.

As the war in Western Europe turned into a stalemated standoff, German forces and those of France and Britain dug trenches for protection and faced each other, in Belgium and northern France, across fields filled with land mines and laced with barbed wire. Attacks across these fields proved futile, and armies that attempted such attacks were mowed down by relentless machine gun and artillery fire from the other side. Efforts to break the deadlock—including mass attacks, sustained artillery fire, and the use of poison gas—likewise proved ineffective. And German assaults in the east, which gobbled up huge chunks of Russian territory at an enormous cost in human lives, forced the Russians to retreat but failed to fully defeat them.

Faced with mounting shortages of soldiers, the warring nations increasingly looked to their colonies to help offset the deficit. Here the British and French fared better by far. More than a million troops from India helped support the British war efforts, serving with distinction in Europe, Africa, and Asia, while British dominions (mainly Canada, Australia, and New Zealand) contributed roughly a million more soldiers to the cause. And at least a half million Africans served the French and British in Africa and in France, some as combat soldiers, some as porters of supplies and ammunition, and some as workers in French factories supporting the war effort. The Germans used colonial peoples far less extensively, but they did mobilize several thousand Africans to help them defend their colonies in Africa.

The involvement of Asians and Africans had some profound effects. Many gained experience in using modern weapons, experience that could later help them fight for their own independence. Many also came to expect that they and their peoples would be rewarded for their service with some sort of self-rule, and later they would feel betrayed and rebellious when such expectations were not met. And many, having seen the supposedly "civilized" white Westerners kill each other by the millions, could never again be expected to accept the myths of European cultural and racial superiority.

Meanwhile, in the midst of the war, several significant events occurred that also gave hope to the colonized peoples. Early in 1917 a rebellion in Russia resulted in the fall of its monarchy, widely blamed for catastrophic wartime losses and mass suffering experienced during the war. But the provisional government that replaced the monarchy, failing to comprehend the depth of popular hostility toward the war, sought to continue the conflict. Seizing the opportunity, V. I. Lenin and his Marxist comrades staged a well-planned coup in November, taking power in the name of the **soviets** (workers' councils) formed by urban workers and others when the monarchy fell. Depicting World War I as an "imperialist war," Lenin's new Soviet regime then pulled Russia out of it, called for a global struggle against capitalist imperialism, and heralded the rights of all oppressed peoples to freedom from imperial rule.

In the spring of 1917 the United States, angered by the Germans' use of submarines to sink US ships taking supplies to Britain and France, joined the war against Germany and its allies. Early the next year, in declaring his war objectives, US President Woodrow Wilson put forth Fourteen Points, many of them based on the principle of **national self-determination**—the right of each nationality to freely decide its own political status. Although Wilson spoke mainly of securing this right for the peoples ruled by his enemies—that is, for nationalities subject to the German, Austro-Hungarian, and Ottoman Empires—the principle clearly had implications for Africans and Asians and others who were subject to the powers on the US side (especially Britain and France).

By autumn of 1918 the arrival of fresh American forces in Europe, along with the devastating impact on Germany of Britain's naval blockade and British deployment of new armored vehicles called tanks, had helped to break the wartime stalemate. In November, the Germans, exhausted and dispirited from hunger and disease, agreed to accept a war-ending armistice based on Wilson's Fourteen Points. Two months later, in January 1919, a conference convened in Paris to decide the terms of peace that would shape the postwar world. Wilson attended as the prophet of peace, a man whose idealism inspired dreams of an end to warfare and imperial rule.

Soon, however, world events dimmed these dreams. At the peace conference, which lasted until June, French and British leaders resisted Wilson's idealism. Bent on punishing their erstwhile enemies and expanding their own empires, they imposed huge reparations payments on Germany and laid claim to territories taken from defeated foes. At Wilson's insistence they agreed to form a League of Nations—an organization of countries worldwide designed to maintain peace through international cooperation—and to rule their newly taken territories as "League of Nations mandates" rather than colonial possessions. Former German colonies in Africa and Asia and former Ottoman provinces in the Middle East were thus entrusted as mandates to victorious nations such as Britain, France, or Japan, purportedly to help prepare the peoples for self-governance. This formula artfully allowed the victors to claim the possessions of the vanquished, enlarging their own empires while paying lip service to the notion of national self-determination.

But some people seeking self-determination took matters into their own hands in 1919. In Ireland, rebels demanding a republic declared independence from Britain, touching off a violent conflict that lasted more than two years. In Egypt, demonstrators called for independence and pressed for the withdrawal of the British, who instead responded by ruthlessly suppressing the unrest. In India, where many believed that self-rule should be granted in reward for the service of Indian soldiers in World War I, a British-led massacre of anti-British protesters helped to ignite a massive independence movement. In China, when the Paris Peace Conference permitted Japan to take over German claims to Chinese territory, angry students began a mass protest heralding the rise of momentous Chinese Nationalist and Communist movements. At the conference itself, when a young merchant seaman and pastry chef who was later called Ho Chi Minh petitioned for self-determination for his native Vietnam, his petition was ignored, and he soon decided to fight for his cause as a Communist. And as violence rocked Syria, Sudan, Trinidad, Jamaica, and British Honduras (now Belize), the world seemed to be seething with anti-imperial unrest.

But conditions in 1919 were not yet fully ripe for successful anti-imperial rebellions, in part because the rebels lacked outside aid and access to advanced weapons, still largely controlled by the imperial powers. Later, after World War II, anti-imperial rebellions could gain such aid and access by exploiting Cold War conflict among the victorious powers, but no such

Cold War conflict existed after World War I. The Soviets, who later would supply some such rebellions with materials and weapons, provided some advice and assistance to nationalist movements in China and elsewhere during the 1920s, but the Soviet regime was still too poor and weak—and still too beset by internal and external foes—to seriously challenge the West's imperial dominance.

As a result, in the years between the world wars (1919–1939), anti-imperial movements met with mixed success. An independent Irish Free State was recognized in 1921, but the British retained Northern Ireland. In India, a mass campaign of nonviolent resistance, led by Mohandas Gandhi and the Indian National Congress, compelled Britain to grant the Indians a measure of self-rule but failed to achieve full independence until after World War II. In the Middle East, where France and Britain held League of Nations mandates over former Ottoman provinces, Arab nationalists made some inroads as the British granted autonomy to Egypt, Iraq, and Trans-Jordan, but the Westerners continued to control the Suez Canal and dominate the region. In Africa, varied nationalist movements were able to organize and even to resist some oppression, but mainly they just planted seeds for independence efforts that would sprout after World War II.

Meanwhile, in the 1930s virulent new forms of imperialism arose in Japan, Italy, and Germany. In 1931–1932 the Japanese took control of Manchuria, a huge region of northeastern China with ample resources and land for them to exploit. In 1935 Italy conquered Ethiopia, as a step toward the creation of a "New Roman Empire" by Italian dictator Benito Mussolini. In 1937 Japan went to war against China and overran its eastern regions, taking control of most of its key industries and population centers.

In Germany, Adolf Hitler and his National Socialists (Nazis), having taken power in 1933, created a racist imperialist realm they called the Third Reich—that is, the "Third Empire."* Asserting that Germans made up a "master race" destined to rule the "sub-human" peoples of Eastern Europe and Soviet Russia, Hitler and the Nazis promoted extreme nationalism and anti-Semitism, borrowing and expanding on ideas used by earlier European imperialists. Acting on such racist imperialist ambitions, Hitler rebuilt the German army into a mighty military force and prepared to engage in a new world war that he hoped would reverse the outcome of the Great War and reassert German global dominance.

These ambitions appeared to put Hitler on a collision course with Soviet Russia, which, despite its anti-imperialist, Marxist-Leninist ideol-

---

*The first two were the medieval German "Holy Roman Empire" and the modern German Empire of 1871–1918.

ogy, was becoming a major imperial and industrial power. Joseph Stalin, who emerged as Soviet leader after Lenin's death in 1924, focused less on spreading communism elsewhere than on strengthening the Soviet state. The country he ruled, called the Union of Soviet Socialist Republics (USSR), or Soviet Union, was allegedly a group of autonomous national republics, but in many ways it resembled the old Russian Empire—especially in its incorporation of numerous non-Russian nationalities. In the early 1930s millions of Ukrainians and others perished in a civil war and famine, both brought on by Stalin's efforts to collectivize farming, build up Soviet industry, and eliminate people who got in his way. By the late 1930s, owing to such efforts, the USSR became not only an industrial powerhouse but also a prison house of peoples, as Stalin executed or imprisoned anyone who might oppose him.

The Western imperial powers, mainly France and Britain, at first sought to undermine and isolate the Soviets but later aspired to join with them in a coalition that could counter Hitler's ambitions. But the French and British, distrusting Stalin's Soviets as much as Hitler's Nazis, sought in 1938 to appease Hitler by letting him take the western borderlands of Czechoslovakia, which he portrayed as national liberation since mostly German people lived there. In 1939, however, as Hitler took over the rest of Czechoslovakia and started to threaten Poland, both France and Britain regretted their appeasement and vowed to defend the Poles. But Stalin, distrusting the Western powers even more than they distrusted him, and desperately fearful of having to fight Germany alone, stunned the West in August of that year by cutting a deal with Hitler. This "Nazi-Soviet Pact" on its surface was a nonaggression treaty between the Soviets and Germans, but it also had secret clauses in which the two sides agreed to divide Poland between them, freeing Hitler to invade that country on September 1, starting what would eventually be World War II.

The next few years proved catastrophic for the Western imperial powers. In spring of 1940, having carved up Poland with Stalin the preceding fall, Hitler turned west and again stunned the world by quickly conquering the Netherlands, Belgium, and France—three of the major Western imperialist powers. That fall, with resource-rich Dutch and French colonies in Asia now open for Japanese conquest, Japan joined with Germany and Italy in a coalition called the Axis Powers. In June 1941, after failing in an effort to knock Britain from the war, Hitler turned eastward and launched a massive invasion of the USSR, breaking his pact with Stalin and gobbling up huge tracts of Soviet territory with appalling brutality. That December, after a stunning surprise attack on the US naval fleet at Pearl Harbor in Hawaii, Japan began a six-month series of conquests that brought most of East and Southeast Asia—including former US, British, French, and Dutch colonial possessions—under Japanese rule. Asians and Africans oppressed by the West could hardly help but take notice: a non-Western nation had won sweeping victories over the imperialist West.

But despite their dramatic successes, both the Germans and Japanese had by this time overreached themselves. In December 1941 Soviet forces had stopped Hitler's armies and prevented them from taking Moscow, the Soviet capital. Japan's attack on Pearl Harbor that same month and Germany's subsequent declaration of war on the United States left both facing a mighty new foe with wealth and resources that far exceeded theirs—and were far beyond their reach. Setting aside their substantial differences for the sake of survival, the British, Soviets, and Americans joined forces, creating a coalition of the world's largest imperial powers. Joined by numerous other nations from all over the globe, this coalition, known as the Allied Powers, eventually would overwhelm its enemies and win the Second World War.

The oppressed and colonized peoples of Africa and Asia, repulsed by the racist imperialism of Germany and Japan, mostly chose to support the Allied Powers as the lesser evil. Although some in India and other Asian countries initially sided with Japan against the West, the ruthlessness of the Japanese eventually turned most other Asians against them. As a result, throughout much of Asia, nationalists and communists and others all worked to undermine their Japanese oppressors, thus effectively aiding the Allied cause. More than two million troops from British India and several hundred thousand more from British colonies in Southeast Asia and Africa fought against the Japanese, Italians, and Germans on the side of the Allies. The Free French Forces, formed by General Charles de Gaulle following the fall of France in 1940 and made up mainly of African troops from various French colonies, also joined the Allied war effort.

Still, the main architects of the Allied victory were two: the Soviet Union, which bore the brunt of the fight against Nazi Germany, and the United States, which helped the Soviets and British beat Germany and used its matchless resources and technologies (including newly developed atomic bombs) to overwhelm Japan. The emergence of these two countries as global superpowers—each ostensibly committed to anti-imperialism and national self-determination—and the roles played by oppressed and colonized peoples in helping to defeat the Axis Powers seemed to bode well for the hopes of these peoples for national liberation in the wake of the war.

But the Soviet Union and United States themselves were both imperial powers, and their outlooks, ideologies, and war aims differed dramatically. Since the Soviets had fought the most crucial battles and borne the brunt of the bloodshed, and since their homeland had been devastated by the German invasion, they felt that they had earned the right to incapacitate Germany and extract reparations to rebuild their country. And since they had freed Eastern Europe from the Nazis, the Soviets felt they had the right to set up friendly governments there, both to shield themselves from future attack and to spread their Communist ways to their nearest neighbors. But the United States, committed to capitalist democracy and fearful that a crippled Germany could again become unstable and dangerous, opposed mass reparations and favored free elections in Germany and Eastern Europe—which might well bring to office anticommunist leaders unfriendly to the USSR. American and Soviet outlooks and aims were thus incompatible.

Unable to resolve their differences, the Allied leaders took steps intended as temporary but destined to have impacts for decades. In Eastern Europe, the occupying Soviets pledged to hold elections and create coalition governments, but they wound up forcibly installing regimes that were Communist-controlled. The USSR annexed most of prewar eastern Poland, so the Poles were given part of prewar Germany, and the rest was divided into occupation zones, with a Soviet zone in the east and British, French, and American zones in the west (map 2.1). The German capital Berlin, which sat in the middle of the Soviet zone, was split into similar sectors, and the Soviets had to settle for reparations from only their own zone in eastern Germany, the country's least prosperous region. Eastern Europe thus became a Soviet stronghold while Germany and its capital were split up into zones, and the German people's future remained unresolved and unsettled.

These unresolved issues were exacerbated by a deep ideological divide between the Communist East and capitalist West. Both the Soviets and Americans saw their values and systems as globally advantageous to all, and both felt they had a historic mission to spread their ideals and virtues to all humanity. Each thus saw the other as a moral and mortal threat: to the Soviet Communists, Western capitalists were oppressive imperialists who sought to use their wealth and power to rule the world; to the Americans and their allies, the Communists were enemies of freedom, bent on establishing a dictatorial, repressive world order. Each side portrayed itself as the promoter of progress and enlightenment, and each side depicted the other side as a purveyor of oppression and inequity. Each saw the other as imperialist, and each could thus justify efforts to expand its own hegemony not only as helpful to humanity but also as essential to thwart the other side's imperialist aspirations. Each thus practiced imperialism in the name of anti-imperialism.

Map 2.1. European Boundary Changes and Occupation Zones, 1945

COLD WAR IMPERIALISM AND ANTI-IMPERIALISM

These divisions and differences would soon help to provoke the Cold War: an intense forty-five-year struggle in which Soviets and Americans confronted each other globally—and often supported opposing sides in regional crises and conflicts—but did not engage in direct, all-out armed warfare against one another. Ironically, while both superpowers claimed to be anti-imperialist, Soviet dominance of Eastern Europe bore almost all the attributes of colonial rule, and American support for Western Europe made the United States an ally of the main imperial powers that had long dominated Africa and Asia. This section provides an overview of Cold War imperialist and anti-imperialist connections; the chapters that follow describe in greater depth the struggle against imperialism as it played out in each major region of the world.[7]

From its onset, the Cold War involved an odd blend of tacit imperialism and anti-imperialism. In 1944–1945, as Allied forces liberated Europe to win World War II, they ended two empires (Hitler's Third Reich and Mussolini's New Roman Empire) only to enhance or resuscitate their own imperialistic inclinations. In the east, the Soviets ended Nazi domination of Poland, Czechoslovakia, Hungary, Romania, Bulgaria, and eastern Germany, but eventually installed in each of these places Communist regimes beholden to Moscow, creating a so-called **Soviet Bloc** that amounted to a westward expansion of Soviet imperial rule. In the west, as American and British forces freed Belgium, France, and the Netherlands from the Nazis, they also freed these nations to try to restore their colonial empires in Africa and Asia. Within a few months of the war's end, the French and Dutch were working to reassert colonial rule in Indochina and Indonesia (see chapter 3).

Despite its own anticolonial roots and long-avowed support for national self-determination, the United States sided with the imperial powers of Western Europe. Alarmed by the expansion of Communism into Eastern and Central Europe, and by the stationing there of vast Soviet forces that could threaten the West, the Americans increasingly sought to counter the perceived Soviet threat. In 1946, as former British Prime Minister Winston Churchill was warning in a celebrated speech in Missouri that an "**iron curtain**" now divided Western Europe from the "Soviet sphere,"* asserting that only the Americans could stand up to the USSR,[8] the United States was simultaneously backing Britain in a dispute over Soviet presence in northern Iran (see chapter 4). In Germany, the Americans and British began to merge their occupation zones in what would prove to be a first step toward creating a unified and fortified West Germany.

Then in March 1947, unnerved by a Communist insurgency in Greece and by Soviet threats against Turkey, US President Harry Truman proclaimed what came to be called the **Truman Doctrine**, a pledge not only to aid Greece and Turkey but also "to support free peoples who are resisting attempted subjugation by armed minorities or outside pressures"[9]— effectively promising US assistance to countries threatened by Commu-

---

*The term *iron curtain* came to signify the boundary between Communist Eastern Europe and capitalist Western Europe, marked by sealed borders that restricted access to the West by those in the East. See map 2.2.

nism. A few months later, following up on this pledge, the United States initiated the **Marshall Plan**, a program that extended vast economic aid to war-torn European nations, fortifying them to resist Communism by reviving capitalist prosperity.

The net effect was to divide Europe, and eventually much of the world, into two highly armed hostile camps, one led by the United States and the other by the USSR. But ironically, although US policy was billed as "**containment of Communism**" and Soviet imperial expansion, it also involved American support for Western Europe's imperialist powers—thus seeming to confirm the Marxist-Leninist identification of capitalism with imperialism and enabling the Soviets to depict themselves as allies of colonized and exploited peoples seeking to free themselves from Western capitalist imperialism.

In September 1947 Soviet spokesman Andrei Zhdanov made this linkage explicit in a speech describing "the division of the political forces operating on the international arena into two major camps," which he called the "imperialist camp" and the "anti-imperialist camp."[10] According to Zhdanov, "the principal driving force of the imperialist camp is the U.S.A., allied with . . . Great Britain and France, . . . [and] supported by colony-owning countries, such as Belgium and Holland.*. . . [The anti-imperialist camp] is based on the USSR and . . . includes countries that have broken with imperialism, . . . Communist parties in all countries, . . . [and] the fighters for national liberation in the colonies and dependencies."[11] Although Zhdanov died the next year, his premise remained a central Soviet theme throughout the Cold War, connecting that conflict directly with anti-imperialism. Indeed, from a Soviet perspective, not only were capitalism and imperialism synonymous but so also were communism and anti-imperialism, merging the Cold War and anti-imperialism into a single global struggle.

In 1948, as the British, Americans, and now the French moved further to unite western Germany and create a common currency there, the Soviets responded by cutting off overland access from western Germany to the Western-occupied sectors of Berlin, which sat in the midst of Soviet-controlled eastern Germany, ninety miles behind the "iron curtain" (map 2.2). During the ensuing **Berlin Blockade**, which lasted eleven months, the United States and Britain supplied West Berlin by airlift, and in 1949 a dozen Western nations formed an alliance called **NATO†** that relied on

---

Holland, the name of the most well-known region of the Netherlands, is a name that is often applied to the whole country.

†NATO, the North Atlantic Treaty Organization, initially included Belgium, Britain, Canada, Denmark, France, Iceland, Italy, Luxembourg, the Netherlands, Norway, Portugal, and the United States, with additional members joining later. Its members are committed to collective defense if one or more is attacked by an outside force.

Legend:
- Postwar Occupation zones in Germany and Austria
- Churchill's original "iron curtain", 1946
- Eventual "iron curtain", 1955-1989

EAST GERMANY

French Sector | East Berlin | EAST GERMANY

British Sector

West Berlin | Soviet Sector

U.S. Sector

Divided Berlin
— Berlin Wall (1961-1989)

NORWAY

SWEDEN

North Sea | DENMARK

Copenhagen

U.S. Zone

NETHERLANDS | Soviet Zone | Stettin (Szczecin)

Amsterdam | British Zone | Berlin

Brussels | EAST GERMANY | Warsaw

BELGIUM | Bonn | POLAND

LUXEMBOURG | WEST GERMANY

FRANCE | French Zone | U.S. Zone | Prague | CZECHOSLOVAKIA

Soviet Zone

SWITZERLAND | U.S. Zone | Vienna

Geneva | Bern | French Zone | AUSTRIA | Budapest

British Zone | HUNGARY

Trieste | ROMANIA

Belgrade | Bucharest

ITALY | YUGOSLAVIA | BULGARIA

Corsica (France) | Sofia

Rome

UNION OF SOVIET SOCIALIST REPUBLICS

0   500   1000 Kilometers
0   500   1000 Miles

Map 2.2.   Divided Germany and Divided Europe, 1945–1955

US military (and nuclear) might to deter a Soviet attack. The Americans thus formally agreed to protect and defend Western Europe's imperial powers, while also extending US power into Europe on a permanent basis.* That same year, as the German occupation zones gave way to

---

*To some extent, US actions in Western Europe mirrored those of the Soviets in Eastern Europe. The Americans maintained military forces in the West, as the Soviets did in the East, and even worked covertly to influence elections in Italy and France to ensure the victory of pro-American, anticommunist parties. In that limited sense, Soviet imperialism in Eastern Europe was countered by a form of US imperialism in the West.

separate capitalist West German and Communist East German regimes, the USSR tested its own atomic bomb, ushering in a nuclear arms race between the Americans and Soviets, adding immensely to the potential dangers of the Cold War.

By then the West's old colonial empires were beginning to recede, especially in Asia, where the Americans, British, Dutch, and French, ousted by Japan during World War II, diverged on how to deal with their old colonies after the Japanese were beaten. In 1946, honoring an earlier pledge, the United States granted independence to its former Philippine commonwealth. In 1947, weary of war and overseas commitments and worn down by Gandhi's nonviolent resistance campaign, the British did the same for India, reluctantly divided into two new hostile states: the Hindu-led Republic of India and Islamic Pakistan. In 1949 the Netherlands, having failed in a four-year fight to reclaim its Dutch East Indies colony, relented and recognized it as the new nation of Indonesia.

Elsewhere, however, the Cold War and Communism complicated the anti-imperial struggle. In Indochina, the French, eager to regain their prewar imperial power status, fought a long brutal war (1946–1954) against the Vietminh, an independence movement led by Vietnam's Ho Chi Minh. Since Ho was a Communist, the United States, which had pressured the Dutch to withdraw from Indonesia, supported France against the Vietminh in what proved an unsuccessful bid to thwart the Communist advance that seemed to be engulfing Asia—especially when in 1949 the Chinese Communists prevailed in a three-year civil war against China's old Nationalist regime. The logic of America's anticommunist crusade led it to side with French imperialism as a lesser evil. This logic also led the United States to maintain a global array of military, naval, and air bases, thereby projecting US power throughout the world. The Americans claimed that these bases were intended to defend democracy against Soviet expansionism and not to defend imperialism per se, but they nonetheless provided a basis for the global extension of US imperial power.

Meanwhile, Communism's victory in China, the world's most populous country, sent shock waves across the Western world and fueled fears in the United States that the West was losing the Cold War. Hence in 1950, when war broke out in Korea, a former Japanese colony that had been divided in 1945 into Soviet and American occupation zones, the United States and its allies sent forces to fight for the US-backed South against the Communist North, which in turn was later aided by troops from Communist China. As the Cold War's first major military conflict, the Korean War (1950–1953) set the stage for a series of limited wars that would follow, and wound up in a deadlock in 1953 with an armistice that kept Korea divided largely along prewar lines (see chapter 3).

By this time, both Cold War superpowers had undergone leadership changes. In January 1953 Dwight Eisenhower, a general who had led Allied forces in Western Europe during World War II, took over as US president. Although he had campaigned on promises to "roll back the iron curtain" and "liberate the captive nations" of Eastern Europe, he and his aides—most notably Secretary of State John Foster Dulles—effectively wound up continuing the "containment" of Communism promised in the Truman Doctrine. Aligning with and aiding anticommunist movements and regimes, they set up a network of client states and allies, while relying heavily on US nuclear might to deter Soviet expansionism. The United States thus accepted the reality of Soviet imperial rule in Eastern Europe, but fought to keep it from spreading, by combating Communist efforts to make inroads in emerging nations seeking liberation from Western imperial rule.

Meanwhile, in March 1953 the death of longtime Soviet leader Joseph Stalin sparked a succession struggle that soon led to the ascendancy of Nikita Khrushchev, who would serve as the main Soviet leader from 1954 to 1964. A crude and boisterous self-educated man with peasant roots, Khrushchev believed that Soviet socialism could prevail in its contest with capitalism—in part by bolstering Soviet strength and in part by supporting the global struggle against Western capitalist imperialism. But he also supported Soviet imperialism with a 1955 alliance called the **Warsaw Pact**, embracing Eastern Europe's Communist regimes and providing cover for continuing Soviet colonial control over them (map 2.3).

As the nuclear arms race continued, with both sides developing thermonuclear weapons and long-range bombers and missiles to deliver them against the other side, Khrushchev, concluding that nuclear war would be unwinnable and unthinkable, called for **"peaceful coexistence"** with the capitalist West.[12] He met with Eisenhower and other Western leaders in Geneva in 1955, traveled through the United States in 1959, and was set to take part in a Paris summit conference with Western leaders in May 1960—until the shooting down of an American U-2 spy plane over Soviet territory on the eve of the summit, combined with Eisenhower's admission that he had ordered this flight and his refusal to apologize, led Khrushchev and the Soviets to scuttle the conference.

At the same time, however, Khrushchev opted for indirect confrontation in what would be called the **Third World***—the nations of Asia, the Middle East, Africa, and Latin America that had emerged or were emerging from Western colonial imperialism—a process often called **decoloni-**

---

*The term *Third World* was used during the Cold War (and hence in this book) for nations and peoples in Asia, the Middle East, Africa, and Latin America that did not belong directly to either of the two main Cold War camps. It has since fallen out of favor, and it is not really useful in the post–Cold War context.

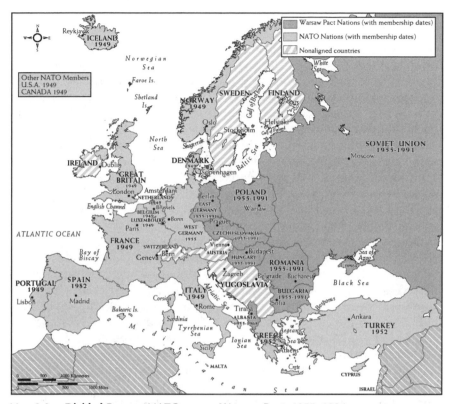

Map 2.3. Divided Europe: NATO versus Warsaw Pact, 1955–1991

zation. He even promoted limited "wars of national liberation," support-ing and aiding various rebellions against Western imperial power.

Under Khrushchev, then, the USSR extended aid not only to Commu-nist China but also to India, Indonesia, and other emerging new nations, even though they were not communist, in efforts to woo these former Western colonies and undermine Western influence. For similar reasons, it likewise gave assistance to Egypt and to various rebel groups and lib-eration movements elsewhere in Africa and Asia. And after Fidel Castro and his movement took power in Cuba in 1959, the Soviets not only supported his efforts to end American domination of that island but also sent troops and weapons to defend it from any potential US bid to oust the Castro regime—as well as to project Soviet power into the Western Hemisphere.

These policies helped the Soviets to win substantial support in the Third World, but they also caused serious problems for the USSR. They helped to drain the Soviet treasury of valuable resources and to engage the Soviets in an "aid to developing nations" contest with the United States, whose wealth and resources the USSR could not hope to match. And Soviet support for Cuba led to a humiliating setback in the Cuban Missile Crisis of 1962, after Khrushchev surreptitiously sent nuclear missiles to that island—in a risky bid to protect Cuba, counter the US lead in long-range missiles, and perhaps get the Western powers out of West Berlin—only to remove them under pressure applied by US President John F. Kennedy (see chapter 6).

At the same time, Soviet aid to new, noncommunist Third World nations rivaled and restrained the aid that the USSR could send to other Communist nations, and thus helped strain relations within the Communist world—especially with Communist China. In the 1950s the USSR provided the Chinese with substantial aid, but also gave ample aid to noncommunist India, which was China's traditional foe. Along with Khrushchev's denunciation of Stalin (who was still revered in China) in 1956 and his call for "peaceful coexistence" with the United States (which the Chinese then perceived as their main global enemy), his visits to India in 1955 and his pro-Indian "neutrality" during border clashes between China and India in 1959 and 1962 contributed greatly to the Soviet split with China in the early 1960s. By the late 1960s and early 1970s hostility with China would undermine Soviet global power and end any sense of worldwide socialist solidarity.

Even more embarrassing for Soviet "anti-imperialism" were revolts against Soviet-installed Communist regimes in East Germany (1953), Poland (1956), Hungary (1956), and Czechoslovakia (1968). Although they were put down, sometimes with brutal force, these rebellions highlighted the inconvenient reality that the USSR was itself an imperialist power, and they were seen by some as similar to the "wars of national liberation" that the Soviets elsewhere aided.* Moscow's hypocrisy was hard to hide, especially after 1968, when Khrushchev's successor Leonid Brezhnev, the top Soviet leader from 1964 to 1982, proclaimed what foes came to call the **Brezhnev Doctrine**: a claim that the Soviets had the right to intervene in other Communist countries to protect the overall interests of world socialism.[13] To the Chinese and others, this amounted to a bald assertion of Soviet imperial dominion, designed to thwart efforts to rebel against Soviet rule.

Meanwhile, Soviet support for Third World anticolonial movements and regimes, combined with US efforts to contain communism and counter Soviet expansionism, created Cold War conflicts and crises in various parts of the world. As both superpowers courted and supported allies

---

*The impulse behind these anti-Soviet revolts—freedom from foreign domination—was similar to the impulse behind Soviet-supported movements and regimes in Vietnam, Indonesia, Cuba, Central Africa, and elsewhere.

and clients throughout the Third World, their conflicts took on a variety of forms in Asia, the Middle East, Africa, and Latin America.

In Asia, after the Korean conflict, the Cold War and anti-imperialist struggle focused mainly in the south and southeast. The Soviets, as noted, provided aid to India—despite its status as a nonaligned democratic nation—while the Americans supported India's main rival, Pakistan— despite its status as a Muslim military dictatorship. In mainly Muslim Indonesia, the Soviets supported Sukarno, the country's founder and first president, who preached nonalignment but accepted Soviet aid—until he was ousted in 1967 by Suharto, a brutal US-backed military dictator. Clearly the Cold War was not simply a contest between Soviet-supported Communists and American-aided democracies.

The deadliest conflicts in Asia occurred in the former French colony of Indochina, which was divided in 1954 into Communist North Vietnam, anticommunist South Vietnam, neutral Laos, and neutral Cambodia. From 1965 through 1973, in a bid to prevent the unification of Vietnam by the Communists, the United States fought on the side of South Viet- nam, while the Vietnamese Communists received substantial aid from the Soviets and Communist China. Both claimed to be aiding their allies in an anticolonial struggle against the United States, depicted as having replaced France as the imperialist power in Southeast Asia. The Ameri- cans withdrew in 1973, but the war resumed the next year, and in 1975 Vietnam was united under Communist rule while Communist regimes also took control in Laos and Cambodia. But Communism's triumph did not end the area's agonies, as Cambodia's genocidal new regime killed perhaps two million of its people—until it was ousted by a 1978 invasion from Communist Vietnam. By 1979, when China briefly invaded Viet- nam, Cold War anti-imperialism in Asia had been replaced by conflicts among Communist countries (see chapter 3).

In the Middle East, made up mainly of Muslim nations in West Asia and North Africa, the struggle against imperialism involved battles not only against the British and French, who had earlier replaced the Ottoman Empire as the region's imperial powers, but also against Israel, a Jewish state formed in 1948 in what had been the British mandate of Palestine. Ironically the Israelis, who had fought for independence from British rule, were perceived by their Muslim neighbors as a new Western imperial power in the Middle East—and one that was backed by the imperialist Americans, British, and French. Defeated in a series of Arab-Israeli wars (1948, 1956, 1967, 1973), some Arab nations (such as Egypt, Syria, and Libya) sought and got Soviet aid—and arms from Communist Czecho- slovakia were used to help Algeria gain independence from France—but the Communists did not win many real friends in the devoutly Muslim Middle East.

Nor did the Western democracies, whose economies increasingly depended on oil from the Persian Gulf region. The United States formed friendships with oil-rich regimes in Iran and Saudi Arabia, but this did not stop these regimes from embargoing oil shipments to the Americans and their allies after they backed Israel in the October Arab-Israeli War of 1973. Nor did it prevent anti-Western Muslim clerics from overthrowing the US-backed regime in Iran in 1979. Perceiving both the Soviets and Western powers as imperialists, and seeing the Israelis as servants of Western imperialism, some Middle East leaders sought to gain by promoting pan-Arab nationalism and playing the Communist East against the capitalist West, while others eventually turned to terrorism and Islamist radicalism (see chapter 4).

In sub-Saharan Africa, most of which in the 1950s was still under European colonial rule, Soviet socialism had real appeal, partly because the Soviets (who had never colonized Africa) supported national liberation movements, partly because communism preached equality of all peoples, and partly because many African leaders saw the socialist command economy as the best and quickest way to modernize and improve their impoverished countries.[14] In their struggles against the British, French, Portuguese, and Belgians—all of whom were America's NATO allies—many African nationalists sought and secured Soviet aid, while seeking also to avoid coming into the Soviet orbit. Anxious to counter communism's spread and stop Soviet influence in Africa, the United States provided aid to African nationalists and nations while also urging its NATO allies to liberate their colonies peacefully and progressively. As a result, while some parts of Africa (such as Congo and Angola) became key Cold War battlegrounds, most African nations gained political independence by 1975. But economic independence was elusive, as impoverished new nations, needing massive aid, relied on outside assistance and support, sometimes even from former colonial rulers (see chapter 5).

The Cold War and the struggle against imperialism took a different form in Latin America than they did elsewhere, partly because most Latin American nations had gained political independence in the nineteenth century and partly because of the proximity of the United States, whose imperialist policies were based not on colonialism but on economic domination and occasional political interference. Determined to keep communism out of Latin America, the United States intervened in Guatemala in 1954, in the Dominican Republic in 1965, in Chile in the early 1970s, and in Nicaragua in the 1980s to combat or remove leftist regimes perceived as Marxist and anti-American. The Soviets at times sought to meddle, but only in Cuba did their meddling have any great significance—especially when Khrushchev sent nuclear missiles there and precipitated the Cuban Missile Crisis of

1962. Khrushchev's gamble failed, but the Castro regime survived. Otherwise, as "America's backyard," Latin America remained vulnerable to US dominance throughout the Cold War and beyond (see chapter 6).

THE END OF THE COLD WAR AND THE SOVIET EMPIRE

By the mid-to-late 1970s, the era of European colonialism was over, as most former colonies in Asia and Africa had gained political independence. But the Cold War and the anti-imperialist struggle nonetheless continued, taking on new shapes and going through new phases for the next decade and a half.

For a time in the 1970s the Cold War also seemed to be subsiding, as **détente**, or easing of global tensions, was pursued by both East and West. In 1972 US President Richard Nixon, seeking to exploit the rift between the Soviets and Chinese, traveled to Communist China, met with its leaders, and opened the door to better relations with them. Later that year, he went to Moscow, where he and Soviet leader Brezhnev signed agreements to curb the nuclear arms race and to enhance their scientific and cultural connections. The US withdrawal from Vietnam the next year, followed by Brezhnev's visit to America, seemed to signal that the Cold War was winding down, as did the 1975 Helsinki Accords—a set of agreements among thirty-five nations (including the United States and USSR) designed to stabilize European security.

Détente nonetheless had its limits, as the superpowers continued to back opposing sides during crises and conflicts in Asia, Africa, and the Middle East. And in 1979 the USSR invaded neighboring Afghanistan—a client state whose Marxist regime was threatened by revolt— shattering what was left of détente. Perceiving this Soviet invasion as a threat to Western oil shipments from the Persian Gulf, the Americans began a vast new arms buildup and sent aid to the Afghan rebels, who went on to wear down the USSR's forces in the lengthy Soviet-Afghan War (1979–1989).

In the early 1980s, then, the Cold War returned with full force. US President Ronald Reagan, a strident anticommunist, denounced détente and accelerated the arms race, hoping thereby to undermine the Soviet economy, which was much weaker than America's and thus much less able to support a costly arms buildup. To counter Soviet support for Third World national liberation movements, Reagan's administration (1981–1989) also aided anticommunist movements in Nicaragua, Ethiopia, Angola, and Afghanistan, supplying modern antiaircraft missiles to the anti-Soviet Afghan rebels. Each side used the other's imperialist behavior to justify its own.

By the mid-1980s, however, leadership changes in the USSR were altering the global dynamic. Brezhnev died in 1982, and his two short-lived successors had little impact, but in 1985 leadership passed to young and energetic Mikhail Gorbachev, who was anxious to make major changes. To improve the weak Soviet economy, he tried to incorporate some capitalistic incentives, freeing businesses and farms to set their own production and prices. In politics, he combated government corruption, encouraged open critical discussion, and even allowed some contested democratic elections.

In global affairs, Gorbachev went even further. To free up funding for his reforms, he cut back on military expenses and on aid for Cold War clients and sought drastic cuts in weapons and forces through negotiations with the West. He met several times with Reagan, and in 1987 the two leaders signed a treaty to eliminate midrange missiles. In 1988 he began withdrawing Soviet troops from Afghanistan and called on all nations to forsake the use of force and not to intervene in other countries. Along these lines, in 1989 he renounced the Brezhnev Doctrine, calling on Eastern Europe's Communist regimes to pursue their own paths without Soviet interference.

In making these changes, Gorbachev inadvertently undermined the Soviet Empire. No longer constrained by the threat of Soviet force, which had held it together for decades, the peoples of the Soviet Bloc initiated their own national liberation movements. Eastern European countries began working to rid themselves of their Communist rulers, and most of the ethnic republics that made up the USSR started seeking some sort of autonomy. Gorbachev vainly sought to hold it all together through persuasion and negotiation rather than by force. The result was a stunning transformation in a few short years: in 1989 the peoples of Eastern Europe overthrew their Communist regimes; in 1990 Germany was reunified under West German rule; and in 1991 the USSR disintegrated into fifteen separate states. One of history's most powerful empires was gone, torn apart by forces that had much in common with the struggle against imperialism elsewhere (see chapter 7).

The Cold War era thus ended with the disintegration of the Soviet Empire, its demise brought about in part by a struggle against imperialism similar to those that had earlier undermined Europe's old colonial empires. Those struggles, which had interconnected and combined with the Cold War in Asia, the Middle East, Africa, and Latin America during this same era, are described and analyzed in the chapters that follow.

3

❧

"Long Live the Victory of People's War"

Anti-Imperialism and the Cold War in Asia

On Wednesday, August 15, 1945, the voice of divinity spoke to Japan by radio. In a prerecorded message, Emperor Hirohito, revered by his people as a god, informed them that his government had decided to accept the Allied Powers' declaration calling for Japan's surrender. The Empire of Japan, which had earlier annexed Korea, occupied much of China, and ousted the French, Dutch, British, and Americans from their imperial possessions in Southeast Asia, was clearly coming to an end. So too, it seemed, was imperialism in Asia.

Or was it? The United States, it is true, fulfilled an earlier pledge of political independence for its former Philippine commonwealth in 1946. And the British, weary of war and of overseas commitments, soon began to dismantle their Asian empire. But the Dutch and French, eager to regain their prewar prosperity and status, sought to recover their resource-rich Asian colonies. Colonial resistance to these efforts, and struggles for power in China and Korea following Japan's withdrawal, soon became entwined with the emerging Cold War, which started in Europe but spread quickly to Asia.

THE COLD WAR'S ORIGINS AND ASIA

The Cold War began in Europe, largely because of the way that World War II ended there, with Soviet forces occupying Eastern Europe, and Germany divided into occupation zones by the Soviets in the east and the British, French, and Americans in the west. Devastated by the wartime

German invasion, and anxious to protect itself against future recurrence, the USSR created a buffer zone of "friendly" (Communist-controlled) regimes in Eastern Europe, using rigged elections and brutal, heavy-handed tactics. Upset by Communism's westward spread, the Americans in 1947 decided to try to contain it by supporting governments resisting Communism (the Truman Doctrine) and extending ample economic aid to war-torn European nations (the Marshall Plan). In 1948, as the Western powers moved toward unifying western Germany, the Soviet army block-aded their occupation zones in West Berlin. This action led the United States and Britain to supply that city by airlift for eleven months, and in 1949, with ten other Western nations, they formed an alliance called NATO that relied on US military (and nuclear) might to deter a Soviet attack. That same year, as the German occupation zones gave way to capitalist West German and Communist East German regimes, the USSR tested its own atomic bomb, ushering in a nuclear arms race between the Americans and Soviets, leaders of the heavily armed and hostile capitalist and Communist Cold War camps (see chapter 2).

The Cold War's origins in Asia, although influenced by these develop-ments, were also rooted in the way the war ended there. On August 6 and August 9, 1945, hoping to end the war quickly without an Allied invasion of Japan—partly to save American lives and partly to preclude the Soviets from occupying part of that country—the United States dropped atomic bombs on two key Japanese cities. The Soviets declared war on Japan on August 8 and then invaded Manchuria* and northern Korea, taking them over from the Japanese, whose forces elsewhere continued to occupy much of eastern China and Southeast Asia when the war formally ended on September 2. Within a few years, all these places would play key roles in the emerging Cold War.

ANTI-WESTERN INSURGENCIES IN SOUTHEAST ASIA

Since the 1800s most of Southeast Asia had been ruled by Western imperi-alists. The Dutch governed the East Indies, now known as Indonesia. The British ruled Burma, Malaya, Singapore, and northern Borneo. A French colony in Indochina embraced Laos, Vietnam, and Cambodia. And the Americans held the Philippine Islands. Anti-imperialist movements had emerged in all these places but had made little real progress prior to 1941.

Then came World War II. In its early stages, in a series of stunning con-quests, the Japanese had overrun and occupied these colonies. Welcomed

---

*A large and resource-rich province in northeastern China, Manchuria had been occupied by Japan since 1932.

at first as liberators by many Southeast Asians, they had soon imposed their own brutal form of imperialist oppression. Their eventual defeat in 1945 gave anti-imperialists in these colonies a chance to assert independence. But their efforts were complicated by the old colonial powers, who sought in many cases to restore their imperial rule, and by Communist involvements that created Cold War connections.

The Western imperialists responded in different ways to the postwar situation. The Americans, as noted above, formally freed the Philippine Islands in 1946. The British, moving to reduce their overseas involvements, reimposed their rule but also claimed to be preparing their colonies for eventual independence. But the Dutch and French, eager to restore their prewar wealth and power, attempted to reassert colonial control. None of these approaches succeeded in averting violence and Cold War complications.

In the Philippines, during World War II under Japanese occupation, a resistance group called the People's Anti-Japanese Army (*Hukbong Bayan Laban sa Hapon*), had formed. After liberation (1944) and independence (1946), now calling itself the People's Liberation Army (*Hukbong Mapagplayang Bayan*), it rebelled against the US-backed government with the support of the Philippine Communist Party. But in the 1950s, with massive US aid, Defense Secretary (and later President) Ramon Magsaysay defeated the "Huk" revolt. Deterred by the American military bases in the former US possession, the Soviets did little to help the "Huks."

In Burma, formerly a province of British colonial India, the liberation movement was led by Aung San, who was also an early Burmese Communist leader. In 1942 he helped Japan oust the British; but by 1945, dismayed by Japan's repressive rule, he helped the British end it and return. The next year, after he broke with the Communists, the British made him premier of its Burma crown colony, and in 1947 Britain agreed to grant Burma independence within a year. That summer, however, Aung San and six of his cabinet ministers were murdered, thereby making him a martyr and national hero. Independence came in 1948 under Aung San's successor U Nu, but it was met by a Communist insurgency, sparking a complex civil war that lasted off and on throughout the Cold War.*

In Malaya as in Burma, after World War II, the British sought to restore colonial rule while granting some local autonomy and also combating Communism. In Malaya as in Burma, the Communists launched a revolt

---

*In 1989 the military regime then in power changed the country's name from Burma to Myanmar. In 1991 the late Aung San's daughter, Aung San Suu Kyi, received the Nobel Peace Prize for her efforts to restore democracy, which finally resulted in free elections in 2015. In 2016 Aung San Suu Kyi assumed the new post of State Counsellor, a position roughly equivalent to Prime Minister. Her government, paradoxically, then intensified persecution of the country's long-oppressed Rohingya minority.

in 1948. In Malaya, however, the rebellion came while Britain was still in control. Responding to a brutal British manhunt, the rebels resorted to guerrilla attacks, which caused great damage but failed to cripple the economy. By 1957 the rebellion was isolated to jungle areas, and in 1956 the British granted independence without incident. By 1960 the insurrection apparently was over.*

Although these revolts had Communist connections and thus Cold War implications, they were triggered largely by local conditions and by local leaders, acting on their own but to some extent inspired by Soviet anti-imperialist assertions and by concurrent Communist advances in China and Indochina. The Americans and British, eager to counter Communism and maintain access to key resources such as rubber and tin, worked effectively to combat and contain the insurrections. The Soviets, although anxious to undermine their imperialist foes and signal their support for anticolonial liberation movements, provided encouragement but little material assistance, treating them mainly as marginal clashes in a complex global conflict. More connected and consequential to the Cold War were the coinciding conflicts, discussed below, in China, Korea, Indonesia, and Indochina.

THE CHINESE CIVIL WAR

The most pivotal and consequential of these conflicts was the Chinese Civil War (1946–1949), pitting Nationalists against Communists, two bitter rival groups contending for dominance in China. The National People's Party (*Guomindang*), founded in 1912, had come to power in 1928 under Jiang Jieshi (Chiang Kai-shek†), its military leader. Commonly called the Nationalists, they had earlier worked with the Chinese Communist Party (CCP), founded in 1921, against Western imperialists and capitalists who dominated China's industrial seaports. But Jiang, who developed close ties with the West, had turned against the CCP in the mid-1920s, staging massacres and extermination campaigns in an effort to destroy it. Led by the charismatic Mao Zedong, a talented young Marxist who sought to inspire a revolution based on China's rural peasant masses, in the mid-1930s the CCP fled on the fabled "Long March" to the wilderness of northwestern China, where it set up a peasant-based socialist society centered at the town of Yan'an. In China's long war

---

*In 1963 Malaya merged with Singapore and the former British colonies in northern Borneo to form the new nation of Malaysia. In 1965 Singapore withdrew and became an independent republic. In 1968 the Communists in Malaysia renewed their rebellion, which lasted until 1989 but achieved no enduring success.

†"Jiang Jieshi" is a modernized (pinyin) version of his name in Mandarin Chinese. Throughout his career he was known in the West as Chiang Kai-shek, an older (Wade-Giles) transliteration of his name in Cantonese Chinese.

against Japan (1937–1945), the Communists and Nationalists outwardly maintained a "United Front" against Japanese occupation forces, while also vying with each other. Once the world war ended, their conflict soon became an all-out civil war (map 3.1).

The US-backed Nationalists at first seemed to gain the upper hand and even captured the CCP's Yan'an base in 1947. But by then the Communists had retreated to Manchuria, where they gained access to tens of thousands of Japanese weapons, which had been taken by the Soviets during their occupation of that province in 1945–1946. These weapons and widespread support for the CCP from local peasants, who were impressed by its earlier reforms in Yan'an, eventually helped turn the tide. The battle for Manchuria

Map 3.1.   The Chinese Civil War, 1946–1949

raged from 1946 through 1948, when the Communists' triumph there gave them the momentum to conquer the rest of mainland China in 1949. The Nationalists fled to the island of Taiwan where, under US protection, their regime survived and continued to call itself China's legitimate government. But reality spoke otherwise: on October 1, 1949, when Mao Zedong proclaimed the formation of the People's Republic of China (PRC), the world's most populous country was clearly under Communist rule.

The Communist victory in China effectively transformed the Cold War from a European standoff into a global confrontation. In 1950 the new People's Republic signed a Treaty of Friendship and Alliance with the USSR, joining the world Communist crusade against the Western "capitalist imperialists" and vilifying the United States—especially when it (and the **United Nations***) continued to recognize the Nationalists on Taiwan as China's rightful regime. The United States, appalled by Communism's rapid spread and racked with Red scares and recriminations over "who lost China," resolved to counter Communism forcefully in Asia as well as in Europe. Japan, America's erstwhile enemy, now became its close Asian ally (as the two nations signed a security treaty in 1951) and a bastion of capitalist democracy, reemerging within a few decades as Asia's preeminent economic power. And the Cold War soon became a shooting war in Korea.

DECOLONIZATION AND COLD WAR IN KOREA

In theory, Korea was decolonized at the end of World War II with the surrender of Japan, which for thirty-five years had been Korea's colonial ruler. In practice, decolonization in Korea, as in other Asian colonies that later achieved political independence, was a convoluted and arduous process that brought neither national unity nor freedom from outside interference. And in Korea, as elsewhere, the Cold War played a key role, as internal factions aligned with and sought support from competing Cold War camps.

Japanese rule in Korea (1910–1945) was exceedingly harsh and exploitative, sparking the formation of several anti-Japanese national liberation movements. As Japan cracked down, many Koreans fled abroad to places such as China and Hawaii, where they often embraced Western democratic and nationalist ideas. Others, however, disenchanted

---

*The United Nations (UN), headquartered in New York, was founded in 1945 to keep the peace, prevent aggression, and promote cooperation in solving world problems among its member nations, which eventually came to include most countries of the world. It has a General Assembly (UNGA), with delegates from all member nations, and a Security Council (UNSC), with five permanent members—Britain, China (initially the Nationalist regime on Taiwan; since 1971, the People's Republic of China), France, the United States, and Russia (initially the USSR)—and a number of rotating temporary members, elected by the General Assembly.

with the imperialist West, went to Soviet Russia, where they started a Korean Communist Party in 1925. Hopes for independence dimmed in the 1930s, as the Japanese occupied neighboring Manchuria and expanded into China, but they brightened in the early 1940s, as Japan overreached its military might by attacking the United States and Britain. In 1945, when Japan surrendered to the Allied Powers, its imperial rule in Korea came to an end.

But the fall of Japan came too quickly for Koreans. The nationalists, still living abroad, did not achieve their country's liberation—that was done by the Americans (who defeated the Japanese) and the Soviets (whose armies moved into northern Korea at the end of the war). Alarmed by this rapid Soviet advance, the United States effectively divided Korea along the 38th parallel of latitude, ordering Japanese troops north of that line to surrender to the USSR, and those south of it to submit to the US Army (soon to have a presence there). Korea, like Germany, was thus partitioned into occupation zones.

As a result, instead of gaining true independence, Korea was split between the two Cold War camps, with a Soviet client state in the north and a US client regime in the south (map 3.2). In the north, Kim Il-Sung, a young Korean Communist who had spent time in the USSR, led a Soviet-supported provisional government that in 1948 became a separate state called the Democratic People's Republic of Korea (or simply North Korea). Ruthlessly repressive and resolute, Kim was determined to unify Korea under Communist rule. In the south that same year, an aging nationalist called Syngman Rhee, a Princeton-educated Christian convert who had lived for decades in US cities and Hawaii, became president of the Republic of Korea (South Korea). An authoritarian anticommunist who used harsh methods to suppress left-wing dissent, he headed a regime that had US backing and held Korea's UN seat.

As each regime hoped to govern all Korea, the situation quickly proved unstable. In 1949, amid recurrent raids by each side against the other, Kim Il-Sung pressed the Soviets to support a North Korean invasion of South Korea. Soviet leader Joseph Stalin initially demurred, reluctant to risk a conflict with the Americans in East Asia. But events in 1949 and early 1950—including the withdrawal of US forces from South Korea, Soviet acquisition of the atomic bomb, American failure to intervene against the Communists in China, and US statements suggesting a similar reluctance to intercede in Korea*—apparently persuaded the Soviet dictator

---

*In a speech in early 1950 US Secretary of State Dean Acheson described an American defense perimeter in Asia that included Japan and the Philippines but not South Korea nor Taiwan, leaving the impression that the United States was perhaps not fully committed to South Korea's defense. See "Excerpts from Acheson's Speech to the National Press Club, 12 January 1950," in Edward H. Judge and John W. Langdon, eds., *The Cold War through Documents: A Global History*, 3rd ed. (Lanham, MD: Rowman & Littlefield, 2018), 85–87.

that such a risk was worth taking. In spring of 1950 he authorized Kim to proceed with his invasion, as long as Kim could get Mao's support as well. Ever the cautious overlord, Stalin agreed to provide war supplies but rejected all-out Soviet armed involvement.

The resulting Korean War (1950–1953) commenced with the North's invasion of the South on June 25, 1950 (map 3.2). Even as the Communist forces quickly overran much of South Korea, however, the Americans promptly came to its defense. Staggered by the recent Communist vic-

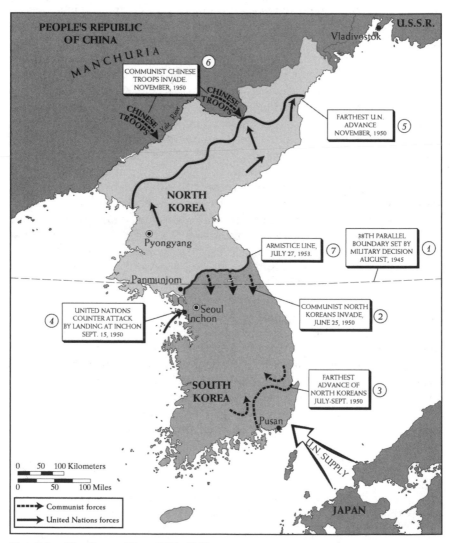

Map 3.2. The Korean War, 1950–1953

tory in China, and badgered by critics for failing to prevent it, President Harry Truman's government decided that it could not stand by and let another nation go Communist. Working through the United Nations,* the Americans assembled and led a multinational UN coalition that, by October of that year, pushed the Communists out of the South and deep into the North. But at that point China's new Communist regime, fearful that the fall of North Korea would pose a threat both to its survival and to the cause of world Communism, sent in several hundred thousand "volunteers" to "assist the Korean people's war of liberation" and "repel the invasion launched by the American imperialists."[1] As the reinforced Communist armies drove the UN forces back toward the South, and the conflict then bogged down into a stalemate in 1951, the Americans opted not to widen the war but to seek a negotiated settlement. After two more years of debilitating deadlock, an armistice was arranged along a cease-fire line not far from the 38th parallel.

Korea thus remained divided throughout the Cold War and beyond. In the North, Kim Il-Sung reigned over a Stalinist police state, complete with state-run industries, collective farms, and powerful military forces, until his death in 1994. Depicting the South Koreans as lackeys of US imperialism and the 1953 armistice as a victory over that imperialism, his regime was backed by both the Soviets and Chinese but fully beholden to neither. He was succeeded by his son (Kim Jong-Il) and later his grandson (Kim Jong-Un), creating the odd anomaly of a Communist dynasty, economically impoverished but militarily powerful, with nuclear weapons and missiles that could threaten South Korea, Japan, and even the United States.

Supported and defended by American arms (and thus to some extent a US client state), South Korea likewise endured decades of dictatorship, including the repressive and corrupt regimes of Syngman Rhee (1948–1960) and General Park Chung-hee (1961–1979).† Unlike the North, however, it achieved economic prosperity, thanks to Park's strong support for industry and trade, combined with US aid and access to global markets. Student-led protests in the 1980s finally compelled the regime to allow free elections, and by the early twenty-first century, despite endemic corruption scandals and dangerous tensions with the North, South Korea had become a flourishing capitalist democracy and global economic powerhouse—in striking contrast to its destitute, despotic northern neighbor.

---

*Earlier in 1950, to protest the UN's refusal to admit the new People's Republic of China in place of the old Nationalist regime (which had fled to Taiwan), the USSR had withdrawn its UN delegation. It was thus not in a position to counter US efforts in the UN on behalf of intervention in South Korea.

†Park Chung-hee was assassinated in 1979. In 2013 his daughter, Park Geun-Hye, was elected president. In 2016 she was impeached on corruption charges, and in 2017 she was removed from office.

Meanwhile, Korea's inconclusive conflict and its continuing division had set a pattern that prevailed—with significant variations—in colonial and postcolonial nations of Asia and elsewhere. Nationalist forces, engaged in the process of national liberation and early nation-building, typically split into conflicting elements supported by opposing superpowers. As often as not, seeking resources badly needed to build their new nations and fight their local foes, one side turned to the Soviets for aid and the other sought US support, combining Cold War and anti-imperial efforts into complex and convoluted conflicts that ravaged Asian nations for decades.

DECOLONIZATION AND COLD WAR IN INDONESIA

Indonesia—known as the Dutch (or Netherlands) East Indies before 1949—had long been a pivotal Dutch possession due to its rich resources, which included spices, coffee, rubber, tin, and petroleum oil. For the Dutch, the East Indies were both a symbol of their maritime supremacy in centuries past and the foundation of Dutch economic strength in the twentieth century—particularly due to the increasing importance of oil and rubber. After military defeat and grinding occupation by the Germans during World War II, the Dutch counted on the Indies to help the mother country recover economically. A Dutch proverb put it succinctly: *Indië verloren, rampspoed geboren,* "if the Indies are lost, misfortune is born." But the Indies would indeed be lost, in a four-year war (1945–1949) that cost the Netherlands more than three thousand dead, a great deal of money, and considerable self-respect.

That was a high price to pay, but the Dutch East Indies seemed worth it. Its strategically crucial location, straddling the maritime passages connecting the Indian and Pacific Oceans, was compellingly attractive to Europeans. But it was also awash in petroleum and laden with renewable commodities like rubber, coffee, indigo, and sugar. The Dutch, who had ruled the region since the 1600s, at first indirectly through their East India Company and then directly after 1816, established a cultivation system designed to produce export crops at the lowest possible cost—intended mainly to benefit the mother country. This system reduced the Indies' peasants to a state resembling serfdom and triggered widespread famine in the 1840s.

From a profit perspective, the suffering of the native inhabitants was immaterial to the Netherlands, which used the cultivation system's revenues to pay off the East India Company's debts and enrich the national treasury. Between 1831 and 1877, profits from the Indies averaged more than 30 percent of total government expenditures, leaving no doubt about the colony's value to the mother country. From a moral perspective, however, many of the Dutch began objecting to the exploitation and degradation of the Indonesians,* and these protests led to the replacement of the cultivation system in 1870 by less onerous alternatives. By the early twentieth century, the Dutch government began educating Indonesians and proposed a number of paternalistic reforms.

An old cliché holds that the most dangerous moment for a bad government comes when it decides to reform. The new Dutch flexibility, especially in education, created a native elite that resented Dutch rule over Indonesians, most of whom were Muslims. Rather than rejecting Islam and adopting pro-Western values, as the Dutch had hoped, this indigenous elite blended Islam with nationalism to create a group of nationalist leaders who turned Western values *against* Dutch colonialism. As a prominent historian has noted, "The whole tradition of Western political and social thought seemed to justify the inclination of nationalistic students to oppose Dutch political and economic subjugation."[2]

In the 1920s several Indonesian nationalist movements arose, including the *Partai Komunis Indonesia* (Indonesian Communist Party, or PKI) and the *Partai Nasional Indonesia* (Indonesian National Party, or PNI), the second of which came to pose a major threat to Dutch rule. Headed by a Dutch-educated civil engineer named Sukarno,† a man with formidable leadership skills, the PNI quickly became the main anti-imperialist force in the Indies, thereby alarming the Dutch. As a result, Sukarno, a gifted speaker and romantic revolutionary who sought to combine nationalism, Marxism, and Islam (the Indies' dominant religion) into a unifying and liberating force, spent much of the 1930s under Dutch arrest and internal exile.

Then in 1940 Nazi Germany overran the Netherlands, and in 1942 Japan conquered the Dutch East Indies, intending to use their resources to fuel Japan's war machine. Impressed by the stunningly swift victory of the Japanese (who were Asians like themselves) over the Dutch imperialists (who were not), local nationalists hailed the invaders as liberators. Japan promptly interned nearly all Dutch citizens living in the Indies, thereby vacating skilled positions that went to the educated Indonesian elites. But their new status was precarious: if Japan lost the war and Dutch rule resumed, these elites not only would lose their newly gained economic status but they also would be condemned by the Dutch as traitorous collaborators with the Japanese enemy.

Indonesians is a modern and general term for the various indigenous peoples who live in the East Indies. We use the terms *Indonesia* and *East Indies* interchangeably.

†"Sukarno" was his full name. A British journalist, fearing that Western readers would think that he had omitted Sukarno's first name, assigned him the name "Ahmad," but this has only served to confuse modern readers.

Sukarno thus worked with the Japanese, as the Indies' new rulers, while also urging them to establish an independent government there. He even helped them to requisition food and forced labor, which caused extensive hardship as the Japanese proved every bit as exploitative as the Dutch had been. But they also offered a bargain to Sukarno and his PNI colleague, the Western-educated Muhammad Hatta: assist Japan's war effort and in return receive its support for Indonesian nationalism, along with a promise of independence once the war was over. The Dutch denounced Sukarno and Hatta as collaborators, which they certainly were, but they were also dedicated nationalists who secretly supported underground resistance movements while agitating for independence throughout the Indonesian archipelago. Their behavior in 1942–1945 defies simplistic categorization.

By March 1945 Japan was losing the war. The United States was moving toward the Japanese home islands, planning to take Iwo Jima and Okinawa for use as staging areas for eventual invasion. But the Japanese, unaware of these plans and fearing a US invasion of Indonesia, tried to buy Indonesian goodwill by setting up an Indonesian Independence Preparatory Committee, led by Sukarno with Hatta as vice chairman. August 24 was fixed as the date for independence, but to avoid being labeled as Japanese stooges, the Committee decided to declare independence on August 17—two days after Japan's emperor agreed to surrender to the Allies. Sukarno thus issued a brief declaration of Indonesian independence, and the next day he became president of the newly proclaimed Indonesian republic.

The Dutch had other ideas. Rejecting Sukarno and Hatta as traitorous puppets of Japanese imperialism, and eager to regain its prewar political and economic status, the Netherlands government decided that the best solution was to restore *Dutch* imperialism!

Doing so would not be easy. Unlike France and Britain, the Netherlands had not been a major world power since the seventeenth century. Taking what little military strength it had and projecting it halfway around the world would be challenging under the best of circumstances. The Dutch had ruled the Indies more by inertia than by coercion, and after the Japanese occupation, Indonesian nationalists deployed a 120,000-man army that Japan had encouraged them to develop in order to defend the islands. No prospect of a *peaceful* resumption of Dutch authority existed.

Nor was there any prospect of Dutch withdrawal. By 1945 the Netherlands claimed that one sixth of its *total* national wealth was invested in the Indies. No other European colonial power was so utterly bound up with its empire. Beyond hard economic realities lay the intangible realm of self-respect. The Netherlands with the Indies was a major imperial power, but without them it would be insignificant in a postwar world dominated by the Americans and Soviets. Given these factors, the only option remaining was war.

But the Netherlands had been occupied by Germany for five years and had no functioning army. It would have to rebuild one. Britain had one, and British forces were dispatched to take over the Indies from the Japanese, but only after the United States, reluctant to become involved in a messy colonial dispute, transferred its jurisdiction in the region* to London. Six weeks lapsed between Sukarno's proclamation of independence and the arrival of British forces. That gave Sukarno and Hatta the chance to consolidate their authority throughout Indonesia. When the British arrived on September 29, they were startled to find an effectively functioning nationalist government asserting its sovereignty over an independent Indonesia and enjoying wide public backing.

The British commanders at once concluded that the Dutch would have no choice but to negotiate with the nationalists. The Dutch at once concluded that the British were questioning Dutch sovereignty over the Indies. The British government assured the Dutch that their suspicions were groundless, but by mid-October it had come to accept the logic of its commanders on the scene. This left British forces in an untenable position. The Dutch considered Sukarno and Hatta war criminals and asserted that their so-called Indonesian Republic was actually a Japanese puppet state. Although The Hague† was willing to consider an evolutionary path to independence, it adopted the unrealistic stance of refusing to negotiate with Sukarno or any other official of the republic's government. So the British were left with the onerous duty of defending a policy they considered foolish, and they were not surprised when fighting broke out in late October.

Now the British were seeking to hand this explosive situation off to the Dutch, who were both unrealistic and militarily weak. The Dutch estimated that seventy-five thousand troops would be needed to regain control of the Indies, but they projected deployment of only thirty thousand by October 1946. This left them dependent on the British, who made it clear that their support was itself dependent on Dutch willingness to talk with the nationalists. Negotiations began in February 1946 and continued sporadically for the next several years.

At this juncture the Indies became a factor in the Cold War. The United States was unwilling to endorse Dutch colonialism, but also refused to

---

*US General Douglas MacArthur's Southwest Asia Command had military jurisdiction over the Dutch East Indies.

†In histories of this era, it is common and convenient to use a country's capital as a short term for its government. The Soviet government is thus often called Moscow, the British government London, and the US government Washington. Here we refer to the Dutch government as The Hague, which is the capital of the Netherlands.

contest Dutch sovereignty over the Indies. Since colonial possession and sovereignty amounted to the same thing, Washington's positions were irreconcilable. As negotiations plodded through the summer of 1946 without progress, the US State Department became concerned that the Soviets would place the Indies question on the United Nations agenda in an effort to embarrass the West. American and British pressure combined to push the Dutch to accept nationalist authority de facto on the Indonesian island of Sumatra, a concession that led quickly to a cease-fire and its institutionalization in the Linggadjati Agreement of November 1946. A few days later the last British forces withdrew from Indonesia. London had pursued a balanced policy and had succeeded in pushing the Dutch into negotiations. Now the power vacuum left by Britain's departure would have to be filled by the United States if further talks were to prove fruitful.

In 1945 Washington had taken a hands-off approach to the Indies, but by 1947 the Cold War had led it to develop a global definition of US security interests. In particular, the colonial war in French Indochina (below), which broke out shortly after the Linggadjati Agreement, gave Southeast Asia a more prominent place in the US assessment of the danger posed by international Communism. A rapid transition to Indonesian independence and stability would deny Communism fertile territory for regional revolution. But with the Cold War intensifying in Europe, suddenly the Netherlands became part of a projected defense against a hypothetical Soviet invasion of Western Europe. It was not in US interests to alienate the Dutch* by bullying them over Indonesia. It would be far better to bring world opinion to bear, and to that end, the Americans began thinking of bringing the issue to the United Nations, which they dominated at that time.

In July 1947, when the Dutch broke the Linggadjati Agreement by launching a full-scale military assault on the Indonesian Republic, Washington was startled and dismayed. The Dutch troops, having grown by then to more than one hundred thousand, made short work of Indonesia's less disciplined army. By this time the United States had announced the European Recovery Program, better known as the Marshall Plan, in an effort to jump-start the economic reconstruction of a continent Americans referred to as "war-torn Europe." The Netherlands was expected to receive ample aid under this program, and the Dutch were desperate for it. Now the Americans had something the Dutch wanted (Marshall Plan aid), and the Dutch could give the Americans something *they* wanted (an independent, stable, non-Communist Indonesia). The bargaining, however, would prove difficult.

---

*The Dutch had been neutral in World War I and had unsuccessfully sought the same status in World War II. Washington did not want to encourage them to be neutral in the Cold War.

On August 1, 1947, the United States sponsored UN Security Council Resolution 27 calling for a new cease-fire in Indonesia. It was the first such directive ever issued by the UN, and its passage testified to the centrality of the Indonesian situation with regard to European recon- struction, at least as viewed by the Western states that dominated the UN. The resolution, and subsequent US offers to mediate the conflict, resulted in the Renville Agreement of January 17, 1948, an accord highly favorable to the Dutch. The United States, while unwilling publicly to endorse Dutch colonialism, saw Indonesia as essential to Dutch eco- nomic recovery and used all available means, both inside and outside the UN, to move the dispute toward a peaceful resolution that would guarantee continued Dutch access to the resources of the Indies.[3] The Cold War had moved US policy toward accepting some measure of continued Dutch imperial presence.

The Renville Agreement was in trouble from the start. The national- ists agreed to it only to buy time for further military preparations, while the Dutch would accept nothing less than restoration of full colonial rule, after which they would be willing to move gradually toward In- donesian independence. Capitalizing on the increasingly ominous Cold War, they repeatedly exaggerated the extent of Communist subversion of the nationalist movement in order to frighten Washington. The US State Department, however, began to suspect that to the extent that such Communist influence existed, its growth was attributable to The Hague's intransigent policy. This belief was strengthened in September 1948 when Hatta moved quickly and forcefully to suppress a Commu- nist uprising in eastern Java. His actions convinced the Americans that the republican government was anticommunist and that the Dutch were crying wolf.

Washington now came to view the Indonesian Republic as a fortress against Communism's spread. Given Mao's repeated victories in the Chinese Civil War (above) and France's lack of success in Indochina (below), this was not a trivial consideration. The United States began implying that if The Hague did not show more flexibility, its posture might negate the impact of Marshall Plan aid. Amazingly, this implica- tion (which diplomatically stopped short of threatening to cut off the aid) made the Dutch *more* rather than less rigid. On December 19, 1948, they shocked everyone by launching a second military assault and quickly captured Sukarno, Hatta, and half of their cabinet. By January 1, 1949, the Dutch controlled all major towns and cities on the Indonesian islands of Java and Sumatra.

This obvious repudiation of the Renville Agreement caused a tsunami of denunciation. Up to this point the crisis in the Indies had been viewed largely through Cold War great-power lenses. Now the Dutch action converted it into a manifestation of the struggle of colonized peoples to break free from imperialist oppression. The leaders of India, the Arab League,* and the newly independent Republic of the Philippines turned Allied wartime rhetoric against the Dutch: if Japanese imperialism was malignant, how could European imperialism be benign? Across the United States, public opinion was strongly pro-Indonesian, and the US government, which till then had tacitly supported Dutch colonialism while publicly maintaining neutrality, began to reassess its policy.

Several factors contributed to this reassessment, all arguably more influential than American public opinion. First, the Dutch offensive soon engendered widespread guerrilla resistance across Indonesia, despite the arrest of the republic's leaders. Second, the US State Department decided that continued Dutch intransigence could lead to the outcome it claimed to be working against: Communist control of the nationalist movement. Third, aroused by the concurrent Soviet blockade of Berlin, the US was moving toward creation of the North Atlantic alliance (NATO). Dutch participation would be essential, but Dutch conduct in Indonesia was embarrassing at best and deeply immoral at worst. Fourth, Dutch defiance of the UN threatened to undermine a cornerstone of US foreign policy. Finally, and most significantly, since US Marshall Plan aid to the Dutch in 1948 was roughly equal to their military expenses in Indonesia, it was difficult to avoid the conclusion that the United States was underwriting their colonialism, not their economic recovery.

Secretary of State Dean Acheson spoke diplomatically but unmistakably on March 31 to Dutch officials who had come to Washington to sign the NATO treaty: negotiate and settle with the nationalists, or face the probable loss of Marshall Plan aid. This threat, coupled with the Indonesian Republic's increasingly effective guerrilla resistance, cut the Gordian knot. Negotiations resumed on April 14, and Indonesian independence was formalized on December 27, 1949. The Netherlands had capitulated in the face of Cold War realities and nationalist perseverance. The sun had set on the Dutch Empire in Asia.

But in Indonesia, as in Korea and elsewhere, the end of an empire did not bring peace and prosperity. Divisions and dissent remained endemic among the diverse peoples of the huge new island nation, as the new regime found it necessary to crush a Communist revolt in 1948 and various separatist uprisings in the 1950s. Poverty endured, and the economy deteriorated under Sukarno, who for all his many gifts had little real grasp of economics. Faced with ongoing unrest and broad discontent, he nationalized Dutch-owned industries and enhanced his own powers in

---

*The Arab League is an organization of Arab-speaking nations in Africa and the Middle East, formed in 1945 to advance their mutual interests.

1956–1957 by instituting "guided democracy"—a form of "consultative" dictatorship—and by declaring martial law.

On the international scene, Sukarno sought to stamp himself as a leader of the "Third World," as new nations belonging to neither Cold War camp were coming to be called. At Bandung, Indonesia, in 1955 he hosted a conference of twenty-nine Asian and African nations, and opened it with a soaring speech urging them to combine as a moral force for liberation, peace, and human dignity.[4] The **Bandung Conference** paved the way for formation in 1961 of a **Non-Aligned Movement**, made up of countries hoping to avoid alignment with either the Americans or Soviets, seeking instead to find a middle way and thus avoid going from colonialism to postcolonial client state subordination.*

But true nonalignment proved elusive. Most of the new post-colonial nations were impoverished and weak, badly in need of economic and often military aid, which they typically sought from one superpower or the other. Some tried to play one side against the other, hoping thus to get aid from both, but in the end often choosing the side opposite the one that aided their local enemies.

Thus it was with Indonesia. Throughout the 1950s and early 1960s Sukarno took aid from both Americans and Soviets, visiting their countries and wooing their support, as each tried to keep him from joining the other camp. But in 1957–1958, after he secured a large Soviet loan, the United States aided a rebellion against him on the Indonesian island of Sumatra, fearful that he was drifting to the Soviet side.† The rebellion failed and Sukarno survived, becoming even more anti-Western as he engaged in conflicts in the early 1960s with the Dutch over New Guinea and with British-backed Malaysia. In 1964, as he drew closer to both the USSR and Communist China and pursued an anti-Western campaign (banning Western books and rock-and-roll music), the United States cut off all assistance, prompting him to famously declare: "Go to hell with your aid!"[5]

Unfortunately for Sukarno, he proved unable to manage an internal conflict between Indonesia's military forces and its Communist Party (PKI), both of whose support he relied on. In 1965, as inflation increased and Sukarno's popularity plummeted, an attempted coup by some military leaders was crushed by a general named Suharto, who soon emerged as Indonesia's new strongman. Blaming the coup on the PKI and armed with American aid, he launched a brutal anticommunist campaign that

---

*Besides Sukarno, the original leaders of the Non-Aligned Movement were Jawaharlal Nehru of India, Gamal Abdel Nasser of Egypt, Josip Broz Tito of Yugoslavia, and Kwame Nkrumah of Ghana.

†Although US aid to the Sumatran rebels was supplied covertly by the Central Intelligence Agency (CIA), this covert aid was publicly exposed by the capture of a US pilot who was flying bombing missions for the rebels.

took at least one hundred thousand lives, deposed Sukarno in 1967, and led Indonesia firmly and forcefully into the Western camp. Happy to have a new Cold War client, the United States ignored the new regime's rampant corruption and repression, as Suharto ruled with an iron fist for the next three decades.

DECOLONIZATION AND COLD WAR IN INDOCHINA

Like Indonesia, Indochina* was a resource-rich region whose exploitation by a European power—in this case France—gave rise to an anticolonial movement with a charismatic leader who combined Marxist and nationalist ideals. Like Indonesia, it included diverse peoples—most prominently the Vietnamese, Laotians, and Cambodians. And like Indonesia, Indochina was occupied by Japan during World War II, following German conquest of its European mother country. But in Indochina, the anticolonial movement sided not with Japan but with the Allied Powers.

That movement, known as **Vietminh**,† was led from its inception in 1941 by Ho Chi Minh, a reserved yet resolute Vietnamese Marxist who had earlier been active in anti-French resistance and had helped found the Indochinese Communist Party. In fighting the Japanese occupying forces from 1941 to 1945, Vietminh aided the Allied cause, and in the process received arms and aid from the United States. Hopeful of continuing American support, as noted at the start of chapter 2, Ho proclaimed Vietnam's independence on September 2, 1945, in a speech modeled on the US Declaration of Independence. But both independence and US support proved hard to come by, in part because France soon sought to reconstitute its colonial empire as a so-called French Union and in part because Cold War considerations led the Americans to support France (which in 1949 would became their NATO ally) against Ho Chi Minh's Communist-led regime.

France's determination to reconstitute its empire involved restoration of French national pride, which had been deeply wounded by World War II. France had lost to Germany in 1940 in a swift and crushing defeat, and much of the country had suffered the indignity of Nazi occupation from then through 1944. These humiliations made any decision to emancipate France's empire extremely unlikely. Defeat by Germany had gravely

---

*The region east of India and southwest of China was known in the West as Indochina. In the 1800s France had acquired a large colony there, encompassing Vietnam, Laos, and Cambodia, that came to be called French Indochina.

†Abbreviated from *Viet Nam Doc Lap Dong Minh Hoi*, or *League for the Independence of Vietnam*, Vietminh was a coalition of anti-imperialist parties and movements committed to independence for Vietnam. It was led by Ho Chi Minh and the Indochinese Communist Party (later the Lao Dong, or Vietnamese Workers' Party).

damaged the self-respect of nearly all French citizens, and eventual liberation by Allied forces, while sincerely appreciated, only increased that damage. France's army, mortified by its defeat in 1940, was in no mood to be kicked out of its own colonies.

Beyond the trauma caused by the war, most French citizens considered the empire important, if not indispensable, to France. Indochina's natural resources—including rubber, tin, coal, zinc, rice, coffee, tea, and pepper—would be no less central to French economic reconstruction than Indonesia's resources were to the Dutch. What the French called *la mission civilisatrice**—the belief that France had a duty to "civilize" the natives of its African and Asian colonies—was a concept taken for granted by the French, few of whom in 1945 could have imagined a France bereft of its empire. These considerations must be borne in mind when evaluating the immediate prospect of independence for France's Southeast Asian empire.

The war in French Indochina, now often called the First Indochina War, also grew out of the circumstances of World War II in Asia. France's defeat by Germany in 1940 left its Southeast Asian colonies open to the Japanese, who occupied Indochina to use it as a staging area for an invasion of British Malaya and the Dutch East Indies and then remained in occupation until 1945. When Japan surrendered that year, no French or British forces were in Indochina, so the resulting power vacuum was filled by Vietminh, which had for four years conducted guerrilla warfare against Japan's occupying forces. By September 1945, however, a detachment of Indian forces commanded by a British general had arrived in southern Vietnam, and Chinese troops were occupying parts of northern Vietnam. French forces followed and rose to thirty thousand men by early 1946. As France insisted on restoring French colonial rule, Vietminh leader Ho Chi Minh and French commissioner Jean Sainteny† worked out a compromise agreement on March 6, 1946, and two lengthy conferences on the subject were held in France that spring and summer.

The talks, however, proved fruitless. Both sides were eager to avoid war, as long as their basic political needs could be satisfied. The problem was that those needs were incompatible. Ho Chi Minh was willing to keep an independent Vietnam in some sort of French overseas union,

---

*Literally, "civilizing mission," embodying the firmly held conviction that knowledge of the French language, familiarity with French culture, and conversion to Roman Catholicism would "civilize" the natives of French colonies in Africa and Asia, whom the French tended to view as backward and primitive.

†As French commissioner for the northern part of Vietnam, Sainteny served as a trusted intermediary between France and Vietminh. Later, during the Paris Peace Talks of 1969–1973 that ended US involvement in the Second Indochina War, Sainteny from time to time turned over his Paris apartment to US National Security Advisor Henry Kissinger and North Vietnamese Special Emissary Le Duc Tho so that they could negotiate without media scrutiny.

provided that Vietnam was actually independent. France was willing to create an Indochinese Federation that would grant Vietminh shared governance in the north while guaranteeing French authority in the south. These minimal requirements could not be reconciled.

So war began in 1946, just as the Cold War was beginning in Europe. France was deeply concerned with the German problem and economic reconstruction, and its people displayed, by and large, a nearly total ignorance of Asian affairs. France fought the war with a combination of volunteer and professional soldiers, leaving conscripts out of Indochina, so many people paid little attention to the region until 1949. Then the end of the Berlin Blockade, the creation of NATO, the Soviet detonation of an atomic bomb, the Communist victory in China, and the escalating cost of the war to a nation struggling to rebuild its war-wrecked economy all combined to bring the Indochina war into sharper focus. Paris appealed to Washington for financial assistance, casting its struggle against Vietminh in the context of a global struggle against Communism. The United States, which was already supporting French efforts indirectly through Marshall Plan aid, responded positively to this appeal, and the outbreak of the Korean War in June 1950 confirmed Washington's belief in the importance of holding the line in Indochina. By 1953 the United States was underwriting 80 percent of French military expenses, and the war was becoming palpably unpopular in France.

Meanwhile, the Vietminh commander, a French-educated former history teacher named Vo Nguyen Giap, proved more than equal to the task. At first he and Ho preferred to use guerrilla warfare, avoiding direct conventional battles against the better-armed French. Later, however, after China fell to the Communists in 1949, Mao's new regime sent aid to Vietminh, allowing Vo Nguyen Giap to go on the offensive. In spring of 1954, as the French grew weary of the bloody and costly conflict, he trapped and defeated their forces at Dien Bien Phu, a remote northern outpost near Vietnam's frontier with Laos (map 3.3). By this time, the French government was looking for the EXIT sign.

It was not that Dien Bien Phu represented a Vietminh conquest of all of Vietnam; it did not. But it did demonstrate that France could not win without an enormous escalation in troops and firepower, which the United States would not fund and France could not afford. Pierre Mendès-France became the new French prime minister, a job no one else would touch because its occupant would have to surrender to Vietminh. But he turned the situation to his advantage by setting a deadline: if an agreement to end the war was not signed by July 20, he would resign and France would lurch into political chaos.

At Geneva, Switzerland, negotiations involving Indochinese, British, American, Soviet, and Chinese officials sought to work out an agreement.

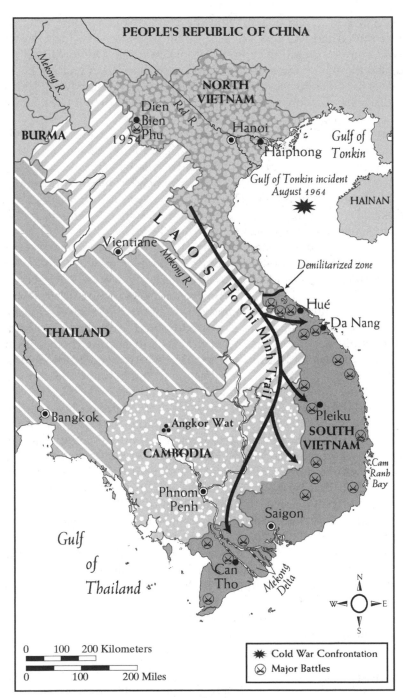

PEOPLE'S REPUBLIC OF CHINA

Mekong R.

NORTH VIETNAM

Dien
Bien
1954 Phu

Red R.

Hanoi

Haiphong

BURMA

*Gulf of
Tonkin*

Gulf of Tonkin incident
August 1964

HAINAN

L A O S

Vientiane

Mekong R.

Ho Chi Minh Trail

Demilitarized zone

Hué

Da Nang

THAILAND

Bangkok

Angkor Wat

Pleiku

**SOUTH
VIETNAM**

CAMBODIA

*Cam
Ranh
Bay*

Phnom
Penh

Saigon

Gulf

of

Thailand

Can
Tho

*Mekong
Delta*

N
W ◄─◯─► E
S

| 0 | 100 | 200 Kilometers |

| 0 | 100 | 200 Miles |

✸ Cold War Confrontation
⊗ Major Battles

Map 3.3. Vietnam, Laos, and Cambodia, 1954–1975

The USSR and China, fearful that the United States would move in if France pulled out without a deal, brought pressure to bear on Vietminh to compromise. Vietminh representative Pham Van Dong resisted to the end, and then, with a member of the French delegation holding back the hands of the clock to prevent it from striking midnight on July 20, bitterly initialed a set of accords that granted Vietminh less than it felt it had won on the battlefield.

The resulting Geneva Accords ended French rule and divided Indochina into four separate states: Laos and Cambodia (slated to have neutral governments), North Vietnam (to be ruled by the Communist-led Vietminh), and South Vietnam (soon to be headed by an anticommunist president named Ngo Dinh Diem). Vietnam's division, like Germany's and Korea's, was supposed to be temporary, with elections to unify the country envisioned for 1956.

Under normal circumstances, Vietminh's victory would have ended the conflict, with yet another set of Asian peoples gaining freedom from colonial rule. But in Indochina, as elsewhere, Cold War rivalries complicated the anticolonial cause. The Soviets and Chinese, distrustful of communists they could not control and fearful of getting dragged into a new war like the one just ended in Korea, supported Vietnam's division, thus undercutting the Vietnamese Communists and leaving them with only the North, unless and until the proposed elections could be held. And the Americans, fearful that Ho's prestige as the liberation leader would ensure electoral victory for him and his comrades, and concerned about a possible "domino effect"* that could result in other Southeast Asian nations falling under Communist rule, refused to sign the Geneva Accords and supported South Vietnam's new regime in preventing the elections.

Vietnam thus remained divided, with the South soon emerging as a US client state under Ngo Dinh Diem. A devout Catholic who repressed his country's Buddhist majority and ruled through corrupt remnants of the old French colonial structure, Diem over time grew increasingly unpopular and dictatorial, ruthlessly repressing communists and declaring martial law in 1963 in the face of widespread Buddhist protests. Disgusted and dismayed, US President John F. Kennedy and his aides turned against Diem, conspiring with his military in a plot to overthrow him. Although the Americans supported Diem's ouster, they apparently did not conspire to have him killed, but his life nonetheless was taken when the coup took place in November of that year, effectively transforming South Vietnam into a US-sponsored military dictatorship. Kennedy himself, ironically, was murdered later that same month.

---

*The **domino theory**, based on a "falling domino" comment by President Eisenhower in 1954, held that a Communist triumph in South Vietnam could cause a chain reaction that would bring the whole region under Communist control.

Meanwhile, taking advantage of the South's increasing chaos, the Communists had launched an armed revolt there, forming "Viet Cong" guerrilla units, eventually supplied from North Vietnam by a patchwork of pathways through Laos and Cambodia known as the Ho Chi Minh Trail (map 3.3). In 1964, further expanding the conflict, the North also started sending its own army units into the fray. Determined to prevent a Communist victory, US President Lyndon Johnson used alleged attacks on a US ship by North Vietnamese patrol boats in the Gulf of Tonkin* near North Vietnam that August to get the US Congress to authorize use of American armed forces. Although Congress did not formally declare war, its Gulf of Tonkin resolution (August 7, 1964) authorized the president to take "all necessary steps, including the use of armed force."[6] Early the next year, he initiated sustained aerial bombing of North Vietnam, and began sending increasing numbers of US combat troops to fight in South Vietnam.

These developments created both problems and prospects for Communist China and Soviet Russia, whose earlier alliance had by this time given way to mutual hostility (see below). Neither fully trusted the North Vietnamese, over whom they had little control, and neither wanted to get dragged into a Southeast Asian land war. Yet, as proponents of national liberation movements and rivals for leadership of the "anti-imperialist" camp, they could hardly turn their backs on Communist comrades fighting for national unification against the "capitalist imperialists." So the Chinese, who after 1965 were focused mainly on their own internal "Cultural Revolution," sent arms to North Vietnam and published a treatise called "Long Live the Victory of People's War," which urged national liberation movements to use guerrilla warfare against the better-armed forces of the Western imperialists.[7] The Soviets tried to have it both ways. They gave North Vietnam substantial aid (surpassing the Chinese in this regard) and championed its cause as a liberation movement, blasting the Americans as imperialist warmongers. At the same time, facing growing hostility from China, and thus hoping to reduce tensions with the United States and end the debilitating US-Soviet arms race, they worked behind the scenes to contain the conflict and promote a negotiated settlement.

The Americans, too, sought a negotiated settlement. Early in 1968 they were caught off guard by North Vietnam's Tet Offensive, a set of simultaneous attacks conducted across South Vietnam (map 3.3) timed to coin-

---

*On August 2 and August 4, 1964, the USS *Maddox*, a US surveillance ship operating in the Gulf of Tonkin off the coast of North Vietnam, reported that it was attacked twice by North Vietnamese patrol boats. Based on subsequent evidence, it seems that an initial attack occurred but a reputed second one did not. See John Prados, ed., "The Gulf of Tonkin Incident, 40 Years Later: Flawed Intelligence and the Decision for War in Vietnam," *National Security Archive Electronic Briefing Book No. 132*, http://nsarchive.gwu.edu/NSAEBB/NSAEBB132/.

cide with celebrations of the Lunar New Year (Tet). The offensive failed militarily, as US forces soon regained the lost ground, but it succeeded psychologically, as it stunned Americans by showing that the Communists were far from being beaten, despite the commitment of immense US resources and half a million US troops. Feeling misled by their own government, many turned against President Johnson, who opted not to pursue reelection and instead opened peace talks in Paris with the North Vietnamese. But the Communists, noting the antiwar protests then rocking America society, concluded that time was on their side and refused to make meaningful concessions. And Johnson was soon to be replaced as president by Richard M. Nixon, elected that fall on a promise to end the war with US honor intact.

Nixon's strategy, called Vietnamization, involved gradually removing US troops while arming South Vietnam's forces to take over the fighting. He also expanded the war, invading Cambodia in 1970 to attack Communist bases there and disrupt the Ho Chi Minh Trail supply lines,* while using diplomatic openings with Russia and China to try to get them to use their influence with North Vietnam to expedite the peace talks. In 1972, when the talks bogged down, he renewed massive bombing of the North. His efforts seemed to bear fruit the next year in the Paris Peace Accords, which suspended the war and allowed for US troop withdrawal. But the North Vietnamese proved resilient and resolute, undeterred by Ho Chi Minh's death in 1969, and resistant to Soviet and Chinese influence. In 1974, with the Americans safely gone, they resumed their war against the South, conquering it in 1975 to unite Vietnam under their rule, while Communist governments also took power in Laos and Cambodia.

These events ended the Second Indochina War (1964–1975), but they did not end Indochina's agonies. Led by a ruthless fanatic who called himself Pol Pot, Cambodia's new rulers, the Communist Khmer Rouge,† launched a mass deurbanization campaign modeled on earlier experiments in Mao's China, including the "Great Leap Forward" and "Great Proletarian Cultural Revolution" (see below). Intent on creating a rural socialist utopia, instead they created a genocidal hell on earth. Urban professionals and other city-dwellers were taken from the cities at gunpoint and forced to work in rural agrarian fields. Those who resisted were murdered by the thousands, while tens of thousands of others died of starvation and exhaustion, over the next several years. Although death estimates vary widely, evidence suggests that perhaps two million of

---

*Nixon's 1970 invasion of Cambodia transformed what Americans called the Vietnam War into the "Second Indochina War" (1964–1975). The First Indochina War was the Vietminh struggle against the French (1946–1964).

†*Khmer* is the name of Cambodia's main ethnic group, and *rouge* is French for "red," the Communist color.

the country's seven million people may have perished in the Cambodian genocide of 1975–1979.

Then Indochina's agonies grew even more complex, with Communist countries fighting each other rather than Western imperialists. As Communist Vietnam, with its large battle-tested Soviet-equipped army, increasingly emerged as a Soviet client, Communist China and Cambodia came to fear that the Vietnamese might dominate the region. In 1978, following earlier Cambodian attacks against Vietnam, the Vietnamese army invaded Cambodia and ousted the Khmer Rouge regime in January 1979, replacing it with a moderate Communist Vietnamese client state called the People's Republic of Kampuchea.* The next month China, alarmed by Vietnam's growing power, invaded Vietnam, only to be rebuffed by its seasoned military forces. Encouraged by China's support, however, Khmer Rouge and other Cambodian rebels conducted an ongoing civil war against the Vietnam-backed Kampuchea regime throughout the 1980s. Only in the 1990s, following the Cold War's end, did the region gain a measure of stability, with Cambodia emerging as a constitutional monarchy, while Vietnam and Laos continued to function as single-party socialist states.

Thus, although the Indochina Wars did liberate the region from French colonial rule and US intervention, they also amply exhibited the complexities and duplicities of Cold War **anticolonialism**. In theory the Americans favored liberation and democratic elections, but in practice—especially when the liberators and probable winners were Communists—they backed repressive leaders who were US clients. The Chinese and Soviets, vying for leadership of the so-called anti-imperialist camp, outwardly aided and encouraged liberation movements but also felt free to undermine or attack them when it suited their interests to do so. And the liberators themselves brought neither freedom nor democracy: indeed, under Communist rule, Vietnam, Laos, and Cambodia became single-party dictatorships, with regimes that could be as repressive as—and in the Khmer Rouge case, more repressive than—the foreign imperialists had been.

DECOLONIZATION AND COLD WAR IN INDIA AND PAKISTAN

India's decolonization began before World War II and culminated in 1947 in political independence for the former British colony and its partition into two new nations: the Republic of India and Pakistan.

---

*Kampuchea is a local name for Cambodia. The official name of the Khmer Rouge regime was Democratic Kampuchea.

Unlike Indonesia and Indochina, India gained independence without a bloody liberation war against its colonial rulers, but like Korea and Vietnam, it was divided into hostile states whose conflicts had Cold War connections.

Much like the Dutch in the East Indies, the British had ruled parts of India indirectly since the 1600s through their East India Company and then directly since the 1800s, when the British government took over control from the company. And like the Dutch in the East Indies, the British had trained and educated a native elite to help them administer their vast and diverse colony. But in 1885, adopting Western liberal and nationalist ideals and applying them to India, some members of this British-educated Indian elite created an organization that came to be known as the Indian National Congress, which eventually grew into a national independence movement.

After World War I, when the British brutally dashed India's hopes for increased self-governance, the struggle for independence was conducted mainly by the Congress, inspired by Mohandas K. ("Mahatma") Gandhi, a British-educated lawyer whose ascetic ways, sparse attire, and insistence on nonviolence made him one of the modern world's most unusual leaders. Beginning in the 1920s, faced with overwhelming British might and feeling that a violent revolt against it would be folly, Gandhi and his followers opted to pursue a path of nonviolent resistance. Through boycotts and demonstrations, which remained nonviolent even in the face of Britain's violent force, they embarrassed the British and undermined their efforts to govern India and exploit its resources. Faced with massive noncooperation and civil disobedience, Britain grudgingly relented, giving the Indians some limited self-governance in the 1930s. It looked as if India was moving toward independence, and that it might get there without a bloody all-out conflict.

In 1937 elections, however, most legislative seats were won by the Indian National Congress. Since the Congress was dominated by Hindus, who made up almost three quarters of India's population, these results caused consternation among India's Muslims, who constituted most of the remaining quarter. Fearful that Hindus would likewise dominate an independent democratic India, the Muslim League, an organization led by a talented Muslim lawyer named Muhammad Ali Jinnah, began to press for an independent state as a homeland for India's Muslims. The issue was placed on hold during World War II, when Britain was led by Winston Churchill, a staunch imperialist and opponent of Indian independence. But at the end of the war, Churchill's government was voted out of office and replaced with a new one, headed by Clement Attlee, that was determined to cut back on Britain's vast overseas commitments. Having thus decided to withdraw from India, it found itself faced with massive Muslim protests and Hindu-versus-Muslim violence, so it grudgingly agreed to Jinnah's partition demands.

As a result, when India became independent on August 14–15, 1947, its mostly Muslim regions emerged as a new Muslim nation called Pakistan ("Land of the Pure"), which was itself split into East and West Pakistan on opposite sides of India. Since the peoples of different faiths were intermingled, however, the split created mass bedlam, as millions of Hindus who lived in the areas that became Pakistan fled to India, and millions of Muslims fled India for Pakistan. These chaotic mass migrations were marred by violent clashes between Hindus and Muslims in which perhaps a million people lost their lives. To make matters worse, a war broke out between India and Pakistan over the northern regions of Jammu and Kashmir, which were claimed by both. By the time a UN truce was arranged in 1949, Gandhi himself was dead, murdered by a militant Hindu who saw him as too eager to accommodate the Muslims.

India and Pakistan were thus born in violence as hostile states at roughly the same time as the Cold War commenced. Starting out as parliamentary democracies and members of the **British Commonwealth**,* both new nations seemed squarely in the Western camp. But as their mutual hostility continued, and as the Cold War became global, both new nations—like most other countries emerging from colonial rule—were compelled by events to take sides.

Pakistan, the smaller and weaker of the two, sought Western aid to shore up its forces for conflicts against India, of which there were three between 1947 and 1971. The British and Americans, committed to the containment of Communism, saw Pakistan potentially as a useful base on the southern flank of the USSR, which they sought to confine by forming alliances with its neighbors. Hence in 1954 the United States entered into a Mutual Defense Agreement with Pakistan, which soon thereafter became a member of **SEATO**, a US-sponsored alliance designed to counter Communism's spread in Southeast Asia.† In 1955 the Pakistanis also joined the **Baghdad Pact**, later called **CENTO**, a somewhat similar British coalition with Muslim Middle Eastern nations.‡

---

*The **Commonwealth of Nations**, initially called the British Commonwealth, is an association of countries that includes Great Britain and many of its former colonies. Intended to maintain cooperative connections among them, it is symbolically headed by the British monarch.

†SEATO (the Southeast Asia Treaty Organization) initially consisted of Australia, Britain, France, New Zealand, Pakistan, the Philippines, Thailand, and the United States. Unlike NATO, it had no structure for collective defense; its members were required only to consult one another in case of attack against one or more by an outside force.

‡The Baghdad Pact initially consisted of Britain, Iran, Iraq, Pakistan, and Turkey. Its name was changed to CENTO (Central Treaty Organization) in 1959 when Iraq (ruled from Baghdad) withdrew. Like SEATO, it lacked an effective structure to assure a collective defense. The United States supported this alliance but did not formally join it.

Pakistan thereby gained substantial military and economic aid, as well as US training for many of its army officers. The Americans gained bases in Pakistan, which they used for intelligence gathering and surveillance flights over the USSR. Pakistan also helped to facilitate contacts between the United States and China, serving as the springboard for a secret visit by Secretary of State Henry Kissinger to the People's Republic in 1971 that paved the way for President Nixon's 1972 visit to that country (see below). And in the 1980s it provided a base for US assistance to rebels in neighboring Afghanistan who were fighting Soviet forces there (see chapter 7). The Americans in turn stood by Pakistan in several disputes with India and also supported repressive Pakistani regimes, overlooking their corruption and human rights abuses. Indeed, despite US consulate reports of genocidal atrocities committed by Pakistani forces in their failed attempts to crush a 1971 revolt in which East Pakistan (with India's assistance) gained independence as the new nation of Bangladesh, the Nixon administration continued to support and aid the Pakistani regime.[8]

India, meanwhile, sought to pursue a neutral course in the Cold War. Jawaharlal Nehru, Gandhi's close associate who served as India's first prime minister from 1947 until 1964, spoke eloquently of the need for nonalignment at Sukarno's Bandung Asian-African Conference in 1955,[9] and emerged as one of the main leaders of the Non-Aligned Movement. Despite India's commitments to neutrality and democracy, however, Nehru and his daughter, Indira Gandhi* (who served as prime minister from 1966 to 1977 and from 1980 to 1984), also sought and received substantial aid from the USSR.

Changes in Soviet leadership facilitated this development. As noted in chapters 1 and 2, Soviet ideology depicted the Cold War as a struggle between the capitalist imperialist camp, led by the United States, and the socialist anti-imperialist camp, led by the USSR. But Soviet dictator Stalin, intent mainly on strengthening the USSR and distrustful of socialists (or anyone else) that he could not control, confined his efforts at expanding Soviet influence mainly to countries on the USSR's periphery. In the early 1950s, even as Nehru strove to implement socialist policies in India, Stalin continued to consider him a reactionary, whose democratic socialism more closely resembled that of Britain's Labour Party than Soviet Marxism-Leninism.

Stalin's death in 1953, however, set in motion a succession struggle that brought to power Nikita S. Khrushchev. A self-educated person of peas-

---

*Although Nehru's daughter Indira had married a man named Gandhi, she was not related to Mahatma Gandhi.

ant stock who was crude and uncouth but highly capable and confident, Khrushchev publicly pushed for "peaceful coexistence" with the capitalist West to forestall the threat of nuclear war, while seeking simultaneously to subvert it by supporting anti-Western national liberation movements and nations newly liberated from Western colonial rule. He thereby hoped and expected that the Soviets would prevail, not through direct confrontation with the West but by winning the support and allegiance of the Third World. And India, as the largest and most influential of the new Third World nations, would play an important part in his approach.

In June 1955, then, Nehru paid a visit to the USSR, where he was warmly received by Soviet leaders. That fall, in return, Khrushchev and his cohorts traveled to India and promised to assist it in its rivalry with Pakistan, which by then was emerging as a US ally. Substantial Soviet aid to India followed, and the Soviets even sided with India during border clashes with China in 1959 and 1962, contributing to a growing rift between China and the USSR (below). Although Nehru died and Khrushchev was replaced in 1964, the Soviet-Indian relationship continued to flourish under their successors. Indeed, as war loomed between India and Pakistan in 1971, India under Indira Gandhi signed a Treaty of Friendship and Cooperation with the USSR, now led by Khrushchev's former protégé and successor Leonid Brezhnev, and then proceeded to use Soviet arms and equipment in defeating Pakistani forces that year in support of the successful East Pakistan revolt that formed independent Bangladesh. In the 1980s, as American aid to Pakistan increased during the Soviet-Afghan War, Indira Gandhi and her son Rajiv—who succeeded her after her assassination in 1984—used Soviet aid to further enhance the strength of India's military forces.

The ironies in these relationships abounded. In aiding India, the Soviets gained some influence in South Asia, but did little to further the Communist cause: as the world's most populous democracy, India retained close cultural and economic ties with Britain and the United States and never even considered becoming a part of the Communist camp. In accepting Soviet aid, India was able to bolster its military forces, but the military equipment it got was generally inferior to that produced in the West. And in aiding Pakistan, the Americans supported repressive dictators who had little use for Western democracy or US Cold War interests and who took the aid mainly to strengthen Pakistan against India. In South Asia as elsewhere, decolonization and Cold War connections helped exacerbate local rivalries and conflicts as emerging nations and regimes sought, with varying degrees of success, to exploit the superpower rivalry for aid and support to strengthen themselves against their regional foes.

THE COLD WAR, ANTI-IMPERIALISM,
AND THE PEOPLE'S REPUBLIC OF CHINA

From its very inception, the People's Republic of China played a key but complicated role in both the anticolonial movement and the global Cold War. After joining the "anti-imperialist camp" by allying with the USSR in 1950, the Chinese Communists saw their main foes as the "US imperialists," fighting them to a standstill in Korea and despising them for continuing to back the Chinese Nationalist regime on Taiwan. In time, however, China's leaders also came to see the Soviet Union as an imperialist power and even as a more serious threat than the United States. They thus increasingly sought to assert themselves as Third World leaders against both the Americans and the Soviets, while also playing those two "hegemonic powers" against one another.

From 1949 to 1976, China's foreign policy was ably guided by Premier Zhou Enlai, a consummate diplomat whose pragmatic flexibility provided a useful counterpoise to the radical idealism of Chinese leader Mao Zedong. In 1950 Zhou helped negotiate the alliance treaty between China and the Soviet Union and later the roles that each would play in the Korean War. In 1954, at Geneva, he agreed to Vietnam's partition, robbing Ho Chi Minh and the Vietminh of the full fruits of their defeat of the French imperialists but serving China's interests by delaying the emergence of a united and powerful Communist rival to its south. In 1955, at the Bandung Conference of Asian and African nations, Zhou called on communists and nationalists to seek common ground in the struggle against colonialism, adroitly identifying China with the emerging Third World nations and deftly defusing concerns expressed by some that communism itself was imperialistic.[10]

Meanwhile, however, the Chinese themselves were coming to consider their Soviet Communist comrades as imperialistic. In the mid-1950s, while still receiving aid from the USSR and outwardly lauding its leadership of the anti-imperialist camp, they watched with dismay as Soviet leader Khrushchev called for peaceful coexistence with the imperialist West and denounced his predecessor Stalin, still widely revered by the Chinese. Mao, who had been willing to recognize Stalin as a senior partner, had no such esteem for Khrushchev and resented the fact that he did these things without first consulting China. Khrushchev's meetings with Western leaders, his twelve-day visit to America in 1959, and his support for India in a border clash with China that same year further rankled Chinese leaders, and his trips to China to try to smooth things over only made matters worse. When Mao's Great Leap Forward (1958–1960), a radical mass mobilization campaign that rejected the Soviet model of economic development,* turned into a catastrophic failure in 1960, the Soviets started withdrawing their technicians and reducing their aid, angering China still further. That same year, the Chinese published "Long Live Leninism," a lengthy article that, without directly disparaging the Soviets, criticized the concept of "peaceful coexistence" as a betrayal of the Leninist obligation to support liberation wars against Western imperialists.[11]

Although Khrushchev vowed in a 1961 speech to support such wars, relations between the two Communist giants continued to deteriorate. At a Communist Congress in Moscow that year, when Khrushchev renewed his attack on Stalin, Zhou Enlai signaled China's disapproval by publicly placing a wreath at Stalin's tomb and abruptly heading back to China. In 1962 Khrushchev's support for India in another border conflict with China, and his compliance with US demands to remove Soviet missiles from Cuba (see chapter 6), triggered a public war of words in 1963 and 1964, during which the Chinese accused the Soviets of collusion with the Western imperialists.

Khrushchev's ouster and replacement by Brezhnev in 1964 eased tensions temporarily, but by the late 1960s they had returned with a vengeance. China's Great Proletarian Cultural Revolution (1966–1969), a new mass mobilization campaign in which tens of thousands of youthful Red Guards sought to transform China by imposing radical Maoist ideals, included verbal denunciations of the Soviet system and attacks on the Soviet embassy in China's capital, Beijing. More damaging still was the 1968 invasion of Communist Czechoslovakia by Soviet forces, undertaken to crush a reform movement there and thus to bring a wayward Soviet satellite back into line. This event brought a vehement response from Zhou Enlai, who in a speech shortly after the assault compared the Soviets to Hitler, charged them with creating puppet states through fascist power politics, and accused them of conspiring to divide up the world with the US imperialists.[12] The USSR's subsequent assertion of its right to intervene in other Communist countries—later dubbed the Brezhnev Doctrine[13]—only served to heighten China's fears of possibly being next on the list. And indeed, although there was no all-out Soviet invasion of China, 1969 brought several bloody border wars between Soviet and Chinese forces along their lengthy frontier.

By this time, China, emerging from its chaotic Cultural Revolution, had come to see the Soviets as a far more immediate threat than the distant

---

*Communist China initially had followed the Soviet model, based on centrally directed "five-year plans," but in 1958 Mao abandoned it in favor of the Great Leap Forward, which called for the creation of huge rural communes intended to accelerate agricultural and industrial production through collective efforts of the masses.

Americans, especially as the latter began to withdraw their forces from South Vietnam. Feeling isolated and vulnerable and seeking to offset the Soviet threat, in early 1972 the Chinese welcomed a visit from US President Nixon, who in turn sought to use his dialogue with China to gain leverage in US relations with the USSR. This latter effort produced an era of Soviet-American détente in the mid-1970s, marked by arms control agreements, cultural exchanges, and other efforts to reduce tensions between the Cold War superpowers.

Superpower détente, combined with US withdrawal from Vietnam and the success of decolonization—through which almost all of Europe's Asian and African colonies had gained political independence by the mid-1970s—prompted the Chinese to provide a revised assessment of the world situation. Speaking at the United Nations in 1974, Chinese Vice Premier Deng Xiaoping, a seasoned and flexible pragmatist, outlined a view that differed radically from the old, bipolar communist versus capitalist Cold War scenario and perhaps provided a better insight into new global realities. In this view, the Americans and Soviets together made up the First World—imperialist powers who used their might to control, subvert, exploit, and interfere with other nations in their quest for global hegemony. The other developed countries, including Japan and the European powers who had lost their colonial possessions, comprised what Deng referred to as the Second World. And the Third World, in his estimation, consisted of the developing nations of Asia, Africa, and Latin America—including Communist China and former colonies that had gained political independence but still suffered from the remnants of imperial rule and the burdens of economic exploitation.[14]

Three years later, following the 1976 deaths of Zhou and Mao and a brutal succession struggle, Deng emerged as China's main leader and took his country in a new direction. Ending China's relative isolation, he opened full diplomatic relations with the United States, patched up relations to some extent with the Soviet Union, and set out to develop his country into an economic power. Over the next few decades, he and his comrades borrowed ideas and technologies from Japan and the capitalist West, experimented with profit incentives and free enterprise zones, sent Chinese students to foreign countries to study business techniques, and flooded Western markets with inexpensive goods produced by Chinese workers with wages far lower than their Western counterparts. By the 1990s, as the Cold War ended and the USSR disintegrated, China was emerging from its Third World status. And by 2010, when it surpassed Japan as the world's second largest economy (behind only the United States), it was well on its way to creating its own economic empire.

CONNECTIONS AND CONCLUSIONS

The anticolonial movements of Asia began before World War II, but that conflict facilitated their success in the years that followed it. Japan's startling string of conquests in 1941–1942 ousted the Western imperial powers from control of Asian colonies but brought no true liberation, imposing instead a new form of imperial rule. Japan's defeat in 1945 then gave oppressed Asians a chance to assert their independence, but internal rivalries and Cold War connections complicated their efforts. As Asian leaders sought outside support against former colonial rulers and Asian adversaries, they typically turned to either the Communist East or the capitalist West and often even framed their struggles in terms of the ideals expressed by one Cold War camp or the other. Anticolonial and postcolonial conflicts in Asia thus combined and coalesced with the Cold War.

In practice this dynamic played out differently in different parts of Asia. Korea, after being freed from Japanese rule, was divided into Communist North and anticommunist South, with the Soviets and Chinese supporting the former and the Americans the latter. Indonesia, after gaining independence from the Dutch, sought nonalignment under Sukarno, but it wound up moving toward the Soviet camp, until Sukarno was ousted and replaced by the US-backed Suharto regime. Indochina, having won independence from France, was divided into four countries, with Vietnam split like Korea into Communist and anticommunist states—until the Soviet-supported North defeated and took over the South in the aftermath of US withdrawal from the Vietnam (Second Indochina) War. India, upon independence from Britain, was partitioned into Pakistan and the Republic of India, with the former emerging as a US ally and the latter accepting Soviet aid. In each of these places millions of lives were lost in violent conflicts, aided and aggravated by the support and involvement of Cold War superpowers.

China's emergence as a Communist country further complicated the agonies of Asia. Aligning initially with the Soviets in the "anti-imperialist camp," the Chinese eventually embarked on a separate path and came to consider both the USSR and the United States as imperial powers. And the Chinese clearly had reasons for doing so. The Soviets, despite their anti-imperial Marxist-Leninist rhetoric, sought to develop Asian client states under the guise of support for anti-imperialism while treating countries under their control as colonies—a posture that they brutally displayed in their 1968 invasion of Czechoslovakia. And the Americans, despite their supposed support for ideals of freedom and popular democracy, allied with the old European colonial powers, and backed heavy-handed dictatorial regimes in South Korea, South Vietnam, Indonesia,

Taiwan, and Pakistan. Although the Soviets and Americans often found it hard to control their Asian clients, their efforts to do so—and their contests for hegemony and influence in Asia—smacked of great-power imperialism. Asians in the Cold War era gained their independence from old colonial empires but found themselves susceptible to new forms of imperial intervention.

4

❧

"We Are Today Free and Independent"

Anti-Imperialism and the Cold War in the Middle East

PROLOGUE: IRAN, 1946–1953

The Cold War's first crisis took place in Iran.

Reza Shah Pahlavi, Iran's monarch, had compensated for British and Soviet interference in his country by drawing close to Germany in the 1930s. After Germany invaded the USSR in June 1941, Reza Shah found himself **persona non grata*** with both Moscow and London. Soviet and British forces occupied the country in August–September 1941 in order to deny the Germans its petroleum resources and strategic location. The Shah was forced to abdicate in favor of his son, and Iran was partitioned into northern (Soviet) and southern (British) spheres of influence.

In 1944 the United States persuaded the British and Soviets to agree to withdraw their forces from their respective spheres no later than six months after the end of the war. That date turned out to be March 2, 1946, by which time the British had withdrawn but the Soviets had not. This caused a crisis, intensified by Stalin's encouragement of the creation of a separate Azeri† state in northern Iran and his pressure on the Tehran government to grant an oil concession to the USSR. Iran complained to the newly established United Nations while simultaneously negotiating with the Soviets. Prime Minister Ahmad Qavam

---

*A diplomatic term meaning "an unwelcome person."

†An ethnic group living mostly in northwest Iran and in Azerbaijan, which was then one of the Soviet Socialist Republics that made up the USSR (see chapter 7).

71

convinced Stalin to withdraw his troops by offering the oil concession and accepting the Azeri state. But in autumn of 1946, Mohammad Reza Pahlavi, who at the age of twenty-two had succeeded his father as shah in 1941, worked with the US ambassador to convince Qavam to change course. Iran's parliament, the **Majlis**, rejected the oil concession, and Iranian troops dismantled the breakaway Azeri state. Stalin, unwilling to risk confronting Britain and the United States over the matter, accepted defeat.

These events checkmated Soviet imperialism but left British and American imperialism intact. Iran's location in the strategically vital Middle East,* coupled with the importance of Iranian oil to Britain, guaranteed the persistence of Western interest in the country. The young Shah was considered well-meaning but weak, and day-to-day authority was exercised by the prime minister, who was responsible both to the monarch and the Majlis. Very soon these governing forces took up the issue of ownership of Iran's oil.

Throughout the Middle East, foreign control of petroleum reserves was deeply resented. The United States deflected this animosity, at least with regard to Saudi Arabia, by brokering a fifty-fifty profit-sharing agreement between the Saudi monarchy and the Arab American Oil Company (ARAMCO). Britain would have done well to conclude a similar deal with Tehran, but the British and their monopoly, the Anglo-Iranian Oil Company (later known as British Petroleum and then BP), refused to recognize the impending collapse of colonialism and underestimated the degree of Iranian hatred for them. Washington's efforts to persuade London to compromise proved fruitless. In May 1951 the Shah and his prime minister, a wealthy physician named Mohammad Mosaddeq, signed a Majlis decree nationalizing the Anglo-Iranian Oil Company.

Britain was shocked and dismayed. American leaders, preoccupied with the Korean War and feeling they had done what they could, were content to let the British simmer in their own oil. But this attitude changed late in the Truman administration, and Dwight Eisenhower accelerated the change when he became US president in January 1953. Eisenhower and his secretary of state, John Foster Dulles (whose brother Allen was director of the US Central Intelligence Agency, or CIA), were anxious to defend the Middle East against Soviet imperialism. They considered

---

*The term *Middle East* is confusing and unhelpful. Rashid Khalidi, in *Sowing Crisis* ([Boston: Beacon Press, 2009], 264 note 3), asks, "In the middle of what? East of what?" Does it extend from Morocco to India, as Roby Barrett suggests? (See "Suggestions for Further Reading.") Is it confined to the eastern Mediterranean? But the term is also indispensable, and here, following Khalidi, we use it to refer "to the area of North Africa and West Asia bounded by the Atlantic, the Caucasus Mountains, Turkmenistan, Afghanistan, and Pakistan."

Mosaddeq a communist dupe, citing his willingness to cooperate with the Iranian communist Tudeh Party against the British, and set in motion a plan to oust him and amplify the power of the Shah, whom they expected to manipulate. The British were only too happy to cooperate, perhaps expecting a reversal of the oil nationalization. But Eisenhower was perfectly content to leave the oil in the hands of the Shah as long as the latter did Washington's bidding. Britain and the United States were on the same side in the Cold War, but when it came to imperial power, their interests did not always coincide.

Accordingly, the CIA hatched a plot and implemented it in August 1953. It failed, and the Shah fled to Rome. Mosaddeq, normally a shrewd politician, became complacent, failing to act quickly enough to forestall intervention by the Islamic Shia **ulema**, the religious leadership body of the nation.* Its head, Grand Ayatollah Boroujerdi, came to the defense of the monarchy, as did General Fazlollah Zahedi, who had been brought out of hiding to support the Shah by Kermit Roosevelt, orchestrator of the CIA plot. The army and security forces refused to fire on pro-Shah demonstrators on August 19.† Mosaddeq was arrested and deposed by the army, and the Shah returned from Rome shaken but with his powers enhanced. He left the oil nationalization in place and cast his lot with the Americans. The CIA later claimed complete credit for the August 19 coup, but evidence indicates the possibility of additional explanations.‡ It must be remembered that the Iranian military, not the US or British military, ousted Mosaddeq.§

Events in Iran between 1946 and 1953 not only demonstrate the challenges to British and Soviet imperialism, the importance of oil, and the centrality of the Cold War, but they also highlight the significance of religious opinion in the Islamic world. That significance would be demonstrated again and again throughout the Cold War, most persistently with regard to relations between Islamic states and Israel.

---

*In Islamic countries, the ulema consists of prominent scholars and clerics who possess teaching authority and interpret the sharia, the holy law of Islam. The Shia branch of Islam claims only 6 percent of Muslims worldwide but is dominant in Iran.

†Boroujerdi and the ulema feared that Mosaddeq planned to remove the Shah and proclaim a secular republic inimical to Islamic interests.

‡Darioush Bayandor, in *Iran and the CIA* (Basingstoke, UK, 2010), makes a compelling case, based on exhaustive knowledge of documents written in Farsi and not consulted by Western scholars, for the central role of the ulema. His account should be contrasted with the equally compelling, self-aggrandizing memoir by the CIA's Kermit Roosevelt, *Countercoup: The Struggle for the Control of Iran* (New York, 1979). A valid explanation for the events of August 1953 should include elements drawn from both accounts. See also the balanced treatments of the coup in Stephen Kinzer, *All the Shah's Men* (Hoboken, NJ, 2003) and in Ervand Abrahamian, *The Coup: 1953, the CIA, and the Roots of Modern U.S.-Iranian Relations* (New York, 2013).

§Explanations that deny Iranian agency and attribute the ouster of Mosaddeq exclusively to Western intervention are overly simplistic.

THE ISRAELI-PALESTINIAN QUESTION

If anything should have convinced the British that their empire would not long survive the war, the loss of India (chapter 3) and Palestine should have done it. After the Balfour declaration of 1917 appeared to have promised a national home in Palestine for the Jewish people,* the inter-war years were filled with increasing strife between Arabs and Jews in Britain's Palestine mandate, which the League of Nations had entrusted to Great Britain in 1922–1923.† Nazi extermination of the Jews of Europe had been rumored since 1941, but conclusive disclosure in 1945 of the existence of death camps placed overwhelming pressure on London to implement Balfour's commitment.

But doing so would be complicated. India's independence in 1947 shifted London's focus to the defense of Egypt and the Suez Canal, through which Iranian and Arabian oil passed on its way to Britain. India had defended that lifeline through two world wars but would do so no longer. Britain sought to keep its naval base at Haifa and two army posts, as well as a major airbase that, in company with similar airbases in Egypt, could be used to launch planes equipped with atom bombs against the USSR in the next world war. The indispensability of oil and the developing Cold War combined to confer on Palestine a value it had not previously possessed.

British Foreign Secretary Ernest Bevin wanted to establish a partnership with Arabs throughout the region, hoping thereby to contain communism and preserve the flow of oil.‡ The issue of Palestine stood squarely in the way. No solution seemed acceptable either to Arabs or Jews. Partitioning the mandate into two states, one Arab and one Jewish, was rejected by Arabs (who wanted to rule the entire area) and Jews (who wanted more territory than any partition plan would give them). A unified, two-nationality state was no better: Arabs feared Jews would eventually take it over, while Jews feared living under Arab rule.

While London lurched from one scheme to another, pressures became unendurable. In 1946 Harry Truman publicly endorsed the admission of one hundred thousand Jewish refugees into Palestine, while a Jew-

---

*The Balfour declaration was issued by British Foreign Secretary Arthur James Balfour on November 2, 1917. It said: "His Majesty's Government view with favour the establishment in Palestine of a national home for the Jewish people, and will use its best endeavours to facilitate the achievement of this object, it being clearly understood that nothing shall be done which may prejudice the civil and religious rights of existing non-Jewish communities in Palestine, or the rights and political status enjoyed by Jews in any other country." Since both Arabs and Jews sought to own the same land, the clause beginning "it being clearly understood…" invalidated the entire declaration.

†After World War I, during which its forces occupied Palestine, Britain received a "mandate" from the newly formed League of Nations to administer that region and prepare it for eventual independence.

‡Or to frustrate Soviet imperialism and amplify British imperialism.

ish underground terrorist group, the Irgun,* blew up British Army headquarters in Jerusalem's King David Hotel and carried out atrocities against Britons and Arabs alike. In February 1947, in the midst of a terrible winter that forced Britain to its knees, London took two momentous steps. Bevin informed Washington that Britain could no longer afford to support Greece and Turkey against Communist subversion,† and he handed the Palestine mandate over to the United Nations with the advice that the mandate was unworkable and that no acceptable solution could be found.‡ Nine months later the United Nations General Assembly (UNGA), by a two-thirds majority, recommended partition, to the horror of Arabs throughout the Middle East (map 4.1).§

Britain completed its withdrawal from Palestine on May 15, 1948. One day earlier, Zionists** in Palestine proclaimed the foundation of the State of Israel. Both Moscow and Washington immediately recognized the new nation. In a sense, they were its parents. A year earlier, Soviet UN representative Andrei Gromyko had come out in support of partition, and Truman had quickly followed suit. Both superpowers then pressured smaller UN members to support partition. Both sought justice for Jewish refugees, while the Soviets also hoped thereby to strike a blow against British imperialism by denying London access to bases in the eastern Mediterranean. In the United States, both major political parties hoped for Jewish votes in the 1948 general election.

Arab states denounced both superpowers, and six of them sent armies into Palestine on May 15. To their astonishment, Israel won its war of independence and annexed additional land while doing so. Three factors made this possible. First, Israel was filled with European Jews who came from highly industrialized cultures and who in many cases had gained combat experience in World War II. Second, the USSR ferried weapons to Israel through Czechoslovakia. And third, King Abdullah of Jordan, whose Arab Legion constituted the strongest of the Arab armies, cut a secret deal with Israeli foreign minister Golda Meir: he would not oppose the Israelis in areas the UN had assigned them, provided that they would not contest Jordanian control of the West Bank of the Jordan River. Well-trained, well-equipped, and unworried about its strongest foe, Israel quickly won the war.

---

*The Irgun was led by Menachem Begin, who became prime minister of Israel in 1977 and, with Anwar el-Sadat and Jimmy Carter, negotiated the 1979 peace treaty between Egypt and Israel.

†This notification led directly to the proclamation of the Truman Doctrine on March 12, 1947.

‡ It is difficult to condemn Britain for its pessimism, since more than seven decades later no acceptable solution has yet been found.

§The United Nations supported the creation of two separate states: one Jewish and one Arab. The Arab state in Palestine was never created because the already existing Arab states never agreed to the partition.

**Zionism is the conviction that the Jewish people must have a land of their own, located in Palestine.

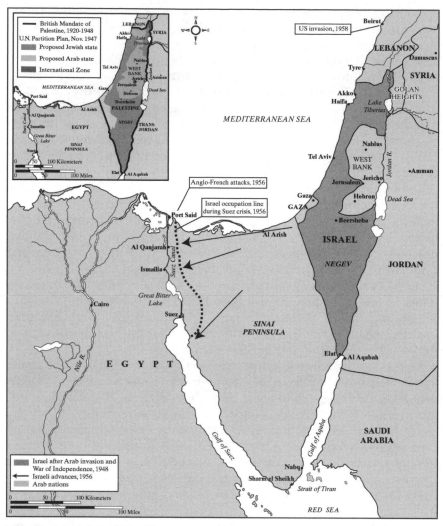

Map 4.1.   Arab-Israeli Conflicts, 1945–1960

From 1949 until 1955, Israel maintained an uneasy truce with its Arab neighbors. No peace treaties were negotiated, because Arab states refused to recognize Israel's right to exist and could not sit at the same table with Israeli diplomats, although Jordan secretly maintained contacts with Israel. And there was a fundamental reason for this refusal: the shock of Israel's victory produced such trauma in Arab states that any government willing to recognize Israel would have been overthrown by its own people. This prompted a search to discover what had gone wrong and how the disaster of 1948–1949* could be rectified. That search, in turn, propelled the Middle East squarely into the arena of the Cold War.

ARAB NATIONALISM AND THE RISE OF NASSER

Israel's defeat of its Arab enemies provoked intense soul-searching across the Middle East. Some concluded that only by returning to the principles of early Islam could Arabs gain the spiritual purity required to defeat Jews. Others held that acquiring modern weaponry would level the balance. Still others contended that Arab governments were weak and inept and that replacing effete monarchs with military regimes would guarantee victory. This third option got its chance in Egypt in 1952, when the Association of Free Officers ousted the dissolute King Farouk and established a military government headed by General Mohammed Naguib and Colonel Gamal Abdel Nasser.

Nasser, the thirty-four-year-old son of a postal clerk, had used his position in the Egyptian army to conspire with the Italians in 1941 in hopes of driving the British from Egypt. His flashing eyes and infectious smile complemented a lyrical, passionate Arabic rhetorical style that enthralled his listeners. Both smarter and more colorful than his colleagues, by 1954 he had replaced Naguib as head of the Revolutionary Command Council and shortly thereafter became president of Egypt.

Most Egyptian army officers hated Britain's indirect imperialistic control of their country. Until 1922 that control had been more overt, with roots extending back to 1882. Now, however, it was exercised more discreetly via a sixty-five-mile-long complex of military and air bases near the Suez Canal and through the Suez Canal Company, which was owned and operated by British and French interests. Occasionally more direct influence had been exerted, most memorably in 1942, when Britain intimidated King Farouk into replacing his prime minister with a man more sympathetic to British interests. Nasser and the rest of the officer corps were deeply humiliated by the incident, and Farouk's removal ten years later was mostly attributable to his weakness in the face of both Britain and Israel.

In order to underscore their superiority to Farouk, the Free Officers would have to expel Britain from Egypt, and Naguib and Nasser set out to do exactly that. They found a British government willing to negotiate. After the Palestine debacle and the development of both the hydrogen bomb and long-range bombers (as well as the prospective deployment of intercontinental ballistic missiles), air bases near the USSR became less crucial to British strategy. London was ready to gradually withdraw all

---

*Called by Arabs *al-Nakba*, "the catastrophe."

but seven thousand of its eighty thousand troops from Suez, provided that it could access the bases in case of war and that Egypt would join the Middle East Defense Organization (**MEDO**), a British-sponsored association designed to oppose a Soviet invasion of the Middle East.

Negotiations soured quickly. Nasser viewed both MEDO and the seven-thousand-man contingent as instruments of British indirect imperialism (which they were). He wanted Britain out completely. The US government, while sympathetic to Britain's position, also saw Egypt through Cold War lenses and feared that London was more concerned with preserving neocolonial leverage than with containing communism. British Foreign Secretary Anthony Eden suspected that Washington intended to replace London in Egypt, while Secretary Dulles feared that unreasonable British demands on both Iran and Egypt might force a reluctant United States to assume expensive commitments it would rather leave to Britain. Dulles in March 1954 threatened that Washington would act independently in both nations unless Britain relaxed its attitude, and this ultimatum got things moving.

On October 19, 1954, thanks to Dulles's cajolery and an unlikely meeting of the minds between Nasser and British negotiator Anthony Nutting,* Egypt and Britain reached agreement on the Suez bases. Britain would withdraw all its forces by June 1956, and the bases could be reactivated in the event of external attack on the region. As Eden had feared, the United States gave notice that after 1956 it would give aid to Egypt and replace Britain there. By this time it was clear that Egypt would not join MEDO, and the United States was looking for other ways to shore up Egypt as an anti-Soviet bulwark. Full implementation of the agreement would end British imperialism in Egypt. Compared to Britain's disastrous withdrawals from India and Palestine, however, the peaceful detachment from Egypt promised by this treaty was a triumph for London.

Nasser, having ousted both Naguib and the British, was understandably euphoric. He took advantage of widespread popular approval to preach a philosophy of pan-Arabism, grounded in four principles:†

1. Arabs are a single people who share a common destiny.
2. They must eradicate European colonialism and imperialism, as well as Zionism, which most Arabs viewed as a form of Western colonialism.

---

*Anthony Nutting was an Arab expert in the British Foreign Office who later became deputy to Foreign Secretary Selwyn Lloyd. Nutting and Nasser became good friends, and Nutting's 1967 biography of Nasser remains a useful and well-respected study.

†Best encapsulated by Salim Yaqub, *Containing Arab Nationalism* (Chapel Hill: University of North Carolina Press, 2004), 31–32.

3. They must eradicate poverty, disease, illiteracy, and all forms of social and economic injustice.
4. They must practice nonalignment in the Cold War.

The development of cheap transistor radios permitted Nasser to use the powerful transmitter of Radio Cairo to disseminate pan-Arabism throughout the Middle East. His stunning rhetorical skills guaranteed him a wide, attentive audience.

There were, of course, those who pointed out that principles 2, 3, and 4 followed from principle 1, and principle 1 was highly debatable. When had Arabs ever constituted a single people? Hadn't the Prophet Muhammad used Islam to develop a community of believers that would replace tribal loyalties and quarrels? Hadn't that faith community (or *umma*) fractured long ago along multiple lines? And wasn't the assertion of "a common destiny" wishful thinking based on a leap of faith? Given this history, how could pan-Arabism succeed?

This logic found little support in Egypt but resonated tellingly in Saudi Arabia, Jordan, and Iraq, where kings opposed Nasser because he had overthrown a monarchy and peoples opposed him for many reasons, including resentment of Egyptian arrogance (among other things, Egyptians refuse to call themselves Arabs, a fact that perplexed those who listened to Nasser's speeches proclaiming Egypt as the leader of the Arabs). Outside the Arab world, pan-Arabism came as a shock—especially in London and Washington.

Britain's Conservative government, now with Eden as prime minister, tried to buttress its influence in the Middle East through the Baghdad Pact. Signed by Turkey and Iraq on February 18, 1955, and subsequently adhered to by Pakistan, Britain, and Iran, it was meant to promote the shared political, economic, and military goals of its five members. The United States supported the Pact as a defensive perimeter against Soviet imperialism but disapproved of London's decision to join and refused to join itself. Nasser agreed with Washington's reasoning: British adherence to the Pact was simply British imperialism in a new form. He refused to bring Egypt into it, and when Eden and Dulles attempted to frighten him with the specter of communism, Nasser simply observed that Soviet Russia had never tried to colonize the Middle East, while Britain had done so and was still exercising imperial influence through Jordan and Iraq. For Nasser, as for most Arab nationalists, anti-imperialism trumped Cold War fears, a position that disturbed Washington profoundly.

By mid-1955 it was clear that both London and Washington were leery of Nasser. It was also becoming clear that France would have its own issues with the Egyptian leader, owing to the latter's support for anti-French rebels in a colonial war in Algeria.

THE ALGERIAN WAR, 1954–1962

France's defeat in Indochina, discussed in chapter 3, emboldened existing independence movements in Morocco and Tunisia, French possessions in North Africa. On November 1, 1954, terrorist attacks in forty-five Algerian cities marked the emergence of a third such movement: the Algerian *Front de Libération Nationale* (National Liberation Front, or **FLN**). Paris moved expeditiously to grant independence to Morocco and Tunisia early in 1956, but Algeria was technically an integral part of France and not a colony. French settlers constituted 10 percent of its population, and neither they nor the French army, having already been defeated by Germany and the Vietminh, were interested in losing yet again. France poured money and troops into a massive effort to preserve French Algeria.

The FLN proved a formidable foe, not so much on the battlefield as in diplomatic and media combat. Carrying out atrocious terror bombings, which provoked vicious French reprisals marked by extensive use of torture, the rebels expertly kept their cause prominent at the UN and in the world. But they fielded only twenty thousand troops against more than five hundred thousand French, and they were constantly desperate for weapons with which to fight hit-and-run guerrilla skirmishes. They obtained those weapons from Nasser, who in 1955 began purchasing arms from Czechoslovakia and running many of them secretly across Libya's desert into Algeria.

This arms deal with Czechoslovakia, arranged by Chinese Premier Zhou Enlai at the Bandung Conference and approved by Moscow, gave Washington nightmares. Here was the stuff of which horror movies were made: Soviet imperialism was encroaching upon the Middle East. Britain and America promptly tried to outbid Moscow by brokering peace between the Arab states and Israel (which would presumably lessen Egypt's need for arms), and by underwriting Nasser's cherished project, a dam on the Nile at Aswan. This bidding war led directly to the Suez Crisis of 1956, which is discussed later in this chapter.

Meanwhile the fighting continued in Algeria, with increasing numbers of French conscripts being sent there. Militarily the French could not be defeated. In an audacious midair kidnapping in 1956, France forced a plane carrying four FLN leaders from Morocco to Tunisia to land at Algiers, where the men were arrested and jailed. The following year the FLN launched a massive campaign of terror bombings across Algiers, but French paratroops clamped martial law on the city, tortured and killed suspected FLN guerrillas, and won this "Battle of Algiers."* The problem was that both French victories, and, for that matter, nearly everything else France did in Algeria, handed victories to the FLN in the court of world opinion. FLN representatives in New York engineered repeated UN resolutions condemning French colonialism and brutality and calling for Algerian independence. The United States, fearful that French insistence on continuing colonial rule was alienating African and Asian states and delivering an invaluable propaganda victory to Moscow, pressured Paris to end the war quickly.†

Gradually the French people turned against the war, but French settlers in Algeria did not. The officer corps of the French army supported the latter, and since most of that army was in Algeria, the possibility that the French government in May 1958 might seek negotiations with the FLN left France open to the appalling prospect of an invasion from Algeria launched by its own army. In what amounted to a coup d'état, France's only living World War II hero and former provisional president, General Charles de Gaulle, became prime minister. He immediately flew to Algiers, told cheering crowds of French settlers, "Je vous ai compris" (I have understood you),‡ and persuaded the French people to pass a new constitution creating a powerful executive branch of government. He then ran for president and won overwhelmingly. No one could imagine that he would let Algeria go. But over the next four years, he did precisely that.

De Gaulle had always been a maverick who never entirely trusted the French army or French political institutions. He trusted only his own vision of France as a great power, and he quickly learned that the Algerian war stood in the path of that status. By 1959 he was convinced that Algeria must eventually govern itself, despite the pain this caused both the settlers and himself. He tried to obtain the best terms possible, but by 1962 the FLN had lost militarily but won politically, and Algeria gained independence. Along the way, de Gaulle survived two military coups and multiple assassination attempts. Both lionized and vilified, he was now free to pursue his vision.

The FLN triumph was hailed by Nasser, but it did not, as Eisenhower and Dulles feared, open the door to Soviet influence. Algeria's Communist Party had played a minor role in the revolution and none at all after independence. In Egypt, Nasser imprisoned and tortured communists while simultaneously accepting Soviet aid. Reality in the decolonizing

---

*The name, widely used at the time, was appropriated by Gillo Pontecorvo as the title of his award-winning 1966 film, *La battaglia di Algeri.*

†The famous 1957 speech by then senator John F. Kennedy calling for Algerian independence was roundly denounced by the Eisenhower administration, less because of any disagreement with its logic than because of embarrassment at a public airing of Washington's impatience with France.

‡Nearly all accounts of this incident fail to note that "Je vous ai compris" also has a colloquial meaning: "I've got your number." Understood this way, it lends a certain ambiguity to de Gaulle's remark.

world was obviously more complex than Cold War thinking imagined. At no point was this complexity more confusing than during the Suez Crisis of 1956.

THE SUEZ TANGLE

Several developments in 1955 intersected and made 1956 a very dangerous year. Nasser was buying arms from the Soviet Bloc and running some of them to the FLN. Britain and the United States agreed to fund the Aswan Dam project. They also launched Project ALPHA, a serious effort to make peace between the Arab states and Israel, which would thereby reduce Nasser's need for weapons. And Britain continued to try to perpetuate its influence through the Baghdad Pact, which the United States endorsed but refused to join.

Into this intricate, volatile situation stepped Israeli Prime Minister David Ben-Gurion. He saw the Baghdad Pact as dangerous to Israel: it connected Britain, which ten years earlier had been the target of Jewish terrorists, with Israel's avowed enemy Iraq. What if London decided to arm anti-Israeli states like Iraq? Weapons earmarked for defense against Soviets could also be used to kill Israelis. Obviously what happened between Israel and Egypt in April 1956 was one consequence of the Baghdad Pact.

By early 1956 Project ALPHA was moribund. Israel agreed to compromise on Palestinian Arab refugees and the status of Jerusalem but refused any territorial concessions. The Arab states of Egypt, Iraq, Jordan, and Lebanon agreed to the Israeli compromises but insisted on territorial concessions. London and Washington tried vainly to break this deadlock while London proceeded with its efforts to strengthen and expand the Baghdad Pact. Nasser, distrusting British intentions, successfully pressed King Hussein to keep Jordan out of the Pact.* The United States, frustrated over the failure of ALPHA, began transforming it into OMEGA, a plan to destroy Nasser's influence, possibly by ousting or assassinating him.† In April, while all this was going on, Egyptian forces killed three patrolling Israeli soldiers. In retaliation, Ben-Gurion launched a large-scale assault on Gaza that killed fifty-six people. Nasser promptly sent hundreds of commandos into Israel, causing another ten deaths. Israel then prepared for war with Egypt, which UN Secretary-General Dag Hammarskjöld

---

*King Hussein's dismissal of the British commander of Jordan's Arab Legion, Sir John Glubb, in March 1956 convinced London that it could not do business with Nasser. Prime Minister Eden incorrectly held Nasser responsible for the dismissal and told the Arab expert Anthony Nutting that he wanted Nasser murdered.

†So it is argued by Tore Peterson, *The Middle East between the Great Powers* (New York: St. Martin's Press, 2000), 63.

managed to prevent through personal diplomacy. The US State Department was so appalled that it recommended involving Moscow in peace negotiations, but Eisenhower would have none of that.

As if this chaos were insufficient, Nasser decided in May 1956 to grant diplomatic recognition to the People's Republic of China. Eden now considered Israel reckless and Nasser implacably hostile, while the United States was disgusted with the entire situation. Both parties decided to withdraw their previously announced backing for the Aswan Dam, a decision made easier for Eisenhower by growing opposition in the US Congress from members representing cotton-producing states that feared Egyptian competition.

Dulles's July 19 statement that Aswan funding would be withdrawn could hardly have surprised Nasser. For some reason, however, his reaction astonished the Western powers.* On July 26, in a dramatic speech in Alexandria, Nasser nationalized the Suez Canal Company, seizing control of it from its British and French shareholders. Canal tolls would henceforth be paid to Egypt, which would use those profits to build the Aswan Dam. The Company's shareholders would be compensated for their loss, but of course the precise value of that property would be a matter for negotiations, which, given the poisonous state of relations, could not be expected to proceed smoothly. Nonetheless, Washington hoped and expected to avoid outright hostilities. It aimed to isolate Israel from the dispute, involve other Arab nations in the quest for a peaceful accommodation, and obtain that accommodation before Moscow could interfere.

This would have been an ambitious but not unrealistic agenda, provided that London and Paris shared Washington's perspectives and hopes. They did not. France recoiled in horror from the prospect that Nasser, flush with Canal revenues, could dispatch unlimited quantities of weapons to the FLN. British Prime Minister Eden, deaf to Kipling's injunction to "keep your head when all about you are losing theirs,"† overreacted catastrophically. Convinced that Nasser would use control of the Canal to cut off Britain's oil imports from Iran and Arabia (highly unlikely, since cutoffs produce no tolls), Eden told the British Cabinet to prepare for military action to overthrow the Egyptian government and reclaim the Canal.

Eden was warned of the probable consequences of his actions. British Minister of Defence Sir Walter Monckton asserted that military action would be widely condemned overseas and would lead to sabotage of British oil installations in the region. He called attention in particular to the

---

*Since nationalization had been feared and denounced for decades by imperialist powers, it is difficult to attribute this shock to anything other than underestimation of Nasser.

†The reference is from Rudyard Kipling, "If."

probable absence of US support; only the explicit approval of the United Nations could mitigate this and avoid serious damage to Anglo-American relations. Eden's law officers (the attorney general and solicitor general) told him bluntly that anyone who said that force was not illegal under the UN Charter was simply wrong, and that if the government tried to assert in public that military intervention to regain the Canal was in fact legal, they would resign. Yet Eden pressed ahead, supported by cooked intelligence and an analogy that preposterously equated Nasser with Adolf Hitler.*

These reactions, which should have led Eden to consider that he might be mistaken, were not necessarily fatal to his plans. What tipped the balance toward catastrophe was his decision to keep his intentions secret from the US State Department. Eisenhower, of course, would have argued against him, but that dispute would have been preferable to what actually happened. The United States set about seeking a diplomatic solution while assuming that Britain and France were open to one, so that when it became apparent that they *weren't*, Eisenhower felt betrayed—a sentiment reciprocated by Eden and most of the British Cabinet, who could not believe that Washington would openly oppose them. These misunderstandings and refusals to communicate led to disaster.

Dulles worked through the late summer and early autumn in pursuit of a settlement, but the British and French worked against him, and Nasser resisted any agreement limiting Egypt's sovereignty. In October 1956, relations between Jordan and Israel deteriorated so sharply that an Israeli invasion of the West Bank appeared likely. In that event, the Anglo-Jordanian Treaty, which bound both nations as allies in a mutual defense pact, would come into play, and Britain would be required to go to war with Israel just as it was contemplating going to war with Egypt. To forestall this preposterous (and dangerous) scenario, Eden addressed both problems by accepting France's suggestion that Israel attack Egypt across Sinai and threaten the Canal. Britain and France would then denounce both belligerents and drop paratroopers alongside the Canal to protect it. Once in Egypt, these forces would coordinate with Israel to overthrow Nasser and return the Canal to Company ownership.

Ben-Gurion, having been prevented by Hammarskjöld from attacking Egypt in April, smiled at British and French hypocrisy and grabbed this new opportunity. London and Paris instituted a news blackout against Washington and set the attack for October 29. When it came, Monckton and Nutting resigned; Lord Mountbatten of Burma, Admiral of the Fleet, attempted to resign but was ordered under naval discipline to remain at his post.† Had the disastrous affair lasted longer, many more would have

---

*It is difficult to decide which of them should have been more insulted by the comparison.

†Mountbatten, the last viceroy of India, was uncle to Prince Philip, Duke of Edinburgh, and second cousin once removed to Queen Elizabeth II.

undoubtedly resigned; some members of parliament thought that Eden had literally gone mad.

Meanwhile the Americans were furious. Eisenhower was in the final week of his reelection campaign and was denouncing the Soviets for their interference in Hungary (see chapter 7). Just when Moscow had apparently decided to accept the Hungarian revolution and withdraw, the Middle East exploded into war. On October 31 Nikita Khrushchev changed his mind about withdrawing,* ordered the Soviet army to crush the Hungarian rebels, and left Eisenhower holding a bag crammed with Israelis, Britons, French, and Egyptians. The US National Security Council concluded on November 1 that if Washington came down on the side of colonialist powers, the entire developing world would look to the USSR for leadership.

The United States therefore opposed its NATO allies in the UN and obtained a cease-fire resolution. By November 2 fighting between Israel and Egypt was almost over, but British and French paratroop drops began on November 5, when there was obviously no need to protect the Canal. At that point the invaders ran into blunt superpower opposition. The Suez Crisis had triggered an investor flight from the British pound, and when London approached the International Monetary Fund (IMF) for financial relief, the Americans, who controlled IMF decisions, would agree to consider it only on condition of an immediate cease-fire. Simultaneously, Soviet Premier Nikolai Bulganin sent telegrams to London and Paris openly threatening atomic warfare if the aggressors refused to withdraw. Moscow couldn't carry out those threats—the Soviets lacked the required missile and bomber capabilities—but the Americans could carry out theirs simply by ignoring Eden's pleas, and on November 6 the British agreed to a cease-fire. Washington then considered the request for aid and agreed only if the British promised to withdraw from Egypt unconditionally. With no feasible alternative, Britain complied and the invasion collapsed.

The Suez Crisis was, in the words of an eminent scholar, "a counterproductive, catastrophic fiasco, marked by deception, hypocrisy, myopia, and confusion, and ending in humiliating failure."[1] It didn't change everything in the Middle East, but its impact was dramatic and extensive. European colonialism, already moribund, was now clearly dead, and indirect imperialistic influence was not far behind. French bitterness at the United States, already raw due to American pressure to settle the Algerian war, became even sharper despite being tinged with a liberal

---

*Khrushchev told the Soviet leadership that the USSR could not afford to be defeated by imperialists in both Egypt and Hungary. Intervention at Suez was out of the question, but the situation in Hungary could still be saved. For his part, Eisenhower was nearly apoplectic over the Suez incident, which distracted world attention from Soviet brutality in Hungary.

dose of Gallic cynicism; after all, what else could one have expected from the Americans? Anglo-American relations would be painstakingly rebuilt over the next several months, but a certain degree of mistrust would persist. Israel, condemned across the globe as an aggressor, was unrepentant, having battered the Egyptian army and occupied the Sinai Peninsula, which it would not relinquish until April 1957 (map 4.1). And throughout the Arab world, two men were heroes for having stood up to colonialism—two men who certainly could not be called either friends or allies: Gamal Abdel Nasser and Dwight Eisenhower.

Clearly this state of affairs could not endure for long, and over the next two years it changed dramatically as the decline of imperialism continued within the context of the Cold War.

THE EISENHOWER DOCTRINE AND ARAB NATIONALISM

Nasser's popularity in the Middle East lasted for years, but Eisenhower's ended in a matter of weeks. Bulganin's rocket-rattling telegrams had played no substantive role in the Suez Crisis,* but Washington feared that, with Britain and France in retreat, the Soviets might now seek a foothold in the region. Joining the Baghdad Pact was out of the question because of its identification with British imperialism. But if Moscow decided, in some future crisis, to send "volunteers" to fight in the region the way China had sent "volunteers" to Korea seven years earlier, how would the United States respond?† Suddenly, in the Middle East, the Cold War was interacting with the decline of imperialism in potentially dangerous ways.

Dulles and Eisenhower decided to capitalize on the latter's newfound popularity with a speech to a joint session of the US Congress on January 5, 1957. In that address, the president asked for (and eventually got) a congressional resolution authorizing military intervention to defend any nation "requesting such aid, against overt armed aggression from any nation controlled by International Communism."[2] This was the **Eisenhower Doctrine**, and it rapidly ended Arab goodwill toward Washington. In its fixation on Communist aggression (which most Arab leaders considered unlikely), it tacitly condoned Israeli aggression (which had actually occurred on October 29, 1956)—and Israeli aggression was widely con-

---

*Khrushchev, however, was convinced that they had forced Britain and France to back down, and several times in the next few years resorted to such intimidation against the United States. Eisenhower's failure to capitulate on these occasions perplexed the Soviet leader but did not dissuade him from repeating his efforts. Many Arab leaders were grateful for the telegrams and tended to overlook Soviet brutalities in Hungary, much to the dismay of Washington.

†Bulganin's telegrams had threatened just such action.

strued as imperialistic.* Thus in attempting to avoid identification with British imperialism by steering clear of the Baghdad Pact, Eisenhower had inadvertently identified himself with Israeli, British, and French imperialism, which his administration had resolutely opposed the previous November.

Despite this, it appeared for a time that the doctrine might succeed. It was never designed to trigger US military intervention, but simply to *threaten* such action, thereby strengthening America's friends and deterring Moscow. In April 1957 King Hussein of Jordan courageously (or impulsively) waded into the midst of troops whose loyalty was questionable, rallying them to the monarchy and giving him the leverage required to oust his nationalist prime minister, whose cabinet was supported by communists. Washington backed Hussein by moving the US Sixth Fleet to the coast of Lebanon. The doctrine's supporters claimed this deterred the Soviets; its detractors suggested that Moscow never noticed what was happening in Jordan.

Encouraged, the US government then tried to use the doctrine to overthrow the Syrian government. The Suez Crisis had broken out on the precise day when a British plot to oust that government, Operation STRAGGLE, was supposed to begin.† The attempt had been aborted, since its timing would have damned it as pro-Israeli, and the Syrians had learned about it. The combination of Suez and STRAGGLE discredited pro-Western Syrian leaders and pushed the government to the left. This in turn alarmed Washington, and Syria's subsequent opposition to both the Eisenhower Doctrine and Hussein's April heroics confirmed the US belief that Damascus was headed for the Soviet Bloc.

According to a group of Syrian army officers, the CIA, working out of the US embassy in Damascus, began in July 1957 to assemble sympathetic officers for a plot to use the army to oust the leftist government. But some of the targeted officers betrayed the plan to their superiors, and the Syrian government monitored its progress before suddenly expelling three US embassy officials on August 13. The relevant documents remain classified, but there is ample evidence that after the expulsions, the Eisenhower administration worked diligently to create an Iraqi-led coalition to invade Syria, at which point Washington would declare Syria under the control of international Communism and implement the Eisenhower Doctrine. Iraq's King Faisal II, fearful that such action would lead to his own overthrow by pro-Nasser elements, declined to take the lead, and the plan sputtered out.

---

*It is not difficult to see why. Zionism was widely perceived by Arabs as imperialistic, and in the Suez Crisis Israel was obviously aligned with British and French imperialism.

†Britain had hoped to install a pro-Iraqi government in Syria that would ally with London's Iraqi protégé, Faisal II.

Clearly the doctrine was not as formidable as it looked. In February 1958 it became even clearer that it would not give the United States carte blanche to defend its interests in the Middle East. On February 1 Egypt and Syria merged to form a United Arab Republic (**UAR**). Although at first reacting negatively, Washington quickly recognized the new regime, having finally accepted the fact of Nasser's hatred for communism. The Egyptian leader could be counted on to block communists in Syria as he had in Egypt—and indeed, one condition of Nasser's consent to the merger was the dissolution of the Syrian Communist Party.* The doctrine obviously did not apply to the UAR.

That summer, however, the doctrine was used to justify military intervention for the first (and only) time. Lebanese President Camille Chamoun, taking advantage of a Congress elected with CIA funds and packed with his supporters, announced on May 8 that he would violate the constitution and seek a second term. Rioting broke out in Beirut; Chamoun attributed it to pro-Nasser elements and informed Washington that he might soon seek military intervention under the Eisenhower Doctrine. The United States advised against it, telling Chamoun that it could detect no evidence of communist involvement in the riots. The crisis deepened until on July 14 Iraqi army officers overthrew that country's pro-Western monarchy, killing the prime minister and the entire royal family.

The bloody events in Baghdad shocked the world and surprised London and Washington. Chamoun used the chaos to claim that he was next on the menu; he formally requested US intervention. Dulles and Eisenhower reluctantly agreed. Even though the doctrine did not apply, as there was no communist threat, they decided to invoke it to avoid loss of US credibility in the region.† King Hussein prepared to invade Iraq to avenge the murder of his cousin, Faisal II; the British managed to dissuade him, but Prime Minister Harold Macmillan, who had replaced Eden in the wake of the Suez debacle, seized the opportunity to send British forces to Jordan to shore up Hussein's regime and reassert British imperial interests.‡ United States marines accordingly went ashore in Beirut on July 15. They found sunbathers and Coca-Cola vendors, but neither communists nor Nasserites (although they nearly got into a confrontation with Lebanese militia units that did not approve of their president's invitation).

Gradually the crisis abated. Nasser urged Khrushchev to issue some sort of ultimatum, but the Soviet leader did not consider Lebanon worth

---

*The initiative for the merger came not from Egypt but from Syria.

†The US government also considered intervening in Iraq to reverse the July 14 coup but decided against it a few days later, when the revolutionary government stabilized the situation there.

‡Hussein was bullied into requesting British intervention and later characterized that request as the greatest humiliation of his life.

a superpower confrontation. American forces left Lebanon on October 25, and British troops pulled out of Jordan the following week. By that time it was apparent that the new Iraqi government was anti-Nasser, and although it cultivated communist support, Khrushchev's reluctance to act reassured the West. If Marx was accurate in his claim that history repeats itself—the first time as tragedy, the second as farce—Suez was apparently the tragedy while July 1958 was the farce.

THE 1967 AND 1973 WARS

For nearly a decade after the 1958 crisis, Middle Eastern issues became less important in the Cold War. Nasser found it impossible to unify the Arab world: Syria dissolved its union with Egypt in 1961, and Iraqis remained allergic to Egyptians. Israeli leadership became more cautious after the Suez Crisis, emphasizing development and accumulation of state-of-the-art conventional weaponry while simultaneously using French technology (provided in consideration of Israeli services during the ill-fated Suez affair) to produce nuclear weapons.* No Israeli government seriously considered a repetition of the 1956 invasion of Sinai.

This did not mean that the region suddenly became calm and peaceful. No Arab state recognized the existence of Israel, and their governments vied with each other in promising to destroy the Jewish state. Border incidents were frequent, and occasional dogfights erupted between patrolling aircraft. Then, in the spring of 1967, tensions escalated between Israel and Syria. In mid-May Soviet military intelligence generated a report that Israeli forces were mobilizing on the Syrian border, and Prime Minister Alexei Kosygin passed this report along to Nasser. The Egyptian president quickly determined that no such mobilization was taking place. But he responded by moving combat units of his army into strategic places in the Sinai Peninsula, simultaneously requesting that the United Nations peacekeeping forces that had been stationed between Israeli and Egyptian forces since 1957 be withdrawn.

What happened next has never been adequately explained. UN Secretary-General U Thant, rather than stalling for time or attempting to negotiate a reduction in tensions, agreed to withdraw the peacekeepers.† Nasser appears to have concluded that he could provoke a war in which the Israelis would strike first, the United Nations would then intervene

---

*Israel has never acknowledged its possession of nuclear weapons, preferring a policy of "opacity" in order to keep other nations guessing. Ever since the 1960s, however, a frequently repeated epigram has been "Israel has no nuclear weapons, and 250 of them are stored in the Negev Desert."

†It is impossible to imagine former Secretary-General Hammarskjöld acting in such an ineffective and potentially disastrous manner.

as it had in 1956, and Israel would be forced to back down while Nasser would regain the popularity he had enjoyed eleven years earlier.* Soviet sources that became accessible after 1991 indicate that Kosygin had no intention of goading Nasser into war, but those sources do not disclose exactly what the Soviet leadership thought would happen.

Israel could not figure out Nasser's objectives and did not feel able to wait around to find out. In a swift predawn raid on June 5, Israeli fighters destroyed nearly all of the Egyptian air force on the ground. With air superiority, Israel then made short work of the armies of Egypt, Syria, and Jordan,† occupying in the process both the West Bank of the Jordan River and East Jerusalem (map 4.2). Nasser resigned his office, but then thought better of it after two million Egyptians poured into Cairo streets imploring him to remain. The United States, preoccupied with the war in Vietnam, played no part in the war; nor did the Soviet Union, whose intelligence report had caused all the trouble.

Despite their lack of participation in the fighting, the superpowers found themselves immersed deeply in the diplomatic aftermath. United Nations Security Council Resolution 242, passed on November 22, 1967, called on Israel to evacuate the lands its forces occupied in the June War in exchange for peace and recognition by its enemies of its legitimacy. The United States and the USSR both supported the resolution, as they had supported Israeli withdrawal after the Suez Crisis. But the conditions for implementation of 242 were not met, as the Arab states refused to make peace with Israel. This led to six years of tension-filled terrorism and animosity, fueled now by the superpowers, with the United States supporting Israel and the Soviet Union supporting Israel's Arab adversaries. That meant that the dispute had become an issue in the Cold War, a fact that placed the Arab states at an even greater disadvantage than the one that had affected them before 1967.

Washington's support for Israel had developed gradually over the previous two decades. Truman's swift recognition of Israeli statehood in 1948 had dismayed many of his closest advisors, who believed that US interests would be poorly served by alienating Arab states.‡ Eisenhower had attempted to implement an evenhanded policy in the region, and Kennedy, aware of Tel Aviv's secret efforts to develop an atomic bomb, had been coolly skeptical of Israeli intentions. But in 1967 Lyndon Johnson, increasingly consumed by the war in Vietnam, was not inclined to

---

*This is the logic deployed in Michael Oren's well-informed account, *Six Days of War: June 1967 and the Making of the Modern Middle East* (New York, 2002).

†Syria and Jordan had joined the war in support of Egypt.

‡Secretary of State George Marshall had gone so far as to threaten to vote for Truman's opponent in the 1948 presidential election if the United States recognized Israel. Because voting in the United States is by secret ballot, there is no way to determine whether he carried out this threat.

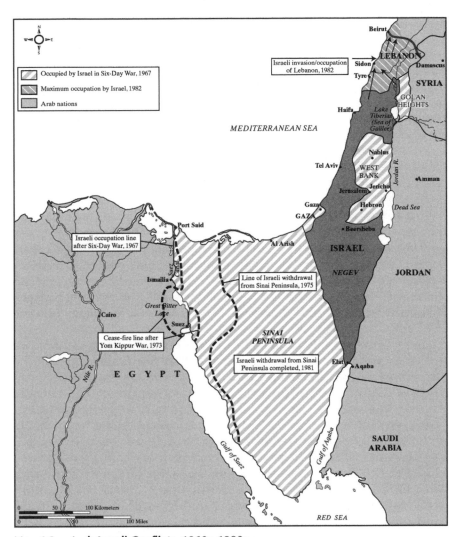

Map 4.2. Arab-Israeli Conflicts, 1960s–1980s

force Israel to surrender the territories it had won in the Six-Day War (although Eisenhower, ten years earlier, had brought enormous pressure to bear upon Israel to relinquish the Sinai Peninsula, which it had conquered during the Suez Crisis). Johnson committed the United States to support Israel against its Arab neighbors, a commitment that Richard Nixon reaffirmed against his better judgment.

The Soviets, who were already supplying weapons to the Egyptian army, responded with a strategy designed to minimize the damage from inter-Arab quarreling by depicting Zionism as the principal threat to the Middle East. Muscovite propaganda explicitly identified Zionism as a form of imperialism and condemned the United States as Israel's financial underwriter. The linkage of Zionism with imperialism carried clear overtones of anti-Semitism, which in turn strengthened Washington's ties to Israel. Ominously, the convergence of these superpower strategies transformed the Middle East into a principal theater of the Cold War.

As long as the superpowers stood clear of the Middle East situation, Israel stood alone against several mortal enemies. This fact contributed to the Israeli decision to develop atomic weapons. But once the situation was framed in Cold War terms, with Israel enjoying strong support from the United States, three additional factors were introduced. First, the United States could project its military power into the Middle East more quickly and easily than could the Soviet Union. Second, the Arab states now became exclusively dependent on Soviet weaponry, which was years behind US weaponry in technological sophistication.* And third, another war between Egypt and Israel would, if not strictly limited in scope and duration, result in a major international crisis and a showdown between the superpowers—a showdown in which the Arabs were likely to come out losers.

These considerations frustrated the Arab opposition to Israel and led to its fragmentation. With the Egyptian military disgraced after 1967, the Suez Canal blocked by sunken ships, and Syria and Jordan having been soundly defeated and deprived of important territory,† conventional warfare against Israel was out of the question for the foreseeable future. This opened the door for the Palestine Liberation Organization (**PLO**), an umbrella group of Palestinian guerrilla and lobbying agencies that had been established by Nasser and the Arab League in 1964 as a way of keeping the Palestinian cause before the world. Under the leadership of an Egyptian-born civil engineer named Yasser Arafat, the PLO initiated terrorist attacks, at first sporadic but later systematic, against Israel. In the process it became embroiled in direct conflict with Jordan's King Hussein, whom the PLO considered insufficiently revolutionary. Hussein unleashed his army on the PLO in September 1970, and Nasser worked day and night to stop the fighting and broker a settlement. He announced the terms of a peace between them on September 28 and then died of a heart attack that afternoon.

Nasser's death propelled his vice president, Anwar el-Sadat, into the leadership of Egypt. Sadat took stock of the changed circumstances of the post-1967 Middle East and recognized that continued hostility to

---

*Before 1967 Israel's enemies could purchase certain types of weapons from NATO nations, a channel that they found closed after 1967.

†Jordan lost the West Bank and East Jerusalem, while Syria lost the Golan Heights.

Israel was weakening the Egyptian economy. He concluded that Washington held the key to peace in the region, and in 1972 he dramatically expelled all Soviet military advisors from Egypt. Then he waited for the United States to notice what he had done and to initiate discussions, but as US National Security Advisor Henry Kissinger later admitted, the US government was preoccupied with extracting the nation from the war in Vietnam, and it paid insufficient attention to Sadat's overture.

Unable to focus Washington's gaze on the Middle East, Sadat moved closer to Moscow, obtaining large quantities of Soviet arms and bringing Syria and Jordan into an alliance dedicated to launching a surprise attack on Israel.* This was the genesis of the October War, a conflict that erupted suddenly on October 6, 1973, a day that happened to coincide with the holiest days of the year in both the Jewish and Islamic calendars. Israeli defense forces were caught by surprise, and the Egyptian army won important victories before Israel was able to mount a successful counteroffensive. The United States and the USSR collaborated to negotiate a cease-fire, embodied in United Nations Security Council Resolution 338, on October 22. But the cease-fire was broken at once, and as Israel drove its forces toward encirclement of the Egyptian Third Army, Washington and Moscow lobbed threats at each other, creating a potentially dangerous situation before finally forcing their clients into a lasting cease-fire on October 25.

Egypt lost the October War, but Sadat had done what Nasser had never been able to do: defeat Israeli forces on the battlefield, however impermanent that defeat turned out to be. This gave him sufficient popularity and leverage to attempt one of the most stunning diplomatic initiatives of the Cold War. With Egypt's economy sinking more and more deeply into bankruptcy, Sadat dramatically opened peace negotiations with Israel, flying to that country on November 19, 1977, to meet with Israeli Prime Minister Menachem Begin and address the Israeli Knesset (parliament). One vestige of British imperialism became strikingly apparent: Sadat and Begin, having both lived under British rule, spoke excellent English and needed no interpreters!

Now it became clear that the United States was the heir to British imperialism in the Middle East. Sadat and Begin, deeply mistrustful of each other, used the good offices of US President Jimmy Carter as an intermediary. With the Soviet Union excluded from the process, Carter, Sadat, and Begin reached agreement on a framework for a peace treaty between Egypt and Israel in September 1978,† and successfully concluded and

---

*For a judicious appraisal of the origins of the October War of 1973, see Craig Daigle, *The Limits of Détente: The United States, the Soviet Union, and the Arab-Israeli Conflict, 1969-1973* (New Haven, CT, 2012).

†These dramatic events are portrayed vividly in Lawrence Wright, *Thirteen Days in September: Carter, Begin, and Sadat at Camp David* (New York, 2014).

signed that treaty on March 26, 1979. For the moment, at least, US diplomacy appeared to have brought Middle East peace closer to realization and to have won a significant Cold War victory over Moscow.

ISLAMIC REVOLUTION IN IRAN

Peace between Egypt and Israel transformed the Middle East power balance. Egypt had been the linchpin of four unsuccessful Arab wars against Israel; without it, a fifth was unimaginable. Arab rage against Egypt was eye-popping, and that fury was not restricted to Arabs. In Iran, a non-Arab Muslim nation that was allied to the United States and had been selling oil to Israel for decades, Sadat was vilified as a traitor to Islam, and it was not coincidental that in 1978, as peace between Egypt and Israel drew nearer, Iran's status as a US ally was called into question by an Islamic revolution.

Since the removal of the nonaligned Mosaddeq government in 1953, the Shah of Iran had planted his feet firmly in the Western camp. He tied both Iran's foreign policy and its economic growth to its status as a client state of US imperialism. Iran was willing to sell oil to Israel, and its strategic placement on the USSR's southern border made it the perfect location for high-tech listening posts whose operators eavesdropped on conversations between Soviet officials and monitored missile tests at the remote, secluded complex at Baikonur in Soviet Central Asia. In exchange for these benefits, the Eisenhower administration granted Iran $78 million in economic aid in 1953 alone, and from 1953 through 1963 US military aid to that country totaled $535 million, making Iran first in that category among countries outside NATO. In 1957 the Shah received CIA help in creating **SAVAK**, the notorious Iranian State Intelligence and Security Organization, and the Israeli intelligence service, Mossad, became SAVAK's close partner. Those who called Iran an ally of imperialism knew whereof they spoke.

This did not mean that the Shah was a backward traditionalist. Most Iranians lived in poverty, landless and illiterate; the Shah, intelligent and well educated, knew he could not rule forever on repression and American clientage. He decided in 1963 to launch a "White Revolution,"* described by one historian as "a systematic process of centrally controlled general mass mobilization and selected socio-economic reforms, largely in line with Westernization, in support of his leadership and rule."[3] In

---

*Since the nineteenth century, revolutions against conservative regimes had adopted the color red, while those regimes often took the color white. The Shah was trying to make the point that conservatives could be revolutionaries, too, and could avoid totalitarianism in the process.

doing so, he aimed to bring Iran into the twentieth century under the protection of a conservative, anticommunist government closely connected to Washington in the Cold War.

Atheistic communism had no more appeal in Iran than in any other Islamic state, but given Iran's experience with Western imperialism, the Shah's bonding with the United States and Israel was risky. Opposition developed almost at once, centered on the same ulema that had undermined Mosaddeq. One of its leading figures, Ayatollah Ruhollah Khomeini, became such an outspoken foe of the Shah that he was exiled in 1963.* From abroad he continued to denounce the Shah as a puppet of Washington and Tel Aviv and the White Revolution as a godless sellout to alien Western values.

Khomeini's critique was compelling, if not entirely fair. The Shah's actions in the early 1970s, when he led a Middle Eastern coalition that succeeded in raising oil prices sharply, indicated that he was more than a puppet. But he was closely tied to the West, and the White Revolution brought with it not merely Western material goods but *materialism*, with all its hangers-on: drugs, rock and roll, sexual promiscuity, equality for women, and jeans. This perspective may seem laughable to persons in the West, but the impact of such values on a traditional Islamic society was corrosive.

By early 1978 Iranian living standards had improved substantially, but the Shah's ties to the West and to Israel, paired with the invasion of alien liberal and materialistic values, destabilized the internal situation. In spring 1978 there were demonstrations and riots in major Iranian cities. Khomeini sent word to his followers to join them, and when some demonstrators were killed, massive memorial services were held forty days later.† This gave further demonstrations a religious veneer, providing camouflage for political and intellectual protesters. The Shah prodded Iraq into expelling Khomeini, who sought refuge in France and inundated Iran with sermons and polemics recorded on cheap, easily smuggled cassette tapes.

Gradually the protests grew into a nationwide movement, and in autumn the Shah's fragile support crumbled. The Cinema Rex, a movie house in Abadan, caught fire and four hundred perished; rumors spread that SAVAK had set the blaze. When mourners packed Jaleh Square forty days later in commemoration, police fired into the crowd, producing more martyrs. A massive earthquake on September 16 killed fifteen thousand and cut the city of Tabas off from water and electricity; the government seemed incapable of providing relief services or restoring power. That same month, Israel and Egypt reached preliminary agreement on a peace

---

*There was a personal dimension to his opposition: Khomeini believed that SAVAK had killed his son.

†Most Iranians are Shia Muslims. In the Shia tradition, martyrdom of believers requires commemorative services forty days after the event.

treaty, infuriating millions across the Middle East. Emboldened supporters of the ousted Mosaddeq (who had died in 1967) publicly demanded
the Shah's abdication, and US President Carter urged him to comply. In
January 1979 the Shah went into exile, and on February 1 Khomeini returned from France to a massive welcome as the leader of what he called
an Islamic Revolution.

Khomeini was underestimated by Carter and most Western and Soviet officials, who considered his appearance and ideas "medieval." All
of them assumed that the Mosaddeq-oriented professional politicians
would outmaneuver the Shia clergy and seize control of the revolution,
but Khomeini outsmarted them all. Vilifying the United States as the
"Great Satan" and the USSR as the "Lesser Satan" and accurately describing both cultures as secular and materialistic, he blended fear of alien
values with hatred of imperialism of all kinds into a foreign policy of
nonalignment. This enabled him to win over Mosaddeq's secular followers *and* deeply devout Muslims, giving him the political base he needed to
create an Islamic theocracy—a development that flabbergasted observers
across the world.

So in 1979 the United States lost its eavesdroppers in Iran, the USSR
found itself demonized, and Israel lost its main oil provider. Imperialism
was in full retreat on all fronts. When the Soviet Union invaded Afghanistan that December (chapter 7), it was at least partially in response to
the unexpected developments that had placed an Islamist regime on its
southern border. If that regime could spread its worldview to the Muslim
majority in Soviet Central Asia, the very existence of the Soviet Empire
would be jeopardized. Israel located oil elsewhere, and Washington
replaced its listening stations with increasingly sensitive espionage satellites, but for the USSR, the threat was existential. Moscow neither understood it nor knew how to defeat it. For decades the USSR had exploited
the struggle against imperialism to advance its Cold War interests, but it
could do so no longer.

CONCLUSION: IMPERIALISM'S LASTING LEGACIES

The Middle East, like Africa and Latin America, is a region of great
diversity and territorial expanse. It is neither entirely Arab nor entirely
Islamic, and its modern history has been shaped by many factors, some
quite contemporary and others centuries old. Western imperialism, a
relatively recent factor, deeply affected Middle Eastern peoples who,
whether Muslim, Jewish, or Christian, had for centuries been part of
powerful, far-flung Islamic empires. The forcible imposition of European colonial rule shocked and traumatized the area, stemming as it

did not from any supposed cultural, racial, or religious superiority, but from a technological revolution that gave Europeans insurmountable military advantages while leaving Islamic regimes baffled and thunderstruck.

World War II left colonial empires in decline, but its aftermath introduced a new European intruder in the Middle East: Israel, a state filled with European Jews and equipped with the same Western technological advantages that had doomed the great Islamic empires. Defeated in the 1948–1949 war, Arab states found themselves whipsawed between traditional monarchism and Nasser's pan-Arabism. The latter approach promised the destruction of Israel, but, crippled by intra-Arab rivalries, it proved incapable of even evicting Britain and France without assistance from the Cold War superpowers. That help, rendered during the 1956 Suez Crisis, brought the Cold War to the Middle East and involved it in the struggle against imperialism. Soon Middle Eastern peoples came to fear not only Israeli but also American and Soviet imperial pretensions.

The Soviet Union never lost interest in either the strategic value or the petroleum resources of the Middle East. But while those factors were *potentially* valuable to Moscow, they were *actually* crucial to the survival of Western industrial states, and Washington left no doubt that it would, if necessary, fight a general war to hold them (as two Persian Gulf Wars later demonstrated). That sufficed to keep the Soviets marginalized throughout the Cold War. But it left the Arab states stuck with a status quo that included Israel, and when pan-Arabism could not deliver on its promises and Egypt defected from the anti-Israeli coalition, some Muslims looked to past glories for a solution through some sort of Islamic revival. Khomeini's Islamic Republic, both Iranian and Shia, repelled Sunni Arabs, but his call for a return to Islamic values resonated among those who saw no hope of defeating the West through conventional military means.

That resonance led to the cul-de-sac of terrorism, which had helped the Jews of Palestine expel the British—but only because London already had one foot out the door. Terrorism is the last resort of the powerless, and it proved less effective against Israel, which, unlike Britain, is located in the Middle East, and against the United States, which continued to define the region and its resources as essential to Western survival. The apparent alternative—mutual recognition and peace between the Arab states and Israel—remained chimerical in the second decade of the twenty-first century, as the persistent legacies of imperialism outlasted the Cold War and continued to plague the Middle East.

5

❧

"Scram from Africa!"

Anti-Imperialism and the Cold War in Africa

PROLOGUE: TWO MEETINGS

It was January 30, 1944. A tall, thin French general stood outlined against a cloudy tropical sky in an open field in the French Congolese city of Brazzaville. Charles de Gaulle, self-proclaimed leader of Free French Forces fighting Nazi Germany, spoke slowly and dramatically to the assembled leaders of France's empire in Africa.

That empire had, in de Gaulle's estimation, rescued the honor of France. After the French government had surrendered to Germany in June 1940, de Gaulle eventually established a government in exile and based it at Brazzaville, which was then the regional capital of French Equatorial Africa and is now the capital of Republic of the Congo. France's African colonies welcomed his forces and contributed tens of thousands of volunteer soldiers to his cause. Now, although the war was still in progress and France itself remained occupied, de Gaulle was summoning French imperial officials to an African conference. He was an aloof, secretive, solitary man, and none of them knew what to expect.

De Gaulle's opening statement startled them. He expressed his gratitude to French Africa and then declared flatly that Africans living under French authority must have the right to participate in determining their own destinies.* The conference then set to work discussing the political,

---

*"This war is about nothing more or less than the conditions of life of mankind and the psychological forces which have been released everywhere that make every individual raise his head, look around him and question his destiny . . . no progress will be possible if the men and women on their native soil do not benefit materially and spiritually and if they are

99

social, economic, and spiritual problems confronting French African territories, where people thrilled to the words of de Gaulle as his message spread. For as long as he lived, Africans would know him as the "Man of Brazzaville," and Senegalese poet and statesman Léopold Senghor would later call de Gaulle the greatest African of the twentieth century.

It might have been even more impressive, of course, had some of the faces at the Brazzaville Conference been black. All of them were white.

Sixteen months later, as the war in Europe was ending, a different sort of meeting convened near Manchester, England. Nearly every face at the **Fifth Pan-African Congress** was black or brown. Convening in a shabby hall that was drafty and chilly, the delegates represented various parts of British Africa, but they had spent the war living either in England or America. Included in their ranks were the most important African nationalist leaders of their day:

- George Padmore, born Malcolm Nurse in Trinidad, a former Soviet agent who had broken with Stalin in 1933
- Jomo Kenyatta of Kenya, another former Soviet agent and skilled journalist who also had abandoned Stalin after 1933
- Kwame Nkrumah of the Gold Coast, a brilliant organizer of incredible drive, who likewise had been drawn to Soviet Marxism
- Dr. Hastings Banda of Nyasaland, a deeply conservative Presbyterian who was so revered for his competence and generosity that patients in his waiting room stood up in respect whenever he entered

The Congress was filled with fiery oratory and passionate anticolonial resolutions, but none of its delegates knew what was going on in Africa, and no one in Africa noticed what was happening in Manchester. Nkrumah reminisced years later, "Nobody bothered you about what you were doing and there was nothing to stop you getting on your feet and denouncing the whole British Empire."[1] The atmosphere could not have been more different from that in Brazzaville the previous year.

These contexts—the cooperative, all-white ambience of Brazzaville, the nationalistic passion of Manchester, the paternalism of de Gaulle, the Marxist tendencies of many African nationalists, and the soon-to-develop Cold War—would all coincide in the next few decades, as the struggle against imperialism engulfed the African continent.

---

not able to raise themselves to the point where they are capable of taking a hand in the running of their countries. It is France's duty to see that this comes about." Charles de Gaulle, Opening Speech at the Brazzaville Conference, January 30, 1944, http://www.charles-de-gaulle.com/l-homme-du-verbe/speeches/30-january-1944-speech-at-the-opening-of-the-Brazzaville-Conference.html.

AFRICAN NATIONALISTS SEARCH FOR A THIRD WAY

The appeal of Soviet Marxism to African nationalists of the 1920s and 1930s was logical. First, their colonial rulers were British, French, Belgian, Portuguese, Spanish, or Italian; the Soviets owned no African colonies and didn't seem to want any. Second, Marxism divided people by class, and not by race; to Marxists there was no such thing as an inferior race. Third, Marxism was international in appeal. The workers had no country; all were brothers and sisters. It was not for Europeans only. Fourth, Marxism preached class solidarity and collective responsibility. These attitudes resonated with Africans, whose traditions were collective, not individualistic. And fifth, the Soviets had a command economy directed from the top. Many African nationalists, aware that their homelands had single-resource economies exploited for the benefit of the mother countries, saw centrally directed economic change as the most efficient way to modernize and industrialize.

Stalin, however, did not rule in the spirit of internationalism. He advocated *socialism in one country*, preferring to fortify the USSR as a bulwark against capitalist invasion. He thus played power politics, allying with some capitalist powers against others. In 1933 he responded to Hitler's ascendancy in Germany by drawing closer to Britain and France, in the process abandoning nationalist movements in their colonies. This led Soviet agents like Padmore and Kenyatta to desert Stalin and focus on anticolonial rather than Marxist agitation.

Once the Cold War began in 1947, US officials looked upon this anti-Stalinist position as a distinction without a difference. A communist was a communist, they believed, and African nationalism was tainted with communism. These officials, many of whom had long opposed European colonialism, now concluded that the need for strong allies in the Cold War trumped America's proud anticolonial heritage. Britain, France, Belgium, and Portugal were founding members of NATO and therefore allies of the United States after 1949, and their support against Soviet Communism could not be won by undermining their control of their African colonies.

Meanwhile, African nationalist leaders were considering their options. Between 1945 and 1957, none of them expected colonialism to end quickly. The most they hoped for was incremental progress over the next few decades.* They understood that the Cold War was transforming international politics into an extremely dangerous standoff between capitalism and communism. They also observed the success of nationalistic movements in Asia, where (as described in chapter 3) India, Pakistan,

---

*Even this timetable was considerably more ambitious than those of the colonial powers. As late as 1956 most European officials anticipated that colonialism would endure into the twenty-first century.

Burma, Indonesia, Laos, Cambodia, and North and South Vietnam all won independence between 1947 and 1954. All the more reason, they felt, to focus mainly on nationalism, and to avoid close identification with an international economic system like capitalism or an international philosophy like Marxism.

The Bandung Asian-African Conference of 1955 (chapter 3) gave them hope. They watched as Nehru, Sukarno, Nasser, and other leaders met to work out a Third Way for the Third World, a nonaligned path between capitalism and communism. Permeating Bandung was the belief that World War II had destroyed the credibility of European civilization without providing any other worldview with which to replace it. The Third World, the newly independent nations, would step forward to provide new leadership. It was exhilarating.

Would it amount to anything more than exhilaration? Only time would tell. In the mid-1950s, African nationalists had reason to feel optimistic. Bandung gave them a glimpse of a brighter future. Khrushchev's ascendancy in the USSR and his focus on peaceful coexistence raised hopes for a thaw in the Cold War. In British Africa, the Gold Coast was moving gradually toward independence, and the French Empire was racked by an anticolonial war in Algeria. In 1956 the Suez Crisis (chapter 4) humiliated Britain and France, caused a temporary rift between them and their American allies, and called into question their ability to retain their colonial possessions. Perhaps independence was closer than anyone anticipated. Perhaps a Third Way might prove more than a dream.

WEST AFRICA GAINS INDEPENDENCE

Colonialism in West Africa began to unravel when London granted its Gold Coast colony a constitution in 1946.* Middle-class African dissatisfaction with that document, which provided only limited autonomy, led to the creation of an anticolonial pressure group, the United Gold Coast Convention, in August 1947. The Convention hired Nkrumah as organizer and all-around dynamo. Gifted with overpowering energy and masterful organizational talents, he soon proved far too radical for the Convention's moderate leadership, and in June 1949 he left it and formed the Convention People's Party (CPP). Within four months he was

---

*Britain's Labour government (1945–1951) granted the Gold Coast a constitution in an effort to establish a representative political system that would serve as the foundation for orderly development in the colony. It was not a framework for independence, which was expected to follow after at least twenty to thirty years of continued British rule over a partially autonomous Gold Coast government.

convicted of sedition and sentenced to three years in prison. But the CPP conducted strikes and protests, and the colony's British governor, Sir Charles Arden-Clarke, decided in 1951 that it was ungovernable without the CPP's assistance. He released Nkrumah, and the two men began to cooperate. By 1953 Nkrumah was Chief Minister of an autonomous Gold Coast government, and London granted full independence to the new nation, now named Ghana, effective March 6, 1957 (map 5.1).

The independence ceremonies turned into an enormous party, attended by delegations from fifty-six countries. Britain held a place of honor: it was liberating Ghana after six years of exemplary collaboration, leaving behind ample currency reserves and a well-educated elite

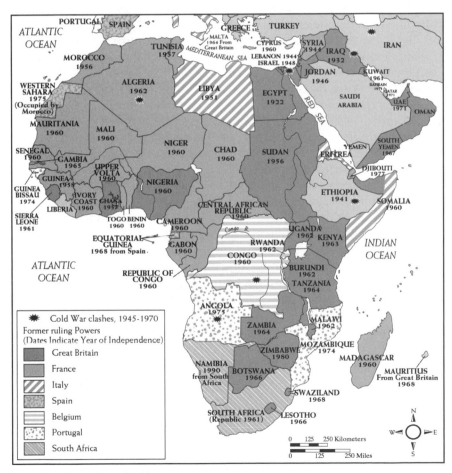

Map 5.1. Postcolonial Africa

prepared for self-government.* In April 1958 Prime Minister Nkrumah, long a proponent of Pan-Africanism,† hosted a conference of African nations committed to that goal. That December an All-African Peoples' Conference, organized by Nkrumah and Padmore, was attended by more than three hundred delegates, some of whom would lead independence movements themselves: Dr. Hastings Banda of Nyasaland, Tom Mboya of Kenya, Kenneth Kaunda of Northern Rhodesia, Joshua Nkomo of Southern Rhodesia, Patrice Lumumba of the Belgian Congo, Holden Roberto of Portuguese Angola, and Amílcar Cabral of Portuguese Guinea. Mboya challenged the European powers in his concluding speech: "It is time to reverse the scramble for Africa. Your time is past. Africa must be free. *Scram from Africa.*"[2]

By this time France was reluctantly doing just that. While Britain worked to give Africans greater autonomy, France worked to give them a role in improving the empire, which had been de Gaulle's intent at Brazzaville. From 1946 to 1958, hoping to recast the empire as a new "French Union," France poured money into Africa, but Ghana's independence, coupled with the Algerian War (discussed in chapter 4), undermined these hopes. After de Gaulle returned to power in May 1958, he sought to convert the Union into a French Community, in which each colony would enjoy local autonomy while Paris exercised full authority over economic, foreign, and defense policy. He might have pulled it off had he not embedded this conversion within a referendum on a new French Constitution scheduled for September 28, 1958. Every French colony and territory was to vote in the referendum.

Most nationalist leaders of French Africa wanted to preserve their association with France into the indefinite future, with independence as their ultimate goal. They were appalled to hear de Gaulle phrase their choice in stark terms: a *Yes* vote on the Constitution was a vote to remain within the French Community forever, with no possibility of eventual independence; a *No* vote would mean immediate French withdrawal, followed by economic and political chaos. In August 1958 de Gaulle toured Africa, where leaders told him that the dichotomy would force at least five colonies to vote *No*. Tacking into the wind, he compromised by assuring Africans that independence would still be possible. This soothed nationalist feeling in every colony except Guinea.

---

*Nkrumah acknowledged Ghana's debt: "We part from the former imperial power, Great Britain with the warmest feelings of friendship and goodwill. . . . Instead of bitterness which is often born of a colonial struggle, we enter on our independence in association with Great Britain and with good relations unimpaired." Nkrumah, *I Speak of Freedom*, 108–9 (see note 1 in this chapter).

†Pan-Africanism is the conviction that all or most of Africa should consist of a single nation organized under a federal system.

There the nationalist movement was led by Ahmed Sékou Touré, a tough-minded former trade union official who deeply resented de Gaulle's bullying tactics. With the French leader looking on impassively, Sékou Touré flayed French colonial policy in an impassioned speech in Guinea, proclaiming, "We prefer poverty in freedom to riches in slavery."* On September 28 Guinea voted 95 percent *No.* The next morning French officials pulled out, taking with them office furniture, telephone wires, lightbulbs, and every other item France had provided. Sékou Touré walked into the executive mansion to find all the crockery broken. Independent Guinea faced a bleak future.

De Gaulle's petty vengeance made Sékou Touré an instant hero throughout Africa, and ironically, his compromise doomed the French Community. By 1960 nearly every French African colony was requesting independence. De Gaulle made the best of the new situation and granted independence freely, accompanying it with generous pledges of continued support—the opposite of what he gave Guinea. Paradoxically, by means of this support, France continued to dominate most of its former African colonies long after they gained independence.

THE COLD WAR AND WEST AFRICA

As West Africans thus emerged from French and British rule, their new nations quickly became part of the Cold War. Prime Minister Nkrumah, who became president of Ghana when its constitution was altered in 1960, had come to realize that communism and African nationalism were incompatible, since Moscow and Beijing demanded direct control of communist parties throughout the world and such control would preclude any movement toward African unity. But he was also a complex and suspicious man who retained his Marxist sympathies and disliked Western consumer-oriented materialism. So he, like others inspired by Bandung, sought a channel between the rocky reefs of capitalism and communism.

He soon found nonalignment no easier to attain than African unity. US Vice President Richard Nixon, seeking to convince the Eisenhower administration that new nations were worth cultivating, attended Ghana's Independence Day ceremonies in March 1957. Eight months later a Soviet mission arrived, although full diplomatic relations were not established until August 1959. By then Nkrumah had visited the United States and was pursuing American support for the construction of a major hydro-

---

*Ahmed Sékou Touré, like British Prime Minister David Lloyd George, preferred to be known by both his middle and last names. The quotation is reprinted in Elizabeth Schmidt, *Cold War and Decolonization in Guinea, 1946–1958* (Columbus: Ohio University Press, 2007), 151.

electric dam on the Volta River, while hinting that he might turn to Moscow for such support if necessary. He thus began a game not of nonalignment but of two-board simultaneous chess, playing against both sides in the Cold War while trying to remain friendly with each. The simple truth was that nonalignment would work only if a nation needed nothing from either Cold War superpower. Ghana, like all newly independent African nations, needed help, and help came not through neutrality but through patron-client relationships.

Dwight D. Eisenhower, suspicious of Nkrumah's Marxist inclinations, deferred consideration of the Upper Volta project. In September 1960 Nkrumah visited the United States again, this time to attend a session of the United Nations General Assembly. The year 1960 was the "Year of Africa," with seventeen new African nations joining the United Nations (map 5.1). World leaders like Eisenhower,* Khrushchev, Nasser, Sukarno, Nehru, and Castro attended parts of the session, seeking Cold War advantages and votes in the General Assembly from the new states. Nkrumah took the opportunity to speak to the General Assembly on the Congo Crisis (discussed later in this chapter) and to meet with both Eisenhower and Khrushchev. His speech was evenhanded, upsetting US Secretary of State Christian Herter, who had hoped for an endorsement of US policy. Rumors spread that Nkrumah had said different things to Khrushchev than he had to Eisenhower, who was only too happy to leave the Volta Dam decision to his successor.

The new president, John F. Kennedy, was favorably inclined toward African nonalignment, feeling that if the Soviets could be denied footholds in Africa, the United States would eventually win the sympathies of the new states. But as his term began, word arrived of the murder of former Congolese prime minister Patrice Lumumba (discussed later in this chapter). Nkrumah, who had backed Lumumba, blamed his death on the CIA and stated publicly that Kennedy was a murderer, even though Lumumba had been killed on the night of January 17–18, 1961, three days before Kennedy took office. Soviet President Leonid Brezhnev flew at once to Ghana and confirmed Moscow's decision to build a smaller dam on the Black Volta River. Ghana was now in the midst of the Cold War.

Kennedy watched while Nkrumah called for the reunification of Germany and diplomatic recognition of the People's Republic of China in

---

*The United States was in a particularly awkward spot between 1957 and 1964, as its intensifying civil rights movement coincided with the decolonization of Africa. How could Eisenhower defend racial equality and justice abroad without alienating both his NATO allies and elected officials in southern states at home? How could any US president effectively rebut Khrushchev's claims that the United States was an intrinsically racist society when African Americans were being set upon by dogs and fire hoses in Alabama? Only the eventual passage of the Civil Rights Act of 1964 brought some relief. See Thomas Borstelmann, *The Cold War and the Color Line* (Cambridge, MA, 2001).

September 1961. Nkrumah was also making pro-Western statements and was trying to pursue a neutralist foreign policy, but the US Congress and State Department believed he had turned communist. Kennedy, less certain, continued to dangle the Volta River project as bait. Moscow, meanwhile, sensing that Nkrumah was no communist, was not sure if it should compete for the Volta Dam.

Nor could the Soviets compete with US consumer goods. Ghana opened an energetic commercial relationship with the Soviet Bloc, with disappointing results. Sacks of Soviet cement arrived underweight. Soap was delivered in buckets instead of boxes. Electrical goods were shoddy and unreliable. Soviet toothpaste tasted and smelled like rancid oranges.* Ghanaians were unimpressed.

Gradually Nkrumah turned toward the West. Kennedy approved the Volta River project on terms highly favorable to American investors, and the completed dam provided an excellent source of cheap hydropower. Washington won the race for Ghana, but its victory proved worthless. Nkrumah, whose regime was rife with corruption, spent an inordinate amount of time and money trying to overthrow neighboring governments in Liberia, Togo, Upper Volta, and Nigeria, all of which were hostile to pan-Africanism. In February 1966 he was ousted in a military coup.† His successors were friendly to America, but Ghana was now impoverished, and its support meant little in the Cold War.

Moscow had higher hopes for Guinea, whose fragile economy was further weakened by France's abrupt withdrawal. Sékou Touré's policy of replacing private shops with state-run stores led to catastrophic shortages of basic foodstuffs like rice, flour, meat, and cooking oil. He turned to the West for help, but France was a US NATO ally, and Eisenhower was not interested in alienating de Gaulle. So Khrushchev, seeing a chance for a Soviet foothold in West Africa, authorized a 1960 food agreement that bailed the young country out. Washington immediately concluded that Guinea's president was a communist, although, like Nkrumah, he was known in Africa for placing nationalism ahead of ideology.

Most Guineans knew little of communism, and some thought that the United States and the USSR were the same country. Sékou Touré himself found socialism attractive as a rapid vehicle for modernization but also saw Marxism as inconsistent with African culture. He was willing to work with both sides in the Cold War and was disappointed by Eisenhower's unwillingness to offend France. His trump card was Guinea's bauxite deposits, the world's largest. Its version of Ghana's Volta River project was the Konkouré Dam, which would provide hydropower to

---

*Since it was made from rancid oranges, this was not particularly surprising.

†Both the CIA and Britain's MI6 were suspected of involvement in Nkrumah's ouster, but no conclusive proof is available.

aluminum plants and which Sékou Touré wanted the United States to build. Kennedy was willing to consider the possibility, but like Nkrumah, Sékou Touré accused the new president of murdering Lumumba, cooling relations even further.

Soviet food aid saved Guinea in 1960–1961, but its consumer goods support was truly eye-popping: a fifty-year supply of canned crabmeat, six tons of quill pens, trucks and buses with service manuals printed in Russian, a radio station that never worked because it was built over a vein of iron ore, and a tomato cannery in a part of the country with neither tomatoes nor water. No wonder Sékou Touré kept hoping Washington would come around. His meeting with Kennedy in the White House in October 1962 gave him hope. Two weeks later, when Moscow requested landing and refueling rights for its planes headed for Havana during the Cuban Missile Crisis (discussed in chapter 6), the Guinean president rejected the plea even before the US ambassador had a chance to object to it. By October 1963 the Soviet Union was so excluded from Sékou Touré's inner circle that Soviet diplomats began consulting with their US counterparts for information concerning Guinean foreign policy. Eventually, disappointed with both sides in the Cold War, Guinea charted its own path, obtaining support from Arab oil-producing countries in the late 1960s.

Americans and Soviets lost interest in West Africa after 1963. Kennedy's murder removed a friend of African nationalism,[3] and his successor, Lyndon Johnson, was far more concerned with Southeast Asia and Western Europe. Khrushchev was overthrown in October 1964, and his successor, Leonid Brezhnev, had never been impressed by the Marxist credentials of any West African leader. Other parts of Africa, however, commanded the attention of both superpowers for years after West Africa's luster wore off.

WHITE SETTLERS AND RACIST REPRESSION IN CENTRAL AFRICA

British Central Africa, composed of Northern Rhodesia, Southern Rhodesia, and Nyasaland, posed unique opportunities and problems. Northern Rhodesia, home to 40,000 white settlers, was rich in copper but in nothing else. Southern Rhodesia, with 135,000 whites, had diverse agricultural and manufacturing prospects but needed larger markets. Nyasaland, with only 4,000 whites, was desperately poor but had a large African labor force. Combining the three into one federation seemed to offer hope for balanced economic growth.

Political problems outweighed these opportunities. Southern Rhodesia, led by Sir Godfrey Huggins, was rigidly segregationist. Northern Rhodesia's white nationalist leader, Sir Roy Welensky, a charming but emotionally turbulent man, was even more devoted to segregation. Many northerners wanted to combine both Rhodesias and create white domination over more than two million Africans. London was skeptical until 1948, when the unexpected victory of the National Party in South Africa led directly to racial apartheid, a brutal and degrading separatist policy that condemned South African blacks to ignorance and servitude.

The British were aghast: apartheid might spread northward to the whites of Central Africa, depriving native Africans of hope and thus pushing them toward communism. Britain now saw a federation in Central Africa as an antidote to this infection. Neither Huggins nor Welensky wanted apartheid; they felt Europeans and Africans could and should work together, as long as whites held all the power.* In 1953 the British House of Commons endorsed the creation of a Central African Federation (CAF).

No sooner had the CAF been created than Huggins and Welensky set out to make it a self-governing dominion, like Canada and New Zealand. That would mean total independence and permanent subjugation for black Africans. African nationalists reacted with dismay, and Dr. Hastings Banda, who had practiced medicine in Ghana for fifteen years, decided to return to Nyasaland. Conservative by nature, he had been radicalized by events: "Throughout the history of the world there is no incident where a so-called moderate has achieved anything. . . . In Nyasaland we mean to be masters, and if that is treason, make the most of it."† His imprisonment in 1959 led to widespread rioting and violence. London established a commission under Sir Patrick Devlin to investigate, and the Devlin Report was scathing: nearly every African in the CAF opposed not only dominion status but federation itself. Its description of Nyasaland as a "police state" humiliated Britain and called London's entire colonial policy into question.

Britain's Conservative government was stunned: it had considered federation a progressive experiment in racial cooperation and had believed Welensky when he claimed that communists caused the riots. Now British Prime Minister Harold Macmillan saw federation as an attempt to

---

Apartheid, as the National Party developed it, was the total subjection of blacks and people of color to white rule. Black educational systems were either rudimentary or nonexistent, and blacks were restricted to menial jobs. No evolution of this system was considered either possible or desirable. *Segregation*, as Huggins and Welensky developed it, was a program to separate blacks from whites so that blacks could gradually be "civilized," a process that was expected to take more than one hundred years. During this time the races would cooperate, with whites in a position of superiority that would slowly erode over time until equality was achieved.

†Sir Hastings Banda, speaking in Blantyre, Nyasaland, July 6, 1958. Banda was paraphrasing the American revolutionary Patrick Henry's challenge: "If this be treason, make the most of it!"

perpetuate white domination. He recognized that communists did not cause the violence, but he also feared that white suppression of African nationalism would open the door to communist subversion. In October 1959 elections he won a substantial majority and then made a six-week African tour with stops in Ghana, Nigeria, the CAF, and South Africa.

Throughout his trip Macmillan spoke of vast changes affecting the continent, but only in Cape Town, South Africa, the home of apartheid, did his words attract global attention: "The wind of change is blowing through this continent, and whether we like it or not, this growth of national consciousness is a political fact. We must all accept it as a fact and our national policies must take account of it."[4]

South Africa accepted the fact the next year, withdrawing from the British Commonwealth and intensifying its racial suppression. But despite Macmillan's fears, the virus of apartheid did not spread, and communism did not benefit. The South African Communist Party sent General Secretary Joe Slovo to Moscow to convince Khrushchev that Cold War opportunities beckoned, but Khrushchev, fresh from his failure in the Congo (discussed below), showed little interest. In the CAF, Welensky continued to raise the specter of communism should African nationalism triumph, but London no longer listened. The fact that Welensky continually insulted Macmillan and the Conservatives, who were actually his only friends, did not improve their hearing. In December 1962 Nyasaland was granted the right to secede from the federation. It later became independent Malawi, with Dr. Banda as president, and Northern Rhodesia become independent Zambia. The CAF died in December 1963.

That left Southern Rhodesia, which took advantage of its self-governing status within the Commonwealth to issue a unilateral declaration of independence in 1965. Overtly modeled on the US Declaration of Independence, it grew out of the 1962 election, which was eerily similar to the 1948 election in South Africa. In 1962 the United Federal Party, which had held power for thirty years, assumed it could not lose to the Rhodesian Front (RF), a haphazard collection of right-wing extremists. It was mistaken. Capitalizing on white fears of black rule (stemming from the Congo Crisis and the riots in Nyasaland), the RF won a landslide victory and immediately demanded independence from Britain, on the grounds that it was the only party capable of defending the values of Western civilization against the twin threat of international Communism and African nationalism.

The RF leader Ian Smith was a man of limited vision but fixed perspective. He contended that if Africans took over Rhodesia, white living standards would decline, whites would leave, and everyone, white and black, would be ruined. To him this was so obvious that he could not see how anyone could disagree. Since London was willing to deal with a white minority government (as it had tried to work with Welensky's), Smith expected no opposition. But Britain insisted on constitutional provisions guaranteeing the eventual repeal of discriminatory laws and the right of Africans to vote, and the RF flatly refused. Rhodesia's Unilateral Declaration of Independence (UDI) in 1965 proclaimed, "We have struck a blow for the preservation of justice, civilization and Christianity."[5]

For several years it appeared that Smith would get away with it. But in 1972 a British investigative commission visited Rhodesia as a prelude to finalizing independence. The commission interviewed a wide range of Rhodesians both white and black, and unexpectedly concluded that "the people of Rhodesia as a whole do not regard the proposals as acceptable as a basis for independence." Smith and most whites, appalled at the finding, blamed black reaction on Communist agitators. The RF then rammed through a series of discriminatory laws equivalent to those in South Africa.

At that point things changed quickly. In April 1974 a coup in Lisbon ousted Portugal's quasi-fascist dictatorship, and within months the Portuguese Empire in Africa crumbled (as discussed later in this chapter). That opened Rhodesia's 760-mile eastern border to infiltration from newly independent, black-ruled Mozambique. The coup called into question the entire structure of white rule in southern Africa. South African leaders looked at the map and realized that, unless they gave Rhodesia unlimited economic and military backing (which they had no intention of doing), white rule there was doomed. Guerrilla warfare in Rhodesia escalated, and by mid-1977 all white men under age fifty were required to serve six months each year in the armed forces. Businesses closed, white emigration exploded, and Smith finally had to agree to "one man, one vote" to undercut the guerrillas. In May 1979 white rule in Rhodesia gave way to black rule in a nation renamed the next year as Zimbabwe. There had never been any serious danger of a Communist takeover; the Smith government had merely used that bogeyman to justify the perpetuation of white minority rule. But Zimbabwe's new president, Robert Mugabe, who at first ruled in a spirit of interracial cooperation, soon justified Ian Smith's worst fears. Mugabe's brutal dictatorship, lasting more than three decades, led to massive white flight and ruined Zimbabwe's economy, impoverishing everyone.

COLD WAR CRISIS IN THE CONGO

As the French and British Empires in Africa dissolved, Belgium decided to emancipate its Congo colony in a collaborative, gradual manner. After more than seventy-five years of colonial rule, only sixteen living Congolese had been allowed to attain a higher education. All physicians, engineers, and lawyers in the colony were Belgians. This systematic neglect had produced a society lacking the well-trained, experienced leaders necessary for a smooth transition to independence. Brussels hoped that transition would take several decades, but Macmillan's "wind of change" blew them away. Rioting and bloodshed in the capital city of Leopoldville in January 1959 frightened Belgian leaders and created a Congolese political elite that demanded immediate independence. Otherwise, armed struggle would erupt, and collaboration would become impossible. Belgium therefore decided to wager on quick emancipation as the only alternative to massive anticolonial violence.

It lost the bet. On June 30, 1960, Independence Day found the enormous Congo governed by a collection of leaders deeply suspicious of each other. None had ever served in government at any level. Every political party except one was based on tribal loyalties, as the Congo's vast extent and lack of decent roads made it difficult to form national movements. Joseph Kasa Vubu, who wanted to revive the fifteenth-century Kongo Kingdom, led the *Alliance des Bakongo* (Alliance of the Bakongo, or ABAKO Party) of the Bakongo people. Moïse Tshombe, of mineral-rich Katanga province, headed the *Confédération des associations tribales du Katanga* (Confederation of Katanga Tribal Associations, or CONAKAT Party), which wanted a degree of provincial autonomy bordering on secession. The only national party, the *Mouvement National Congolais* (Congolese National Movement, or MNC), was led by Patrice Lumumba, at age thirty-five an outstanding organizer, prolific author, and spectacular public speaker. Belonging to a small, relatively powerless tribe, Lumumba wanted to submerge tribalism in a unified national state. At first, Belgium preferred him to the secessionists Kasa Vubu and Tshombe, but in December 1958 Lumumba returned from Nkrumah's All-African Peoples' Conference determined to transform the MNC into a mass movement modeled on Ghana's Convention People's Party. Belgium then stood aloof as nationwide elections in May 1960 returned a parliament in which MNC held 33 of 137 seats. Although it was the largest party, it had no support in Leopoldville (Congo's capital) or in the southern provinces of Katanga and Kasai. Lumumba was named prime minister with Kasa Vubu as president. This delicate situation called for prodigious coalition-building skills, which neither Kasa Vubu nor Lumumba possessed.

Everything quickly fell apart. A Congolese army garrison mutinied on July 5, and by July 11 internal security had collapsed. Tshombe declared Katanga independent the same day. Brussels now saw Katangese secession as a way to protect European commercial interests in the potentially wealthy province. It could not actually recognize a secessionist government there, since the government in Leopoldville would have immediately expropriated all Belgian investments in the rest of the Congo. But it encouraged Tshombe at every turn, sent in troops to protect European lives and destabilize the Congo further, and helped Katanga recruit white mercenary forces from Europe.

The loss of Katanga's mineral riches left the Congo economically nonviable. Those minerals (uranium, cobalt, chromium, titanium, and diamonds)* also made the region attractive to the superpowers, which pitched the Congo into the Cold War. Lumumba and Kasa Vubu, flying from one part of the Congo to another in an effort to restore order, agreed to intervention by Belgian troops and then appealed to the United Nations. The deputy prime minister asked for US help, a request that Lumumba denounced. Then he and Kasa Vubu, surrounded by Belgian troops at the Kindu airport and fearing for their lives, sent a plea to the Soviet Union on July 14.

Khrushchev had paid little attention to the Congo situation until the arrival of Belgian troops, which took him by surprise. He viewed Katangese secession and Belgian intervention as part of a European conspiracy to continue to control the Congo's mineral deposits and sharply denounced those actions on July 12, 1960. The next day he agreed not to veto an African-sponsored UN Security Council resolution calling on the United Nations to send forces to the Congo to replace the Belgian troops. Then the Congolese government's July 14 telegram arrived.

Khrushchev replied quickly and sympathetically, but he did not commit to any specific action. At this point he was willing to work with the UN, provided it would remove the Belgians from the Congo. He feared American intervention if the UN force proved inadequate, and he warned Washington off in strong terms. Eisenhower and Secretary Herter discounted Khrushchev's rhetoric, but they were apprehensive of Soviet intentions and hopeful that the UN could settle the matter. Complicating their position was Belgium's status as a NATO ally. The Americans hoped the Belgians would leave Africa, the Soviets would stay out, and the Congo would calm down, leaving the NATO alliance intact and the minerals at the continued disposal of the West.

This left matters up to the United Nations, and Secretary-General Dag Hammarskjöld acted decisively. A slightly built, sandy-haired bachelor who combined the characteristics of a Scandinavian mystic and a riverboat gambler, Hammarskjöld saw the Congo Crisis as an opportunity for the UN to assert its moral leverage on behalf of emergent African nations.

---

*The Congo supplied significant percentages of global production of all of these strategically crucial minerals. Exact percentages are available in the *United Nations Statistical Yearbook* for 1962, with the exception of uranium. Because of its use in the production of atomic weapons, actual global production of uranium was not disclosed to the public.

He wanted to keep the Congo out of Cold War politics, get the Belgians out, negotiate a settlement with Katanga, and restore the country's fragile unity. To do all that, he was willing to take the unprecedented step of committing UN troops.

This willingness angered both Khrushchev and Lumumba. By mid-August, Moscow was sending Lumumba modest military aid and portraying Hammarskjöld as a Western stooge: although Belgian regulars had withdrawn, European mercenaries remained, and Hammarskjöld insisted on negotiating with Tshombe rather than using force to end Katanga's secession. Lumumba, increasingly intemperate, called Hammarskjöld a Belgian puppet,* while Hammarskjöld came to see Lumumba as a threat both to Congolese stability and to the United Nations. Lumumba's acceptance of Soviet aid made the Congo a potential Cold War battlefield and earned him Washington's mistrust. On August 18 the CIA was authorized to plot his assassination, and the American embassy in Leopoldville worked to oust him from office. In September Kasa Vubu fired him, and in turn he fired Kasa Vubu.† Colonel Joseph Mobutu, who had been Lumumba's personal secretary and who was close to CIA station chief Lawrence Devlin,‡ orchestrated a military intervention that restored but marginalized Kasa Vubu, leaving Lumumba in the lurch and gaining Washington's approval.

All this chaos infuriated Khrushchev, who believed that Hammarskjöld was conniving with the Americans to remove Lumumba. The mutual firings occurred as the Soviet leader was sailing to New York to address the UN General Assembly in an attempt to rally African and Asian support for both Lumumba and the Soviet position. At the UN he demanded Hammarskjöld's resignation and, when he didn't get it, proposed replacing the secretary-general with a *troika*§ of three officials, one socialist, one capitalist, and one neutral. Eisenhower, convinced that this proposal would render the UN impotent, lobbied forcefully against it but needn't have worried. African and Asian countries were in no mood to see Europeans replaced in Africa by Russians and Americans; they endorsed

---

*Lumumba, like Sir Roy Welensky, seemed unable to refrain from insulting those who had originally been well disposed toward him and his cause.

†The Congo's constitution seemed to indicate that Kasa Vubu had the authority to replace Lumumba, but its language was ambiguous.

‡The CIA's efforts to manipulate events during the Congo Crisis are vividly catalogued in Lawrence J. Devlin, *Chief of Station, Congo* (New York, 2007). Devlin was a colorful figure whose cover was a position as agricultural attaché at the US Embassy in Leopoldville but who seemed to have difficulty distinguishing between a cow and a horse.

§A *troika* was a traditional Russian sled pulled by a team of three horses, one looking right, one looking left, and one looking straight ahead. The Cold War implications were obvious. The analogy, however, was flawed: the troika driver directs the horses to their ultimate destination. Khrushchev's proposal would replace the troika driver (Hammarskjöld) with three driverless horses that would make effective UN action unlikely.

Hammarskjöld's policies, backing a resolution from Ghana that passed 70–0. The Soviet proposal was dead. Although Khrushchev made the best of it by arranging a well-publicized meeting with Cuba's Fidel Castro, he sailed home empty-handed.

None of these developments helped resolve the Congo's problems. It was difficult to imagine that events there could become more turbulent, but they did. Lumumba tried to get to his base of support in Stanleyville to set up a rival regime, but he was arrested in late November 1960 and imprisoned. The rival government was then established without him. By December the Congo was divided into four parts: a government in Leopoldville with Western support; a secessionist government in Katanga with Belgian support; a "Free Republic" in Stanleyville backed by the Soviet Union; and another secessionist government in South Kasai, also with Belgian support. Only the presence of UN forces kept the state together. To make matters worse, the Stanleyville government conquered Kivu province in the eastern Congo and then captured a city in northern Katanga. Fearing that Lumumba would ride Stanleyville's victories back into power, the Leopoldville government turned him over to Tshombe. On January 17, 1961, he and two of his officials were tortured and killed in the presence of Belgian officers and Katangese officials.

Lumumba's murder, which remained undisclosed until February, led to widespread African denunciations of Kennedy, the new US president. Moscow expressed sympathy for Lumumba and renamed its People's Friendship University as Lumumba University,* but avoided deeper involvement. Khrushchev's troika proposal had failed, and his air force could not match US airlift capability, essential for moving troops and supplies into central Africa. So he stepped back and watched warily as Hammarskjöld and Kennedy grappled with the crisis.

Lumumba's death blunted Stanleyville's offensive; deprived of his leadership, his successors proved inept. The Americans, who feared eventual Soviet intervention if the Congo were not reunited, engineered a coalition government in Leopoldville under Cyrille Adoula, a former trade union official. All factions were represented except Katanga, where Tshombe sat supported by mining revenues, European mercenaries, Belgian weapons, and behind-the-scenes backing from certain European officials. Hoping to end secession, Hammarskjöld flew to the Congo in September 1961 to negotiate with Tshombe. He was killed there in a plane crash,† mourned throughout the world, and posthumously awarded the Nobel Peace Prize.

---

*This university offered full scholarships for study in Moscow to students from Third World countries.

†Several investigations over the decades have failed to clarify the cause of the crash. Susan Williams of the University of London makes a compelling circumstantial case for the responsibility of white supremacists, in *Who Killed Hammarskjöld?* (Oxford, 2011).

But peace was no closer, and his negotiations could probably not have produced it without more force than the UN alone could provide.

Force was the key to persuading Tshombe, and Hammarskjöld's death helped convince the United States to provide it. Kennedy authorized a massive airlift of reinforcements and equipment, and UN troops occupied Katanga's capital in December. For another year Tshombe tried to outmaneuver both Hammarskjöld's successor, U Thant of Burma, and the Leopoldville government. By December 1962 Washington concluded that further talks were futile and that, if secession continued, Adoula might be replaced by a pro-Soviet cabinet that would invite Moscow to reunify the country. Kennedy then provided the UN with all the military force it needed to end secession in January 1963.

The reincorporation of Katanga left America's reputation high among African nations, and its NATO allies were finally convinced that colonialism was a spent force. But although colonialism was dead, imperialism was not. Adoula's government proved incompetent and corrupt; by April 1964 it had lost half the Congo to Simba rebels who claimed magical powers. As pro-Soviet revolutionary regimes were established in Stanleyville and Kwilu province, and with defeat looming, the Kasa Vubu government turned to—Moïse Tshombe! He returned from exile, accompanied by his European advisors and mercenaries, and as prime minister led a campaign to reunify the Congo, with massive Belgian and American assistance. His chief military advisor, Major Mike Hoare of South Africa, hired the most vicious thugs he could find in Rhodesia and South Africa. The Kwilu regime quickly collapsed, and Moscow sent Stanleyville nothing but good wishes. The regime there took more than three hundred Belgian and American hostages in November 1964, threatening to kill them unless the assault ended. On November 24, hundreds of Belgian paratroops dropped into Stanleyville from American planes. Fifty hostages were killed and sixty more were wounded as the "People's Republic of the Congo" was overthrown.

The United States was the military winner in the Congo Crisis. But it was immediately vilified by Africans for its embrace of Tshombe and its support for Belgian, Rhodesian, and South African mercenaries. In 1965 Kasa Vubu sacked Tshombe but then was ousted by Mobutu, who seized and held power until 1997. His corrupt and repressive regime was solidly endorsed by Washington. The United States had never been a colonial power in Africa, but it built imperialistic control of the Congo on the ruins of colonialism.

THE COLLAPSE OF THE PORTUGUESE EMPIRE

As the British, French, and Belgian Empires crumbled, Portugal soldiered on. Lisbon's African empire of Mozambique, Angola, and Portuguese

Guinea dated from its pioneering exploration of the African coasts during the fifteenth and sixteenth centuries. Like Belgium, it had done nothing to prepare its colonies for independence; unlike Belgium, it was ruled by a quasi-fascist dictatorship. Convinced of Portugal's civilizing mission in Africa, its dictator, António de Oliveira Salazar,* had no intention of surrendering Portuguese rule. In 1951 he had abandoned the concept of colonialism and decreed that all Portuguese-held territories throughout the world were part of a single, unified nation. Portugal was economically dependent on its colonies, which Salazar now called "provinces." Letting them go was unthinkable to him. Then a 1961 rebellion in Angola took him by surprise.

The Bakongo people of the lower Congo basin populated not only the western Congo but northern Angola as well. Belgium's flight from the Congo in 1959–1960 suggested to them that Portugal similarly might prefer to withdraw rather than to resist the surge of anticolonialism. They were poorly informed. The União das Populações de Angola (Union of Angolan Peoples, or UPA), led by an exiled Congolese accountant named Holden Roberto, sought, like Kasa Vubu did, to restore the old Kongo Kingdom. Roberto had attended Nkrumah's African nationalist conference in December 1958 and had met Patrice Lumumba, who in 1960 let him broadcast to Angola from a Congolese radio station. He had not, however, met Salazar, and the Portuguese ruler would rather fight than flee. The 1961 UPA-led rebellion was brutally suppressed at a cost of seven hundred Portuguese and twenty thousand African lives; the western Congo was inundated with tens of thousands of refugees. But the revolt stunned Portugal, an American NATO ally, causing Cold War complications.

Since 1943 the United States had leased part of Lajes Field, an air base in the Portuguese Azores Islands, 990 miles west of Lisbon and 2,290 miles east of New York. Transport aircraft had limited fuel capacities until the late 1960s, so Lajes was an indispensable refueling station, crucial to the projection of US power into Europe, Africa, and the Middle East. Washington thus maintained friendly relations with Lisbon's fascist government, and when the UPA rebellion erupted in 1961, with the Lajes lease soon up for renewal, President Kennedy was in a delicate position. He wanted to support African nationalism and decolonization, without offending a NATO ally and losing access to a vital air base.

Kennedy encouraged Salazar to make concessions to African nationalism, while secretly supplying CIA support to the UPA. Salazar cooperated up to a point: he abolished forced labor in Angola and introduced

---

*Salazar (1889–1970), a professor of economics who had studied law and had once thought of becoming a priest, became dictator in 1932 and remained in power until 1968, when he was incapacitated by an injury to his brain. In 2007 he was voted the greatest Portuguese of all time by the Portuguese people.

social, economic, and educational reforms. But since he considered the colonies part of Portugal, he refused to make *political* concessions, which were central to the agenda of African nationalism. Moscow watched with interest but did not play an active role: Salazar was staunchly anticommunist, Lajes was well outside the Soviet sphere of influence, and Khrushchev had recently been burned by the Congo Crisis. Kennedy's successors, Lyndon Johnson and Richard Nixon, strongly supported Portugal, and the Lajes lease was repeatedly renewed.*

Meanwhile, with the UPA's defeat and retreat to Congolese base camps, other nationalist groups emerged to compete with it: the *Movimento Popular de Libertação de Angola* (Popular Movement for Liberation of Angola, or MPLA), founded in 1956 among the Kimbundu people of northern Angola and led by a Communist-influenced poet, Agostinho Neto; and the *União Nacional para a Independência Total de Angola* (National Union for the Total Independence of Angola, or UNITA), founded in 1966 among the Ovimbundu people of the central highlands and led by Jonas Savimbi, a former associate of Holden Roberto. These three guerrilla movements, essentially tribal in nature, competed for power for decades. Elsewhere in the empire, the *Frente de Libertação de Moçambique* (Mozambican Liberation Front, or FRELIMO), created in 1962 among the Makoude people of Mozambique, was led by Eduardo Mondlane, the first Mozambican to study at the University of Lisbon. Mondlane was also a UN officer and anthropology professor at Syracuse University before helping found FRELIMO. The most effective of them all was the *Partido Africano para a Independência da Guiné e Cabo Verde* (African Independence Party of Guinea and Cape Verde, or PAIGC), established in 1956 in Portuguese Guinea by a Portuguese-educated agronomist, Amílcar Cabral. By 1963 Portugal faced revolts in all its African "provinces."

Salazar was determined to crush them. Portugal did what France had done in Indochina and Algeria: draft hundreds of thousands of men for colonial combat. It deployed fifty thousand soldiers in both Angola and Mozambique, and forty thousand in Portuguese Guinea, a territory of no value economically or strategically but apparently important to Lisbon's prestige. Portugal's counterinsurgency tactics were initially effective in Africa, and Portuguese secret police assassinated Mondlane in 1969 and Cabral in 1973. But the insurgencies continued, and the Portuguese army grew restive. Its junior officers, mostly draftees, began to sympathize with the people they were fighting, and their concerns drifted upward to the army's general staff. Young people in Portugal increasingly resented its fascist dictatorship and economic backwardness. Salazar was replaced

---

*The lease remained in effect in 2017. The base at Lajes remains strategically important both to the United States and to NATO's ability to project its air power into areas of conflict.

in 1968 by Marcelo Caetano, who promised modernization but failed to promote it.

In early 1974 General António de Spínola, a war hero who implemented reforms in Portuguese Guinea, published a small book, *Portugal and the Future,* asserting that military victory was impossible in Africa. Caetano fired Spínola, but many key officers secretly agreed with his analysis. Every April, the army's general staff returned from Africa to brief the government on the progress of the wars. On April 25, 1974, instead of briefing Caetano, they arrested him and his entire cabinet. Spínola led this military junta, which was supported by the leftist Armed Forces Movement (AFM), a group of radical majors and lieutenant colonels. But Spínola proved too conservative for them, speaking as he did of a twenty-five-year transition to democracy, so they ousted him in August. The new leaders then recognized the independence of Portuguese Guinea* and turned Mozambique over to FRELIMO in 1975.†

That left Angola, where the situation turned chaotic. Internal quarrels distracted the Lisbon government: several members of the AFM were Communists, and Portugal's NATO allies feared that their military secrets would be passed to Moscow. Not until 1976 was the situation resolved by a democratic government that expelled the Communists. Meanwhile, the three Angolan nationalist groups jockeyed for position, and civil war broke out. Virtually the entire white population of three hundred thousand emigrated, and Angola found itself a centerpiece of Cold War tensions. Neither the United States nor Russia had vital interests there, but their prestige was on the line, and any alteration of the global balance of power frightened them.

Moscow backed the MPLA, as did Cuba (with military instructors) and former Katangese troops hoping to destabilize Mobutu's government in the Congo (now renamed Zaire). Washington and Zambia (formerly Northern Rhodesia) supported UNITA. The UPA, now renamed the *Frente Nacional de Libertação de Angola* (National Front for the Liberation of Angola, or FNLA), gained assistance from *both* the United States and China, Cold War partners against the USSR since Nixon's trip to China in 1972. China sent weapons and trainers, America sent CIA personnel, and Zaire sent military units. Tribal divisions accentuated the rivalries. In 1975 Cambodia and South Vietnam fell to the Communists, and US Secretary of State Henry Kissinger saw Angola as a place to recoup lost US prestige.

To further complicate matters, South Africa secretly intervened against the MPLA, which supported a guerrilla movement fighting to gain independence for South African–occupied Namibia and gave that movement

---

*Known after that as Guinea-Bissau.
†For details of the collapse of Portugal's empire, see Norrie MacQueen, *The Decolonization of Portuguese Africa* (London, 1997).

refuge in southern Angola. So South Africa secretly ran weapons to the FNLA and helped train FNLA and UNITA fighters. Chaos might be too mild a term for Angola in 1975.

Matters came to a head in August. Cuba and South Africa both decided to intervene openly with army units.* By November several thousand from each nation were in combat, with the Cubans supported by Soviet arms shipments. CIA funds to support the FNLA and UNITA ran out, and in December the US Senate refused to provide more money. South Africa felt betrayed by Washington, and other African nations, viewing Soviet and Cuban involvement as preferable to South African and CIA imperialism, threw their support to the MPLA. In January 1976 fifteen thousand Cubans were actively deployed, and the war ended the next month with an MPLA victory. Finally the Soviets achieved a Cold War triumph in Africa.

CONCLUSION: AFRICAN TRANSITION

By 1980, then, almost all of Africa was politically independent, and Europe's colonial empires were gone. Decolonization had triumphed, but the hopes and dreams inspired by Brazzaville, Manchester, and the Year of Africa had been dashed by the persistence of poverty, disease, lack of education, and tribal rivalries.

The Cold War was also partly responsible, as it had magnified Africa's inherent challenges. Neither Moscow nor Washington lacked altruism: Khrushchev really *did* see socialism as the correct road for emerging African societies, while Eisenhower and Kennedy really *did* see freedom and democracy as essential to improving African lives. But altruism was trumped by geopolitics. New African nations were seen as providers of rare minerals and as votes in the UN General Assembly. The superpowers manipulated those states economically, politically, and—when they could—militarily. The legacy for Africa was arrested development, characterized by the persistence of one-man rule and single-resource economies.

These characteristics, combined with Africa's economic poverty and its mineral wealth, helped to ensure that Western industrial powers—and later China—would continue to exercise economic dominance and political influence through investments, assistance, and coercion. The empires were gone, but in many less formal ways, imperialism in Africa would live on.

---

*Controversy has raged for decades over which country intervened first. The available evidence supports the Cuban position that South Africa struck first, but the decisions to strike were likely taken independently of each other. Reasons for the Cuban intervention are discussed in chapter 6. For an extensive account of these events, see Piero Gleijeses, *Conflicting Missions: Havana, Washington, and Africa, 1959–1976* (Chapel Hill, NC, 2002).

6

~&

"So Far from God . . . So Close to the United States"

Anti-Imperialism and the Cold War in Latin America

PROLOGUE: CHAPULTEPEC AND RÍO

As World War II entered its final few months, the nations of the Western Hemisphere convened in Mexico City's Chapultepec Castle to discuss issues of hemispheric security in the postwar world. This Inter-American Conference on the Problems of War and Peace was designed to fulfill the prewar Declaration of Lima, which had authorized pan-American consultation in case of threats to the "peace, security, or territorial integrity" of any state in the hemisphere.* The Lima declaration had been directed against German and Italian espionage or aggression; now the Act of Chapultepec (March 3, 1945) updated it by transforming its anti-Axis features into anticommunist ones. In effect, Chapultepec replaced monarchy with communism in the implementation of the Monroe Doctrine of 1823, which had barred European ideologies and regimes from exploiting Western Hemisphere nations.

In March 1945, of course, the Soviet Union was a member of the Grand Alliance, fighting Germany alongside Britain and the United States. The Act's anticommunist thrust therefore predated the Cold War by at least a year. By 1947 that conflict was well under way, and on September 2 the Act of Chapultepec was made permanent in the Inter-American Treaty

---

*Declaration of Lima, December 24, 1938. Readers in the United States are accustomed to referring to their country as "America," a designation that could be applied to any state in North, Central, or South America. In this chapter, we avoid the terms *America* and *American(s)* in favor of *United States* or *US*.

of Reciprocal Assistance, often called the **Río Treaty**.* The United States thereby served notice: in the developing Cold War, Latin America was off limits to Soviet ideology and interference.† The Western Hemisphere was to remain the backyard of the United States.

US IMPERIALISM IN LATIN AMERICA

The United States never had any intention of colonizing Latin America in the way England had colonized the eastern seaboard of North America in the seventeenth century: by sending settlers to displace indigenous peoples and claim distant lands for the British crown. From 1823 on, the United States wanted to exclude European powers from the Western Hemisphere and claim it not for colonization but for economic exploitation.

For most of the nineteenth century, that economic exploitation was carried out by US entrepreneurs like William Wilson and Minor Cooper Keith and by corporations with little or no direct assistance from the US government. The US victory in the Spanish-American War of 1898 changed all that. Washington intervened directly and formally in Cuba through the Platt Amendment of 1902 and in Latin America at large through the Roosevelt Corollary to the Monroe Doctrine in 1904. Repeated military interventions in Mexico, the Caribbean, and Central America ensured the survival of pro-US governments, and the opening of the Panama Canal in 1914 gave those regions strategic significance. The canal expanded exponentially the economic and military power of the United States, so its defense became essential to US security, and that defense required cooperation from local pro-US regimes.

President Franklin Roosevelt changed the nature of US imperialism with his "Good Neighbor Policy,"‡ but he did not dismantle it. The United States depended on Latin America for raw materials (copper, tin,

---

*So named because it was signed in Río de Janeiro, Brazil.

†The term *Latin America* is widely used to refer to the nations of the Western Hemisphere south of the Rio Grande, including the Caribbean basin. It is an incomplete term, because although it is intended to refer to all those nations, the appellation *Latin* refers only to areas colonized by peoples speaking Latin-based languages (French, Spanish, and Portuguese). This would exclude areas colonized by English and Dutch speakers. In this book, we use the term *Latin America* in its broadest sense, including states originally colonized by people who did not speak Latin-based languages.

‡In his inaugural address on March 4, 1933, Roosevelt stated: "In the field of world policy I would dedicate this nation to the policy of the good neighbor—the neighbor who resolutely respects himself and, because he does so, respects the rights of others—the neighbor who respects his obligations and respects the sanctity of his agreements in and with a world of neighbors."

manganese) and foodstuffs (coffee, bananas, sugar). Large German and Italian communities in countries like Argentina and Brazil, as well as the presence of fascist regimes in Spain and Portugal, raised the possibility of fascist subversion within the Western Hemisphere. This concern led to US efforts to promote hemispheric solidarity (hence the Declaration of Lima mentioned earlier), a task facilitated by the Good Neighbor Policy. The transition from an Axis to a communist threat was occasioned by Germany's defeat and the coming of the Cold War.

In the early years of the Cold War (1946–1953), neither Washington nor Moscow paid much attention to Latin America. They were focused on Germany, Eastern Europe, China, and Korea. Latin America was clearly a US sphere of influence, and Moscow could see nothing to be gained by interfering in it.

GUATEMALA: THE OVERTHROW OF ÁRBENZ

What little attention Washington paid to Latin America in those years centered on Guatemala (map 6.1), whose president from 1945–1951, Juan José Arévalo, was a nationalist who wanted to transform Guatemala from US satellite to US ally. To do that, he needed to restrain US companies

Map 6.1.   Cold War Clashes in Central America and the Caribbean

that controlled most of Guatemala's economy.* Arévalo was a strong anticommunist, Eastern Europe was far away, and Moscow was not interfering in Guatemala, where there was only a handful of communists. The United States distrusted Arévalo but never moved against him, reasoning that in the event of a crisis, the Guatemalan army would never risk its privileged status by permitting a Communist takeover in a US sphere of influence. Using similar reasoning, it was prepared to tolerate Arévalo's leftist successor, army officer Jacobo Árbenz.

Árbenz, however, turned out to be neither cynical nor opportunistic but an idealist who spearheaded agrarian reform and drew close to the tiny Guatemalan Communist Party. As he did so, he lost touch with his power base in the army. Árbenz found explanations in Marxism that he could find nowhere else and which seemed to explain the troubled history of Guatemala. He was attracted to the USSR for three reasons: it was governed by a class that had previously been oppressed; it had defeated illiteracy; and it had never harmed Guatemala.

Árbenz was convinced that capitalism was doomed. According to Marxist doctrine, history assured the triumph of communism. Nevertheless, he never became a party member while he was president, because had he done so he would have had to submit to party discipline. But after 1952 he considered himself a communist, and he spoke as one to his closest friends. No communist held a key governmental post, but communists exercised influence over Árbenz far beyond what their numbers warranted. He could rely on no other party, since only the communists shared his commitment to agrarian reform.

Had Árbenz not been overthrown, communist influence would have continued to increase. But it could not have been turned into control because there were no communists in the army, and the army would oust any president who tried to install a communist regime. The Eisenhower administration accepted this logic but turned it on its head, using it to remove Árbenz. In 1953 it authorized the CIA to use covert action against him, and the CIA's Operation PBSUCCESS proceeded from the assumption that only the Guatemalan army itself could oust him. The CIA used psychological warfare tactics to convince Guatemalan officers that the United States would invade if they didn't remove Árbenz first. In this way his ouster could be justified as a nationalistic, anti-US, and anti-Soviet action rather than a US-supported intervention.

In October 1953 Árbenz learned from a spy that Washington was plotting his overthrow. Desperate, he decided to import arms from Czechoslovakia and hold some of them in reserve to arm workers' militias in

---

*US investment in Guatemala was concentrated in three companies: Empresa Eléctrica de Guatemala, International Railways of Central America, and United Fruit Company.

case of invasion. But this put him further out of touch with his military power base. He envisioned an armed militia (which he knew the army would never accept), yet ironically, he imported weapons that the army could use to crush the militias should the latter materialize. On top of this, importation of arms from Czechoslovakia lent credibility to the US claim that Árbenz was a secret communist.

In June 1954 a few hundred Guatemalan exiles led by Lieutenant Colonel Carlos Castillo Armas invaded Guatemala from Honduras with CIA support. Both Árbenz and the army knew that this force was pathetically small and could be defeated easily. But they feared the consequences of victory: if Castillo Armas were beaten, the United States might invade and do the job itself. On June 25, military leaders told Árbenz he must resign, and on June 27 he did so, hoping that a military government could preserve some elements of his agrarian reform and block both Castillo Armas and the United States. But by July 7 the military had gone over to Castillo Armas and installed him as president.

US opposition to Árbenz was conditioned by its economic interests in Guatemala but cannot be fully explained without reference to the Cold War. As of 1954 no Latin American president had ever been as sympathetic to communism as Árbenz, and communists were more influential in Guatemala than anywhere else in the hemisphere. These were obvious facts that any US government would have noticed, with or without corporate prodding.*

The impact on the CIA was significant and troubling. The Guatemalan operation was fortunate to succeed, given the CIA's failure to plan beyond the first stage of the invasion. Moreover, the Iran operation against Mosaddeq (described in chapter 4) was puffed up in retrospect. These "achievements" made the Agency giddy with success and led it into the Bay of Pigs fiasco, in which Fidel Castro, unlike Árbenz, would have the army firmly on his side.

CUBAN COMMUNISM AND
THE ALLIANCE FOR PROGRESS

Watching the resignation of Árbenz in 1954 was a young Argentine physician, Ernesto "Che" Guevara, who was working in Guatemala and

---

*Washington decided not to tolerate Árbenz because of his opposition to US economic imperialism and his pro-Communist sympathies. Both objections worked in tandem, and accounts that favor one at the expense of the other understate their symbiosis. In particular, accounts from the 1950s and 1960s that attribute the intervention to the machinations of the United Fruit Company are reductionistic and untrustworthy. For extensive treatment of the Árbenz government and Operation PBSUCCESS, see Piero Gleijeses, *Shattered Hope: The Guatemalan Revolution and the United States, 1944–1954* (Princeton, NJ, 1991).

studying Marxism.* He joined a group of Cuban exiles in Mexico City in 1955. Guevara's horror at Árbenz's overthrow taught him the importance of revolutionizing the army, a conviction he then conveyed to the leader of the Mexico City exiles, Fidel Castro.

The United States had helped liberate Cuba from Spain in 1898–1899, only to exploit the island economically and politically.† Cuban dictator Fulgencio Batista ruled the island from 1952 through 1958 in cooperation with US organized crime leaders Meyer Lansky and Charles "Lucky" Luciano. In those years Cuba was a playground for wealthy North Americans, complete with casinos, brothels, nightclubs, and race tracks. Batista and his cronies received lucrative kickbacks from these businesses, while most Cubans worked in related low-wage service jobs or on sugar plantations.

This situation offended many young Cubans, including Fidel and Raúl Castro, Jesuit-educated sons of a plantation owner. Fidel earned a law degree and promptly ended up on the wrong side of the law, organizing a hopeless assault on the military base at Moncada on July 26, 1953. The date of the assault gave Castro's revolutionary movement its name: the 26th of July Movement, or **M-26-7**. Convicted of treason, the Castro brothers had their prison sentences commuted by Batista in 1955; he knew their family, and the Cuban Catholic Church intervened on their behalf. The brothers were exiled to Mexico, met Guevara and other young people there, and returned to Cuba by boat on December 2, 1956. Batista's troops caught them on the beach and killed sixty-five of the eighty-two-person landing party. The remaining seventeen, including Fidel, Raúl, and Che, escaped into the Sierra Maestra mountains, where they began recruiting fighters to overthrow Batista.

Over the next two years, the rebels grew into a formidable force. Batista's army, riddled with corruption, low in morale, and unable to locate and defeat M-26-7, gradually melted away through desertion. The Castros received sizable financial contributions from upper-class Cubans, which they used to purchase weapons in US cities such as Galveston and New Orleans. On January 1, 1959, Batista resigned and fled the country. One week later M-26-7 entered Havana, and Fidel Castro took over the government.

Neither the United States nor the USSR knew how to interpret Castro's victory. He had given a stirring speech denouncing Batista's dictatorship

---

Che is an Argentine expression roughly equivalent to the Canadian expression "eh," asking if your listener understands what you've been saying. Guevara's frequent use of it amused Cubans, who then used it as his nickname.

†Authority for such exploitation came from the Platt Amendment, which passed the US Senate in 1901. It restricted Cuban foreign policy and commercial relations to avenues acceptable to the United States.

at his 1953 trial, but afterward his public statements became sporadic and vague. The Soviets, who were preoccupied with a crisis over Berlin and their disagreements with China over the direction world Communism should take, paid no more attention to Castro than they had to Árbenz. Washington was worried: Vice President Richard Nixon's "goodwill" trip to Latin America in 1958 had been disastrous,* and Batista, for all his faults, had been a reliable US ally. President Dwight D. Eisenhower invited Fidel to Washington in April 1959 to sound him out but then refused to see him because the revolutionary government had begun executing Batista's former supporters. Instead, Castro met for three hours with Nixon, who concluded that he was not a communist and that the United States should make every effort to convince him to remain its ally.†

The Eisenhower administration and M-26-7 probably never could have come to terms. Raúl Castro was a classical Marxist, Che Guevara was moving toward communism, and Fidel Castro was a Cuban nationalist and charismatic political opportunist who despised US imperialism. None of them was, however, a Communist Party member, in part because none would ever have submitted to party discipline originating outside Cuba and in part because the Cuban Communist Party was dominated by elderly radicals who had disapproved of Castro's reckless revolution. The 26th of July Movement wanted to expel all vestiges of "Yanqui imperialism"‡ from Cuba, and whether or not the movement was Communist, such actions would not have been accepted in Washington. The Castro government's actions in expropriating plantations, industries, refineries, and businesses owned by US citizens only intensified the Eisenhower administration's suspicions.

In February 1960 Soviet Deputy Premier Anastas Mikoyan visited Cuba and concluded a trade and assistance pact between the two countries. The Castro brothers had concluded that the only safe way to cut Cuba off from the United States was to seek Soviet protection. The agreement affected the US government as negatively as had Árbenz's 1954 decision and Nasser's 1955 decision to purchase Czech weapons. In March 1960 Eisenhower authorized the CIA to draw up plans for covert action to overthrow Castro.

Meanwhile, Moscow was slowly awakening to the possibilities inherent in a close relationship with Cuba. The Soviets were skeptical of the Communist credentials of the Cuban leadership (with good

---

*In Lima, Peru, Nixon's car was pelted with eggs, tomatoes, garbage, and rocks, and he was nearly killed by a mob in Caracas, Venezuela.

†Nixon's later statements that he had urged the administration to take a tough stance against Castro are contradicted by the memorandum of their conversation, which contains his recommendations as outlined here.

‡*Yanqui* is a Latin American term for US residents.

reason), but Khrushchev, surrounded by US client states in Japan, Pakistan, Iran, and Turkey, was willing to gamble on Cuba's becoming an "unsinkable aircraft carrier" stationed ninety miles south of the Florida Keys. After the collapse of the Paris summit in May 1960* and the intensifying Congo crisis later that summer, he drew closer to the Cuban Revolution, embracing Fidel in September when both were in New York to address the UN. Two months later, John Kennedy edged out Richard Nixon for the US presidency and inherited the plans to remove Castro.

Kennedy initiated a two-track Latin American policy. In March 1961 he announced the **Alliance for Progress**, a ten-point program to transform Latin America through political and social reform, economic development, and the alleviation of poverty, illiteracy, and disease. The next month he approved a covert operation to land exiles in Cuba in an attempt to spark an uprising against the Castro regime. The removal of M-26-7 and the modernization of Latin America would immunize the hemisphere against the Marxist virus.

Both tracks failed. The April 17 landing at the Bay of Pigs† was an unmitigated disaster. The CIA, self-assured after its 1950s triumphs in Iran and Guatemala, designed a plan predicated on the disloyalty of the Cuban army. When that army backed Castro, the invasion force was cut to pieces on the beaches. The debacle placed Kennedy at a disadvantage in his June 1961 summit with Khrushchev, and the latter's subsequent miscalculations led to two more dangerous crises: Berlin in 1961 and Cuba again in 1962.‡ As for the Alliance for Progress, it failed as badly as the invasion. It was based on an internal contradiction: its prescriptions for political, social, and economic reform would have crippled the very elites whose cooperation was essential to its success. By the time President Lyndon Johnson acknowledged its failure in 1965, it had been moribund for more than two years.§

---

*As noted in chapter 2, the four-power summit in Paris (United States, USSR, Britain, and France) was broken up by Khrushchev, who was indignant over Eisenhower's admission that he had authorized espionage flights over the Soviet Union by U-2 spy planes.

†The location is the Bahía de Cochinos, translated inaccurately at the time as "Bay of Pigs." A *cochino* is a tropical fish found off the coast of southern Cuba, but given the utter failure of the operation, the inaccurate name seems more appropriate.

‡The Vienna Summit of June 3–4, 1961, between Kennedy and Khrushchev brought about nearly catastrophic consequences. Kennedy was poorly prepared, Khrushchev bullied and underestimated him, and the dangerous confrontations over Berlin and Cuba resulted. Either might have led to nuclear war, but neither did.

§The best concise analysis of the Bay of Pigs can be found in Howard Jones, *The Bay of Pigs* (New York, 2008). The best analysis of the failure of the Alliance for Progress can be found in Stephen G. Rabe, *The Most Dangerous Area in the World* (Chapel Hill: University of North Carolina Press, 1999), chapter 7. On the latter point, it should be noted that the difficulties encountered by the Alliance for Progress reflected the inherent contradiction between US anti-imperialist ideology and its imperialist behavior, which we have noted elsewhere in

So both US responses to Cuba's Cold War challenge were stillborn. Frustrated, Kennedy authorized CIA efforts to destabilize the Castro regime and assassinate Fidel. The US circumstances notwithstanding, however, Khrushchev was anything but triumphant. His unsinkable aircraft carrier survived the botched invasion but remained vulnerable to what both Fidel Castro and the Soviets feared would be a full-scale amphibious assault led by US marines rather than poorly trained exiles, an attack that Kennedy repeatedly promised to the exile community in the United States. Early in 1962 Khrushchev devised a plan to defend Cuba and simultaneously address two other problems: Soviet inferiority in nuclear intercontinental ballistic missiles (ICBMs) and the recurring aggravation of the US presence in West Berlin. The plan would station medium-range nuclear missiles in Cuba, which could either be left in place or exchanged for a US withdrawal from Berlin.

Khrushchev's scheme was, as the best historical account of it asserts, "one hell of a gamble."[1] Fidel Castro realized it at once and accepted the missiles only because doing so would strengthen the socialist camp against US imperialism. He knew the deployment would create an enormous Cold War crisis, and when a U-2 spy plane detected the missiles on October 14, the Cuban Missile Crisis began.* Initial secrecy was essential to the plan's success, and once the missiles were discovered prematurely, the United States could bring to the table its absolute conventional superiority in the Western Hemisphere.

The question was how to use that superiority, and the US government took a week to decide. Deferring the options of air strikes or invasion, Kennedy opted for a naval quarantine of Cuba that would prevent the Soviets from transporting any more military matériel to the island. Since the Soviet navy did not have the force required to break the quarantine, Khrushchev would have to negotiate a way out or proceed to nuclear war. Without consulting Castro, he cut a secret deal with Kennedy: he would withdraw the missiles in return for a US noninvasion pledge and the removal of NATO missiles from Turkey. As things turned out, the United States was the clear winner, since the Turkish missiles were obsolete† and the noninvasion promise was valid only if the Cuban government permitted on-site inspections to verify that the missiles had been removed.

That would never happen. Castro was furious: he had incurred a huge risk in accepting the missiles only to have Khrushchev abandon him. When he visited Moscow in April and discovered that Khrushchev had

---

this book. Washington was always more comfortable working with established elites than with radical nationalists who harbored varying degrees of sympathy for Marxist analysis.

*The crisis is known in Russia as the Caribbean Crisis and in Cuba as the October Crisis.

†For a full discussion of the US missiles in Turkey, see Philip Nash, *The Other Missiles of October* (Chapel Hill, NC, 1997).

been bluffing with a losing hand, his anger turned to contempt. The following year, the Castro brothers consolidated their rule by reconstituting the Cuban Communist Party as an organization more radically revolutionary than its Soviet counterpart. They also realized by the end of the decade that other Latin American nations were resistant to Cuban-style revolution, and that the United States would crush any Communist movement that might somehow take root in the hemisphere.

Accepting these realities, Castro turned his attention to Africa. Che Guevara had gone to Zaire and Angola in 1965 and had found the local revolutionary movements poorly organized, badly led, and impervious to Cuban advice. His execution by the Bolivian army following his capture in the Andes Mountains in 1967 ended his meteoric career as an international revolutionary. Eight years later, when the Portuguese Empire in Africa collapsed, Castro sent combat units to Angola to fight on the side of the Popular Movement for Liberation of Angola (MPLA) against South African forces.* Cuban intervention in Africa, undertaken against the advice of the Soviets (who wanted to maintain détente with the United States), was a way to actively oppose European and US imperialism without risking the immediate US retaliation that intervention in the Western Hemisphere would have guaranteed.

As the Cold War ended, the USSR collapsed, and China moved toward a capitalist economy, Cuba soldiered on, with the aging Castro brothers "made weak by time and fate, but strong in will to strive, to seek, to find, and not to yield."†

US REACTIONS TO HEMISPHERIC
DISTURBANCES IN THE 1960S

Washington's inability to dislodge Cuba's Communist government left it forced to coexist in the same hemisphere with Fidel. His avowed intention to turn other Latin American nations Communist didn't make coexistence easy. For a few years it appeared that Brazil, the largest nation in South America, might be susceptible to a Communist takeover; the abrupt resignation of President Jânio da Silva Quadros in August 1961 brought to power his vice president, João Goulart, a prominent landowner and former minister of labor who was also inclined toward Marxism. At the time of Quadros's resignation Goulart was in Beijing on a state visit to the People's Republic of China. The Brazilian Congress and army con-

---

*These events are discussed in chapter 5 and in Piero Gleijeses, *Conflicting Missions: Havana, Washington, and Africa, 1959–1976* (Chapel Hill, NC, 2002).

†Alfred, Lord Tennyson, "Ulysses" (1842), lines 69–70. Fidel Castro, "made weak by time and fate," relinquished power to his brother Raúl in 2008 and died in 2016.

sidered prohibiting his return to Brazil because of his leftist tendencies, but a compromise was reached and he became president a few days after Quadros left office.

Goulart was viewed skeptically by Washington from the outset of his presidency. His reform efforts in Brazil were consistent with the aims of Kennedy's Alliance for Progress, and in the 1962 Cuban Missile Crisis, he played a behind-the-scenes role on behalf of the United States. But his appointments of leftists to high positions in his government, his opposition to international sanctions against Cuba, and his sponsorship of legislation reducing the amounts of money that could be transferred out of Brazil by large multinational corporations all drew US disapproval. US Ambassador Lincoln Gordon supported internal opposition to Goulart and gave Washington advance notice of an impending military coup one week before it was implemented in April 1964. Available documentation indicates that the Johnson administration was prepared to support the coup with military aid, but that such intervention proved unnecessary. Goulart's resignation two days after the coup began brought to power a harshly repressive military regime that surprised observers by remaining in power for twenty-one years. Nevertheless, the coup was carried out by generals who were anti-Marxist for domestic political and economic reasons rather than for reasons directly related to the Cold War.*

One year later, when a revolution erupted in the Dominican Republic in April 1965, Johnson interpreted it in Cold War terms and sent US military forces to put it down. The actual situation was considerably more complex and had little to do with either Castro or Communism.

The United States exercised political imperialism in the Dominican Republic throughout the twentieth century, beginning in 1903, when corrupt leaders brought the country to financial ruin and Washington took over the customs houses in an effort to imitate British rule in Egypt. The US military occupied the nation from mid-1916 to late 1924, and six years later the chief of the National Police, General Rafael Trujillo, became president. He ruled as a dictator until his assassination in 1961, turning the Dominican economy into his personal empire and pleasing the United States with his hatred for fascism and communism. His murder, followed in November 1961 by the flight into exile of his son and heir, opened the prospect of a turn toward democracy. Elections in December 1962 brought to power a longtime enemy of Trujillo, a writer and poet named Juan Bosch.

Inaugurated in February 1963, Bosch steered through the Dominican Congress a modern, democratic constitution in April. Five months later a

---

*For a reliable account of the Goulart years and the 1964 coup, see W. Michael Weis, *Cold Warriors and Coups d'Etat: Brazilian-American Relations, 1945-1964* (Albuquerque, NM, 1993).

military *golpe de estado* (Spanish for coup d'état) sent him into exile. The nation's upper classes collaborated with military officers and the National Police to impose a three-man executive "triumvirate" headed by Donald Reid Cabral. But Bosch retained a following within the country and the armed forces, and on April 24, 1965, Reid was driven from office by a group of military officers determined to restore the 1963 constitution and permit Bosch to complete the remainder of his four-year term.

This constitutionalist counter-*golpe* might have succeeded if Castro had never taken power in Cuba or if the US embassy in Santo Domingo had interpreted the events accurately. The Communist takeover in Cuba had left Washington both unwilling to risk any more such regimes in the hemisphere and predisposed to see any incipient revolution as Communist-inspired. This bias could easily have been corrected by the embassy staff, but the ambassador was in Georgia visiting his ill mother and the team on-site completely misread the situation. At first it predicted that Reid would be able to defeat the rebellion. Then, after he was ousted, it refused to believe that the rebels actually wanted to restore the constitution and recall Bosch. Instead, the embassy concluded that since the rebels were military officers, they would naturally seek to install a military junta, which Washington could live with. So for two days the embassy took no position on the constitutionalist counter-*golpe*, misleading both the Johnson administration and the Dominican army, the latter assuming that silence meant that the United States was adopting a neutral posture.

By April 26 a split had developed within the armed forces, with pro- and anti-Bosch units fighting each other. Now the embassy woke up to reality: the rebels meant to restore Bosch, and that was against US interests. Ironically, the Dominican Communists opposed the return of Bosch, whom they considered a Dominican version of Rómulo Betancourt, the democratically elected president of Venezuela from 1958 to 1966, a former Communist who had become a left-of-center anticommunist and had been the target of Cuban assassination attempts. Such a figure should have been viewed favorably by Washington, which had resolutely backed Betancourt in Venezuela. But the United States believed erroneously that Communists were supporting Bosch, and on April 28 the embassy, convinced that the revolt was on the verge of success, begged for US marines to stabilize the situation. The intervention was officially described as an action to protect US citizens, but it was actually an invasion to prevent the restoration of a democratic constitution and the return of a president who was opposed by the same Communists the US embassy thought were supporting him (map 6.1).

The pacification of the Dominican Republic took several months, and the last US military units left in December 1966. What had begun as an indigenous constitutionalist revolt had evolved quickly into an incident in the Cold War. Two factors—Castro's survival despite US efforts to remove him, and his commitment to bringing Communist regimes to power elsewhere in Latin America—had led a poorly informed US government to invade a Caribbean nation in order to perpetuate its political imperialism there. Meanwhile, Dominican Communists proved to be as opposed to Bosch's return as was Washington, and the USSR stood aloof, unwilling to intervene in a US sphere of influence and uncertain as to which side it would support if it *did* step in.

The Dominican intervention ensured that political power in that nation would remain in the hands of the upper classes and those military officers willing to cooperate with the United States. As mentioned earlier, the Alliance for Progress had been dead since 1962, but this incident buried any thought of its eventual revival. As long as the Cold War lasted and Castro remained in power, the United States would avoid the risks inherent in supporting democratic governments in the Western Hemisphere if there were even the most remote possibility that such regimes might be subject to Communist subversion. Indeed, the United States, under intense pressure from its community of Cuban exiles, installed a strict economic boycott of Cuba in an effort to destroy the Castro regime, an effort that continued in place long after the Cold War ended. Bosch might or might not have actually emerged as the Betancourt of the Dominican Republic, but neither he nor any other similarly inclined politician would be given the opportunity.*

One year after the Dominican intervention, Che Guevara left Cuba for Bolivia. He had just returned from Africa, where his efforts to foment a Communist revolution in the Congo had brought him nothing but frustration. After a brief stay in Cuba he left for Bolivia, hoping to ignite a Castroite revolution there. Arriving in Bolivia under a false name in November 1966, Guevara disappeared from public view and began building a guerrilla army in the southeastern part of the country, near the western border of Paraguay (map 6.2).

Nothing went right for Guevara during the eleven months he spent in Bolivia. He sought support from the Bolivian Communist Party, but that organization distrusted the Castro brothers and did nothing to assist him. He hoped for supplies of aid and recruits from local peasants but failed there as well; Che was preaching the virtues of a social revolution in a nation and society that had already experienced one,† and those peasants who opposed the Bolivian government had little desire to exchange

---

*The best accounts of the Dominican intervention are Abraham Lowenthal, *The Dominican Intervention* (Cambridge, MA, 1972), and Piero Gleijeses, *The Dominican Crisis* (Baltimore, 1978).

†The *Movimiento Nacionalista Revolucionario* (Revolutionary Nationalist Movement, or MNR) had taken power in 1952 and instituted universal suffrage, agrarian reform, and nationalization of the tin mines.

Map 6.2.   Cold War Clashes in Latin America

their domestic dictatorship for a Cuban one. Unlike the Cuban peasants ten years earlier, who had kept Castro's guerrillas apprised of the Cuban army's movements, Bolivian peasants alerted the government as to Guevara's whereabouts. Finally, Guevara had bad luck. He expected to be fighting the Bolivian army, a poorly equipped fighting force riddled with corruption. Instead he found that that army was being advised by a commando unit of the Special Activities Division of the CIA, aided by an elite force of US Army Rangers proficient in jungle warfare.

Guevara's fifty-man guerrilla force, isolated and starving, was surrounded in October 1967, and Guevara himself was captured. He was executed on October 9 on orders of Bolivian President René Barrientos, in contravention of the US government's request that he be transported to Panama and turned over to US forces stationed there. Che Guevara thereupon became a martyr, not only in Cuba but to revolutionaries throughout the world, a status derived more from his achievements in Cuba than from his failures in Africa and Bolivia.

MARXISM IN CHILE

By 1967 the fates of Goulart, Bosch, and Guevara made it clear that the United States would not permit another Cuban-style revolution, or any remotely left-wing government, in the Western Hemisphere. Castro himself understood this and directed his revolutionary activities at first inward, toward a ten-million-ton sugar harvest, and then, as mentioned earlier in this chapter, outward toward Africa.* After Khrushchev's removal from office in October 1964, his successor, Leonid Brezhnev, concentrated on difficulties with Eastern Europe and China and left Latin America alone. The cost of subsidizing Cuba's economy in the face of a US-orchestrated boycott was significant enough to deter even someone like Khrushchev from supporting another such venture.

On the other hand, it was gradually becoming clear that the United States might end up with another Marxist government in its sphere of influence, not through violence but through the democratic process. In 1958 a Marxist physician, Salvador Allende, had lost Chile's presidential election by only 33,500 votes. He was widely viewed as the likely winner in 1964.† The United States had never exercised the sort of political imperialism in Chile that it had in Cuba and the Dominican Republic. Indeed, Chile is so remote that it is difficult to consider it in a US geographic sphere of influence: Communist Prague, clearly within the Soviet sphere, was six hundred miles *closer* to Washington than Santiago, Chile, while even *Moscow* is closer to Washington than is Santiago(!) (map 6.2).

Chile's principal resource was its wealth of minerals, particularly copper. Its rich deposits were largely controlled by US-based multinational companies like Anaconda and Kennecott. Its communication infrastructure was dominated by the US-based conglomerate ITT (International

*The 1970 sugar harvest was 8.5 million tons, and Castro took full responsibility for the failure.

†Chile has a six-year presidential term and prohibits immediate reelection.

Telephone & Telegraph), which owned Chiltelco, the Chilean Telephone Company. The country was heavily dependent on New York banks for its credit. This sort of economic imperialism was resented by many Chileans and helped explain Allende's political appeal.

Beyond economics lay the Cold War implications of an Allende victory. No country had ever elected a Marxist government in a free and open election. Propaganda from the United States hammered the theme constantly: Communism can only come to power by force. A Marxist electoral victory in Chile would invalidate that contention and serve as an example for others to imitate. Both political and economic concerns led Washington to attempt to influence the 1964 election.*

As things turned out, the CIA needn't have bothered. Allende came so close in 1958 because it was a three-way race between leftist, centrist, and rightist candidates. In 1964 the right-wing contender was a token for those who could not bring themselves to vote for the centrist Eduardo Frei.† That left only two viable prospects, and Frei soundly defeated Allende by 56 to 38 percent. A strong rightist opponent would have weakened Frei and probably would have elected Allende.

No sooner did Frei take office than Washington started worrying about the 1970 election, and this time the concerns were aptly placed. Frei's moderate reforms, which he called a "Revolution in Liberty," gave the Chilean government a 51 percent share in all copper operations and initiated redistribution of large landed estates. But private investment declined, inflationary pressures increased, and a coalition of communists, socialists, and moderate parties elected Allende president of the Senate in 1967.‡ The US government was relieved when rightist Jorge Alessandri, president from 1958 to 1964, agreed to run again in 1970. His candidacy weakened the centrist Christian Democrats, who inexplicably nominated a left-of-center candidate who repudiated Frei's moderate policies. Many Christian Democrats thereupon defected to Alessandri, whom Washington assumed would win.

He lost, and it is not difficult to see why. Allende started with a solid Marxist base of 30 percent and, in a three-way race, he didn't need a majority to win.§ He gained 36.2 percent of the vote to Alessandri's 34.9, and the US government was appalled. The CIA spent $250,000 bribing mem-

---

*The CIA spent approximately $2.5 million to help elect Frei, a significant sum even for a US presidential election of that period.

†Frei, the leader of the Christian Democratic Party, was an observant Catholic and too religious for some Chileans.

‡Allende was not a communist but a socialist. In Chile, the Socialist Party was far more radically left-wing than the Communist Party.

§If the leading candidate had a plurality but not a majority, the Chilean Congress would determine the winner. In practice, the legislature had always elected the popular-vote leader, as with Alessandri in 1958.

bers of the Chilean Congress, who took the money and elected Allende anyway.* So the first freely elected Marxist president in world history took office on November 4.

US President Richard Nixon feared that Allende would convert Chile into a communist dictatorship. Allende swore that he would leave office when his term expired, whether or not a Marxist succeeded him. Instead of reassuring the United States, this prospect proved even more frightening: no communist government had ever left office peacefully. If Allende did so, it would mean that people throughout the world could vote for Marxist parties without fear of dictatorship. This might be even worse for the United States in the Cold War than the imposition of a proletarian dictatorship in Chile, a country whose strategic significance was mocked by US National Security Advisor Henry Kissinger, who called it "a dagger pointed at the heart of Antarctica."[2] Either way, Nixon was in no mood to wait until 1976 to learn how Allende would act. He gave orders to do everything possible to cripple the Chilean economy and drive Allende from office.

How could this be done? The CIA, backed by promises of money from ITT, proceeded cautiously. Economic imperialism gave the imperialist power a sizable stake in the fiscal health of the target nation: if the Chilean economy actually collapsed, US investors would lose their holdings. Economic pressure from the United States took the form of efforts to deny Chile credit in global markets. This reduced but did not eradicate Chile's access to credit from US and international lenders. Allende was able to obtain significant credits from Europe and Latin America as well as favorable terms of trade from Communist nations. Foreign private investment, of course, dried up entirely: who would be foolish enough to invest in a country governed by committed Marxists? But for the Latin American left, foreign investment meant an increase in economic imperialism. This could be avoided if the government itself became the principal source of new investment. And this logic, not US sabotage, doomed Allende's experiment.†

Allende nationalized Chilean industries, banks, and mines, simultaneously enacting wage increases and measures to redistribute income. He intended to pay for these actions with revenues from nationalized companies. But industrial production declined steeply while prices increased sharply because of wage hikes. In 1971 the United States offered an agreement on compensation: US companies nationalized in

---

*During the 1970 election campaign, the CIA spent approximately $425,000 to help Alessandri, while the Soviets spent about $568,000 in support of Allende. The CIA's largesse in bribing Chilean Congress members may have been attributable in part to feelings of chagrin over having been outspent in the election itself.

†This argument is made compellingly by Paul Sigmund, *The Overthrow of Allende and the Politics of Chile* (Pittsburgh, 1977).

Chile would be offered compensation in twenty-five-year bonds backed by the US Treasury. It was a reasonable bargain, but Chilean socialists wanted no compensation whatsoever and forced Allende to reject it. Meanwhile, in rural areas, the radical leftist *Movimiento de Izquierda Revolucionaria* (Movement of the Revolutionary Left, or MIR) encouraged peasants to take farmland by force, checkmating Allende, who had preferred a gradual approach.

By 1972 Chile suffered widespread shortages of consumer goods and uncontrollable inflation. Allende's leftist coalition held a minority of seats in Congress, where the majority did everything possible to block implementation of his program. Now a constitutional crisis emerged: constitutional revisions in 1970 had abolished the Chilean Congress's right to override a presidential veto by a two-thirds vote, without prescribing any substitute procedure. With Congress deadlocked, supporters of both sides launched massive street demonstrations in Chile's principal cities. Strikes by engineers, architects, lawyers, dentists, doctors, and truckers coalesced in October 1972 into work stoppages that idled seven hundred thousand Chileans. Allende was able to restore order only by reorganizing his cabinet to include military officers, since the armed forces were now the only institution enjoying a modicum of trust on both sides. General Carlos Prats became minister of the interior, a post that placed him in control of Chile's police.

The military now shared responsibility for carrying out governmental policy. It quickly realized that the constitutional crisis, coupled with increasingly confrontational strikes and demonstrations, might lead to chaos that could only be resolved by ending civilian rule. In March 1973 Allende's coalition won an unexpectedly high 44 percent of the vote in congressional elections and promptly overreached itself by introducing a National Unified School Curriculum that was opposed by both the military and the Catholic Church. Prices rose more rapidly than in 1972, industrial production continued to fall, and by August the country resembled an armed camp, with both sides openly carrying weapons.

Obviously this state of affairs could not continue indefinitely, a fact that Soviet General Secretary Brezhnev repeatedly pointed out to Allende. The Soviets could offer him little besides goodwill and advice: their principal international problems involved China, Vietnam, Egypt, and Cuba, with Chile well down the list. Brezhnev advised Allende to compromise with the United States over compensation for expropriations, but Allende, whipsawed between the opposition and the MIR, made no move in that direction. The United States funneled money to finance a second truckers' strike in July 1973, and when several professional associations joined them the following month, Carlos Prats resigned as army commander and left the cabinet.

A military *golpe* was clearly imminent, and the waiting ended on September 11, 1973. The navy occupied Valparaiso, Chile's chief port, and the army and air force laid siege to the presidential palace in Santiago. Allende, offered the traditional choice of deposed Latin American leaders—the airport or the cemetery—chose the latter and committed suicide. The complicity of the United States in the *golpe* was widely rumored, and both Nixon and Kissinger were delighted to see Allende go, but apart from funding the truckers' strike, no further intervention was necessary. Allende's economic ineptitude destroyed him, and Chile spent the next seventeen years submerged in a military dictatorship that perpetuated US economic imperialism.* Guatemala's military, fearing a US invasion, had deserted Árbenz in 1954; Cuba's military had stood by Castro in 1961; now Chile's military, taking matters into its own hands, ended a constitutional impasse by ousting a democratically elected Marxist government.

THE CHALLENGE TO
IMPERIALISM IN CENTRAL AMERICA

Chile's remoteness left it on the fringe of US influence, but the same could not be said for Central America. After the overthrow of Árbenz, US political and economic control of the region seemed assured, especially once the administration of President Jimmy Carter concluded an agreement in 1978 to return the Panama Canal to Panama and pro-US sentiment in the region soared.

Beneath the seemingly placid surface, however, Central America was not completely stable. In Nicaragua, where two generations of the Somoza family had since 1936 ruled a country in which the US military had intervened eleven times, a powerful earthquake had wrecked much of the capital city of Managua on Christmas Day 1972 (map 6.1). Humanitarian aid had poured in from all over the world,† but most of it was diverted into President Anastasio Somoza's personal accounts and never directed to suffering people. In early 1978 downtown Managua remained in ruins, and a full-blown revolutionary movement was working to oust Somoza.

---

*Most scholarly accounts conclude that while Washington did everything it could think of to undermine Allende's presidency, the CIA did not orchestrate the *golpe* of September 11. See Kristian Gustafson, *Hostile Intent: U.S. Covert Operations in Chile, 1964–1974* (Washington, DC, 2007); Hal Brands, *Latin America's Cold War* (Cambridge, MA, 2010); Stephen G. Rabe, *The Killing Zone: The United States Wages Cold War in Latin America* (New York, 2016); and Tanya Harmer, *Allende's Chile and the Inter-American Cold War* (Chapel Hill, NC, 2014).

†The Hall of Fame baseball player Roberto Clemente was killed in a plane crash while trying to bring food and supplies to Managua.

The radical wing of the opposition centered on the **Sandinistas**,*
the *Frente Sandinista de Liberación Nacional* (Sandinista National Liberation Front, or FSLN) founded in 1961 and inspired by Cuba's M-26-7.
Moderates focused on the editorials of Pedro Joaquín Chamorro, a
reform-minded Conservative politician and editor of the opposition
newspaper *La Prensa*. Chamorro was assassinated on January 10, 1978,
and Managua blew up in weeks of rioting, culminating in a two-week,
highly effective general strike led by business leaders, who demanded
Somoza's resignation.

At this point the moderates expected the United States to step in and ar-
range for Somoza's departure. That was the way it had acted in the 1930s,
and it was the way imperialistic powers were supposed to act. But the
Carter administration, which had made human rights violations a focus
of its foreign policy, was reluctant either to break with Somoza, a loyal
Cold War ally, or to condone his repression of the upheaval. Congress
was equally conflicted. So for more than a year Washington refused to
tilt to one side or the other, thereby driving the moderates into the arms
of the Sandinistas. In July 1979 Somoza left for exile in Miami, and a Sandinista government that owed nothing to the United States took power.

Meanwhile, public order was breaking down in nearby El Salvador,
a tiny nation of minimal strategic or economic value, but one in which
US political and economic imperialism had long been exercised. A
military junta governed the country, but its authority was opposed by a
left-wing coalition, the *Frente Farabundo Martí para la Liberación Nacional*
(Farabundo Marti National Liberation Front, or FMLN),† and compromised by right-wing "death squads" that roamed through the country
murdering leftists, moderates, and Catholic clergy. The Carter administration tried to build up a moderate, reform-minded political center as
an alternative to these extremes, but that option failed, and Washington
decided to forestall a guerrilla victory in 1980 by arming the right-wing
military establishment.

Up to this point the Soviet Union had demonstrated little interest in
Central American affairs. Communist efforts there had been thwarted in
1932 (El Salvador), 1948 (Costa Rica), and 1954 (Guatemala), while the
outcome of the Cuban Missile Crisis left no doubts in the Kremlin that the
United States would intervene militarily if that was required to defend
its sphere. Carter's failure to do so stimulated Brezhnev's curiosity, but
Soviet involvement in Afghanistan‡ precluded meaningful commitment
elsewhere.

---

*Named for Liberal Party leader Augusto César Sandino, assassinated on the elder So-
moza's orders in 1934.
†Named for an El Salvadoran communist leader of the 1930s.
‡See chapter 7.

Then Carter lost the 1980 presidential election to the committed Cold Warrior Ronald Reagan, and what is often termed the Second Cold War began in earnest. The Reagan administration viewed Asia, Africa, and Latin America primarily as cockpits of Cold War combat. Its UN ambassador, Jeane Kirkpatrick, was a scholarly exponent of the argument that Washington should support dictatorships against totalitarian Communist regimes, on the grounds that the former might eventually become democratic while the latter would not.* Castro's Cuba, which had remained aloof from the insurgencies in both Nicaragua and El Salvador, began sending arms to Nicaragua in late summer 1980 and to El Salvador after Reagan's election in November. Castro assumed that Reagan would be hostile to Cuba no matter how that nation behaved, and his assumption proved correct.

For the next eight years, Washington placed Central America squarely in the midst of the Cold War in an effort to maintain imperial control in the region. The Reagan administration faced several obstacles: the reputation of its death-squad allies in El Salvador; its avowed enemies, the FMLN and FSLN; and the US House of Representatives, controlled by the opposition Democratic Party and deeply skeptical of intervention in Central America. White House efforts to fund anti-Sandinista "contra" rebels in Nicaragua were frequently scaled back or rebuffed by Democrats in Congress.

Despite the opposition of the House of Representatives, the Reagan administration continued to funnel secret support to the "Contras" in Nicaragua. Indeed, US covert operations designed to destabilize the Nicaraguan government provoked an increase in Soviet aid to that country, which the White House then offered as evidence that the Sandinistas were actually Communists. This "evidence" strengthened the resolve of President Reagan and his closest advisors, and in 1985, with the House refusing aid to the Contras, the Reagan administration hit upon a method of circumventing a congressional prohibition on spending. For several months, Israel had been selling antitank missiles to Iran, which was embroiled in a bloody war with Iraq, in return for an Iranian promise to release US hostages held by the militant group Hezbollah and a US commitment to replenish Israel's missile inventory. This unusual, highly secret three-way exchange was modified by several administration officials into a way to fund the Contras. The United States would sell the weapons to a private company, which would then peddle them to Iran at exaggerated markups. Profits from such sales would be banked in a "reserve fund" that could then channel money to the Contras in violation of congres-

---

*See her seminal article, "Dictatorships and Double Standards," *Commentary*, 68, no. 5 (November 1979): 34–45.

sional directives. It was a blatantly illegal operation, and when news of it broke in November 1986, it became known as the **Iran-Contra Scandal**.

The controversy threatened to provoke a resolution to impeach Reagan, but only twelve years after the resignation of Richard Nixon, few in Washington had the stomach for that. Reagan simply denied any knowledge of the scheme, and Congress chose to believe him (although most of his fellow citizens did not).* Dramatic congressional hearings were held, resolutions disapproving further aid to the Contras were passed, and the fighting in Central America went on. President Oscar Arias of Costa Rica brokered a peace plan in 1987 that was agreed to by all six Central American presidents, including those of Nicaragua and El Salvador. It won Arias the Nobel Peace Prize, but the fighting in Central America continued.

Then a highly unlikely development changed everything: the Cold War began to end (as related in chapter 7).

After 1985, as the Cold War thawed, Moscow dramatically increased aid to the Sandinistas in an effort to establish Nicaragua as a counterweight to Afghanistan in case a "spheres of influence" trade could be worked out, by which the United States would stop interfering in Afghanistan if the Soviets did the same in Nicaragua. Then, when the USSR began withdrawing Soviet forces from Afghanistan in May 1988, the entire commitment to Nicaragua was rethought. When George H. W. Bush replaced Reagan as US president in 1989, the US commitment to Central America in general was rethought as well. Bush considered relations with the USSR, Eastern Europe, and the Middle East to be more important to US security than Central America—a pointed reversal of the priority accorded the region by Reagan.

In August 1989, as the "iron curtain" was being dismantled in Hungary, the Sandinista government startled everyone by reaching a sweeping agreement with the Contras and the moderate opposition parties. The regime made far-reaching concessions for two reasons: first, because with the Cold War ending, its aid from the Soviet Bloc would dry up; and second, because it expected to win the upcoming elections. Why it expected to win is difficult to understand. Ten years of Sandinista rule, internal rebellion, and confrontation with Washington had pulverized Nicaragua's economy, and it would have been astonishing had voters not held the incumbent government responsible. In February 1990 the opposition coalition won the presidency and a majority in the National Assembly. Startled, the Sandinistas gracefully surrendered power and took up a new role as an opposition party.†

Washington Post and CBS-*New York Times* polls taken in summer 1987 showed that about 60 percent of respondents thought Reagan was lying.

†Sandinista leader Daniel Ortega was defeated in the 1990 election by Violeta Chamorro, widow of the newspaper editor slain in 1978. Ortega converted the Sandinista movement

In El Salvador the path to peace was preceded by a bloody crime. The FMLN launched a new offensive on November 11, 1989. Five days later the head of the Salvadoran military academy ordered the murder of six Jesuit administrators at Central American University, along with their housekeeper and her fifteen-year-old daughter. This outrageous act caused the government and the army to lose support at precisely the moment when the Sandinista electoral defeat and the demise of Communism weakened the FMLN and removed El Salvador from the Cold War arena. On January 16, 1992, a peace accord was signed in Mexico City, with Salvadoran President Alfredo Cristiani shaking hands with the FMLN's high command. Both sides then took up a cause they could agree on: the necessity of taming the Salvadoran armed forces.

CONCLUSION: THE COLD WAR'S IMPACT ON LATIN AMERICA

Geography doesn't explain everything in world affairs, but we ignore it at our peril. The vast expanses and enormous resources of the United States have permitted it to treat the Western Hemisphere as its own backyard. It replaced European imperialism with economic and political imperialism of its own, dominating weaker Latin American nations and exploiting them for its own benefit.

The Cold War came to Latin America in a different way than to Africa and the Middle East. In the latter two regions colonialism was dead or dying, and European powers were looking to preserve their control by indirect, often neocolonial means. But in Latin America after 1945, US imperialism was by no means in decline. When it was confronted, the challenges came not from the USSR but from indigenous leaders and movements: Árbenz in Guatemala, the Castro brothers and M-26-7 in Cuba, Bosch and the constitutionalists in the Dominican Republic, Allende and his coalition in Chile, and the FMLN and FSLN in Central America.

Washington responded to these challenges using Cold War logic and terminology in defense of its political and economic interests. It was successful in Guatemala, the Dominican Republic, Chile, and the Caribbean island of Grenada (where a quick US military strike in 1983 toppled a Marxist government), and unsuccessful in Cuba. In Central America, the end of the Cold War settled the issues. But in each of these instances, Moscow, Washington's main Cold War adversary, found itself unable to exert meaningful pressure in support of its clients. In the Dominican Republic,

---

into a "loyal opposition," and his efforts were rewarded in 2007, when he won that year's presidential election and returned to power.

of course, it had no clients at all and was baffled by Lyndon Johnson's reaction to a Communist threat that did not exist. Moscow's sole attempt to project its power into the Western Hemisphere came in 1962, when Khrushchev placed nuclear missiles in Cuba. That experiment led the world to the brink of nuclear war, a disaster averted when Khrushchev, faced with the overwhelming conventional superiority of the United States in its own backyard, agreed to a deal that resulted in the removal of the Soviet missiles.

So the Cold War did not deter US imperialism in the Western Hemisphere. The gradual ebbing of that influence came about for other reasons, among them the decline of manufacturing in the United States, the rapid development of the information superhighway, and the consequent outsourcing and internationalization of information-based service jobs. These and other factors made US economic imperialism less pervasive. And ironically, the *end* of the Cold War lessened the relevance of US political imperialism, as the absence of a global adversary made outright political domination less crucial. In order to understand this fully, we now need to examine the way in which the Cold War ended.

7

&

"Every Country Decides Which Road to Take"

The End of the Soviet Russian Empire

The era of decolonization and Cold War, which lasted from the end of World War II until the early 1990s, witnessed not the end of imperialism but rather its transformation. As colonized peoples gained their independence from Europe's old colonial empires, they found their independence both bolstered and limited by the Cold War between the United States and Soviet Union, each of which preached anti-imperialism while seeking to impose its ways and visions on the rest of humankind. Eager to acquire skills and resources needed for security and economic growth, leaders of Third World nations—in Asia, the Middle East, Africa, and Latin America—typically sought aid from one or the other of the Cold War superpowers. Such aid was frequently forthcoming, but it came at a rather steep price, as Americans and Soviets each expected that the client states they aided would at least outwardly profess to adopt their vision of the road to modernity: Western-style consumer-capitalist electoral democracy or Soviet-style single-party socialism with central economic planning. These visions, like the "civilizing missions" of the old European empires, provided a pretext and a pattern for interventions and impositions by the superpowers, each of which justified its actions as not only bringing enlightenment and progress but also thwarting the other side's imperialistic designs. Mixing high-minded idealism with brutal, self-serving pragmatism, each side practiced imperialism in the name of anti-imperialism, as Third World leaders scrambled simultaneously to exploit the Cold War to their advantage and to keep from being controlled or engulfed by it.

In their efforts to gain and maintain independence from old and new forms of imperialism, as well as to unite their peoples against poverty and local foes, Third World leaders often found it useful to appeal to nationalist sentiments, stressing ethnic, cultural, linguistic, and sometimes religious connections. In the long run, these connections and sentiments frequently proved stronger than the ideologies and visions that the superpowers sought to impose. Realizing this, the Americans and Soviets, committed in theory—though often not in practice—to national self-determination, strove to woo emerging new nations by endorsing their nationalist aspirations. Americans portrayed their aid and interventions as defending national freedom and democracy, while Soviets depicted theirs as support for national liberation movements and newly liberated nations. Each promoted nationalism—the enemy of imperialism—to undermine the imperial efforts of the other side. But in so doing, they each ran the risk of undermining their own imperial efforts. In the end, this risk proved particularly real for the Soviet side.

As we have seen, in the Cold War era, both the Americans and Soviets practiced informal imperialism, by maintaining client states that depended on them for economic and military aid, and by intervening (clandestinely or openly) in these client states to keep them in line (or at least to keep them from joining the other side), as well as by maintaining far-flung networks of naval, air, and military bases. This form of imperialism, which the Chinese called "hegemonic," did not involve the creation of formal colonies and thus differed in form from Europe's old colonial empires, which during the Cold War were largely dissolved through national liberation and decolonization. Likewise, the United States, which had earlier acquired a modest colonial empire, did away with its main colonial possessions through political liberation (as in the case of the Philippines) or by incorporating them as states (as with Alaska and Hawaii).* By the late 1970s, with the old nineteenth-century US continental land empire (see chapter 2) long since incorporated into the federal union, and with most of Europe's old colonies having gained political independence, all that remained of the once vast Western colonial empires were some relatively minor territories, mostly islands. Many former colonies, to be sure, remained culturally and economically connected with their former mother countries—a phenomenon sometimes referred to as **neocolonialism**. But large colonial empires, by and large, had become a thing of the past—except for the one that we might call the Soviet Russian Empire.

For in many ways the Soviet state was itself a re-creation of the old Russian Empire, with numerous non-Russian nationalities directly under

---

*The United States retained a number of island territories, the largest of which is the Commonwealth of Puerto Rico.

Russian rule, bordered by a string of satellite nations in semicolonial status. The Soviets had sought quite creatively—and perhaps even quite sincerely—to reckon with this reality by creating the USSR. Recasting their realm in the 1920s as a "Union" of Soviet Socialist Republics, each with its own national identity and language, they also depicted the largest of them—the massive Russian republic—as a federation of autonomous republics and regions. And in the 1950s, maintaining their control of Eastern Europe arising out of World War II, they entered into a formal alliance with their satellite regimes, portraying them as allies rather than subservient nations. But despite these efforts, much as France's ill-fated "French Union" was in most respects largely a reconstitution of the former French colonial empire, the Soviet Union remained in many ways a reconstitution of the old tsarist Russian Empire.

THE EMPIRE OF ALL THE RUSSIAS

In some respects, at least in its origins, the Soviet state was unique. It began not as a traditional realm or conventional nation-state, but rather as a revolutionary regime. Led by V. I. Lenin, a Marxist group called the **Bolsheviks**, which later became the Russian Communist Party, seized power in Russia in 1917, not simply to replace one regime with another but rather as a "spark" to set off a global Communist revolution. They withdrew Russia from World War I and made it clear that their goals were to ignite a worldwide revolt of the exploited and oppressed masses, to lead a revolution that would overthrow capitalist imperialism the world over, and to create a new world order based on the Marxist vision of a classless society where equality and justice would prevail. As time went on, and as the Soviet regime began to act more and more like a traditional state, hopes for attaining these goals would continually be pushed further into the future, but the vision would not fully disappear until the Soviet state collapsed.

In other respects, however, the Union of Soviet Socialist Republics was itself a re-creation of the old tsarist Russian Empire, with Russians ruling over a wide array of non-Russian nationalities. That old empire, which had roots going back to the fourteenth and fifteenth centuries, had come to be ruled by a monarch designated as the "Emperor and Autocrat of all the Russias"—even though many of the "Russias" being ruled were places actually populated by non-Russians.

Historically, what became the Russian Empire had begun as the principality of Moscow, a city-state that started expanding in the 1300s, a time when the region was still indirectly under the rule of the mammoth Mongol Empire. Taking advantage of its central location, its commercial connections, its astute princes and their collaboration with the Mongol overlords, and its status as the home of Russia's main religious leader, Moscow gradually extended its sway over most other Russian principalities. By the end of the reign of Grand Prince Ivan III the Great (1462–1505), its most effective and expansive ruler, Moscow had become a sizable state and an important regional power.

But Ivan the Great did more than expand his realm to triple its former size; he also laid the basis for—and took on the trappings of—imperial rule. In 1472 he married the niece of the last Byzantine (East Roman) emperor, whose realm had fallen in 1453 to the Islamic Ottoman Turks, and began to call himself "tsar"—apparently a Russian adaptation of the title "Caesar"—that had been used by Roman and Byzantine rulers for many centuries. He thus claimed succession to the emperors of Rome and Byzantium (Constantinople), continuing a concept of imperial rule that dated back 1,500 years. He also put an end to the final remnants of Mongol dominion in Russia, and he built a grandiose palace and cathedrals to emphasize his majestic imperial status.

Shortly after Ivan's death, a Russian Christian cleric named Filofei put forth the premise that Moscow was also the "**Third Rome**."[1] According to this concept, the First Rome, in Italy, had become not only the hub of the great Roman Empire, but also the center of the Christian faith in the centuries following the life of Jesus Christ. By the time Rome fell to Germanic peoples in the year 476, however, the center of the empire and the true faith had shifted to Byzantium, or Constantinople, which thus became the Second Rome. But following the fall of that city to the Muslim Turks in 1453, Moscow effectively succeeded it as the Roman imperial and Christian spiritual center, and hence became the Third Rome. Not everyone accepted this premise, to be sure, but it did affirm Moscow and its imperial rulers as not only successors to the Caesars but also as protectors and promoters of what they saw as the one true faith—the Eastern Orthodox Christian religion—thereby providing them with a holy mission and vision.

Ivan III's grandson, Ivan IV (1533–1584)—later called Ivan the Terrible—had himself crowned tsar and expanded the realm of Moscow even further. In the 1550s, momentously moving to the east and south, he conquered and annexed the Mongol khanates of Kazan and Astrakhan. And in the early 1580s, after being rebuffed in his efforts to conquer territories to the west, he sent Cossack adventurers eastward to attack the Mongol khanate of Sibir, whence comes the name Siberia. In the course of the next two centuries, these Cossacks and their successors steadily moved eastward to the Pacific Ocean and beyond, claiming all of northern Asia, and much of northwestern North America,* for Moscow.

---

*After crossing from Siberia to Alaska in the 1700s, Russian explorers moved south along the North American west coast as far as northern California. Their presence that far south did not last, but the Russians claimed Alaska and held that huge region as an overseas colony until 1867, when they sold it to the United States.

This colossal eastward expansion had momentous consequences. The realm that was ruled from Moscow emerged as history's largest contiguous land empire, stretching six thousand miles from west to east and almost two thousand miles from north to south. And portentously, it included many people who were neither Russians nor Christians. In what became a sort of civilizing mission, the Orthodox Church sent out missionaries, and the government sent soldiers and officials, to convert, Christianize, and Russianize these people—a task they pursued with rather mixed results as they ran into stubborn resistance.

In the mid-1600s the realm again began expanding to the west and south, taking what is now eastern Ukraine and gradually extending its authority into the region to the north of the Black Sea. And in the early 1700s Tsar Peter I (1682–1725), eager to modernize and Westernize his realm and enhance its connections with the West, fought a long war with Sweden (1700–1721) to acquire lands along the Gulf of Finland and the Baltic Sea—lands that likewise were peopled mainly by non-Russians. Peter also built a new capital, which he named Saint Petersburg, and formally began to call his country the Russian Empire, taking for himself the grandiose title of Tsar Peter the Great, Emperor and Autocrat of All the Russias.

Peter's successors, especially Empress Catherine II the Great (1762–1796), expanded the realm even farther to the west and south, annexing a huge swath of lands from the Black Sea to the Baltic Sea. Included in this swath were non-Russian lands with a wide diversity of languages, cultures, and creeds, including Lithuania, most of eastern Poland and what is now Belarus, almost all of central and western Ukraine, and the whole northern shore of the Black Sea. Although the majority of the people in these lands were Christians, many were from Western branches of the Christian faith (Roman Catholics and Protestants) that were hostile and unreceptive to the Russian Orthodox Church, while sizable communities of Jews and Muslims also resided in these regions. Indeed, by this time, at least half of the empire's peoples were non-Russians, and most of the non-Russians were also non-Orthodox as well.

Although Peter and Catherine were far more focused on adapting Western ideas and ways than on spreading Russian culture and beliefs, their nineteenth-century successors eventually reverted to the earlier mission. In the 1830s, at a time when new ideologies such as liberalism, socialism, and nationalism were pervading and beginning to transform the West, Sergei Uvarov, the minister of education for Russian emperor Nicholas I (1825–1855), devised a new Russian ideology. Known as the Official Nationality, it sharply rejected the new Western beliefs and instead focused on the formula Orthodoxy, Autocracy, and Nationality.* The implication

---

*For a detailed discussion of this ideology, its implementation, and its impact, see Nicholas V. Riasanovsky, *Nicholas I and Official Nationality in Russia 1825–1855* (Berkeley, CA, 1959).

was that officials and educators throughout the realm should focus on instilling these three interlocking loyalties—to the Orthodox Christian faith, to the imperial autocratic regime, and to the national character of the Russian people. This imperially sanctioned ideology eventually gave rise to efforts at Russification—attempts by influential Russians and officials to impose Russian ways and Orthodox beliefs on the non-Russian peoples of the realm.

By the reign of Emperor Nicholas II (1894–1917), an indecisive ruler opposed to reform and committed to Russian imperialism, it was clear that these efforts had backfired. Not only did they fail to insulate the realm from the new Western ideologies, which inspired the emergence in Russia of reformist and revolutionary movements, but they also further alienated many of the myriad non-Russian peoples, some of whom began to form nationalist organizations and liberation movements of their own. By 1914, when Russia became engaged in World War I, the empire was seething with rebellion and unrest among its burgeoning exploited working masses and its increasingly alienated non-Russian nationalities.

At first the outbreak of war seemed to still the unrest, but as Russian losses and casualties mounted, and as German invaders drove deeper and deeper into the Russian domains, rebellion and unrest resurfaced with a vengeance against the increasingly ineffective and discredited imperial regime. In March 1917, as the empire's capital Petrograd (formerly Saint Petersburg)* ran short on food, bread riots and protests by striking workers there led Nicholas II to abdicate his throne—once he learned that the soldiers called in to suppress the riots had refused to follow orders to fire on their fellow citizens. A provisional government was hastily assembled to manage the transition to a new form of government; workers, peasants, and soldiers began electing "soviets" (councils) to champion their needs; and various non-Russian nationality groups sought to use the chaotic situation to achieve their independence. In the course of the next few years, as Russia was racked with revolution followed by civil war, Finns, Poles, Estonians, Latvians, Lithuanians, Ukrainians, Georgians, Armenians, Azerbaijani Turks, Central Asian Muslims, and other non-Russians asserted independence from Russian rule. It looked as if the once great Russian Empire had totally and permanently unraveled.

---

*In 1914, after entering World War I against the Germans, the Russians decided that "Saint Petersburg" sounded too Germanic, so they changed it to Petrograd, a Russian-rooted name that likewise meant "city of Peter." It was changed again to Leningrad ("city of Lenin") from 1924 until 1991, when the original name Saint Petersburg was restored.

THE IMPERIAL SOVIET STATE

In November 1917, as the Russian realm descended into chaos, Lenin and his Bolsheviks staged a new revolt that overthrew the short-lived provisional government and replaced it with a "Soviet" regime, supposedly centered on the soviets elected by the working classes. Although portrayed mainly as a working-class revolt to create a Marxist soviet socialist state, this revolution also had a very strong nationalist component, as non-Russian nationalities, encouraged to some extent by Lenin, exploited the ongoing chaos to assert their independence.

As noted above, the Bolsheviks (or Communists) who seized power in November 1917 did so with the aim of sparking a worldwide socialist revolution, without which they did not expect that their new Soviet regime could long survive. In a bid to gain support for their movement from workers everywhere, they instituted radical socialist reforms and pulled Russia out of World War I. But the global revolt they hoped for did not materialize, and they found themselves faced with governing the Russian realm they had won. Their leader, Lenin, who identified imperialism with capitalism and championed the principle of national self-determination, had claimed the non-Russian nationalities as allies with the Russian working classes in their joint revolution against the old Russian Empire. Neither Lenin nor his party had any intention of re-creating that empire.

But re-create it they did. As their hopes for world revolution faded into the future, they set about ruling the Russian realm, including the many non-Russian nationalities who wound up under Soviet sway. Instrumental in this regard was Joseph Stalin, who served as "Commissar for Nationalities" in Lenin's new Soviet government from 1917 to 1924. Himself a non-Russian,* Stalin initially worked with Lenin to remake the old empire into a multinational socialist state, with each of the main nationalities retaining its own language and culture and (at least in theory) exercising regional autonomy. By 1922, victories in the Russian Civil War (1918–1920) and in conflicts with national separatist groups had left the Soviet leaders in control of most, but not all, of the old Russian Empire.† That year they renamed their realm the Union of Soviet

---

*Joseph V. Djugashvili, who adopted the Russian pseudonym Stalin (meaning "man of steel"), was born and raised in Georgia, a country in the mountainous Caucasus region in the southern part of the old Russian Empire. As a non-Russian who had written about problems faced by non-Russian nationalities in the tsarist era, he was appointed as People's Commissar for Nationalities in 1917 and held that post until its abolition in 1924.

†Finland, Poland, Lithuania, Latvia, and Estonia, formerly parts of the Russian Empire, emerged as independent nations after World War I. During World War II, however, the last three were reincorporated into the Soviet Union.

Socialist Republics (USSR), with four constituent national components: the Russian Soviet Federative Socialist Republic (RSFSR), and the Ukrainian, Belorussian, and Transcaucasian Soviet Socialist Republics (SSRs). This arrangement, reaffirmed by subsequent Soviet constitutions, gave each republic its own language(s) and the right to leave the union but also made the USSR government preeminent, with the power to overturn the actions of any republic. As new republics were added, some by division of old republics* and some by World War II territorial gains,† the Soviet Union grew to fifteen (and at one point sixteen) republics. Adhering to the form of a multilingual, multinational union, on the surface it seemed to show how nationalist identities could be preserved in a unified socialist state.‡

But this unified socialist state was also a multilingual, multinational empire that was ruled from Moscow, the imperial metropolis, which served as capital of both the Russian republic (RSFSR) and the Soviet Union. Stalin, as General Secretary of the Soviet Communist Party from 1922 to 1952, and as the dominant Soviet leader§ after Lenin's death in 1924, eventually curtailed the earlier emphasis on regional and cultural autonomy for non-Russians. Instead, embracing the Russian language and culture as unifying forces for the Soviet peoples, he began promoting Russian nationalism and repressing non-Russian nationalities. In the early 1930s, for example, he conducted civil war and imposed a forced famine in the Ukrainian SSR, effectively murdering millions of Ukrainians, allegedly for resisting his efforts to collectivize farming. In an effort to rally his peoples during the Great Fatherland War (1941–1945), as World War II is known in Russia, he actively encouraged Russian nationalist sentiment and glorified pre-Soviet Russian history while brutally uprooting and displacing non-Russian nationalities whose loyalty he suspected. The Soviet Union thus became an imperial Russian realm, in which non-Russians (who made up roughly half the population) were relegated to secondary status, despite their supposedly equal stature in the Soviet constitution.

---

*In 1936, for example, the Transcaucasian republic was divided into Georgian, Armenian, and Azerbaijani SSRs.

†These included the Estonian, Latvian, Lithuanian, and Moldavian SSRs.

‡In 1945 Stalin demanded that each of the SSRs be admitted to the UN General Assembly as a separate member nation. The result was an odd and rather inconsistent compromise, in which Ukraine and Belorussia (now Belarus) became UN members (as did the USSR itself), but the rest of the SSRs did not.

§As General Secretary from 1922 onward, Stalin gained full control of the Soviet Communist Party. Since the USSR was a single-party state and the Communists controlled the government with no opposition, he was the realm's most powerful leader, even though he did not become head of government (Chairman of the Council of Ministers, or "Premier") until 1941. Subsequent Soviet leaders, such as Khrushchev, Brezhnev, and Gorbachev, likewise attained and exercised power as heads of the Communist Party Secretariat.

World War II also helped the Soviets extend their sway over even more nationalities. Lithuania, Latvia, and Estonia, parts of the old Russian Empire that had gained independence at the end of World War I, were now incorporated into the Soviet realm as SSRs. Eastern Poland, with millions of Poles, Belorussians, and Ukrainians, was annexed by the USSR, as were territories taken from Germany, Finland, Czechoslovakia, and Japan.* Bessarabia, a former Russian imperial province that went to Romania in 1918, was added to the Soviet Union as part of a new Moldavian SSR (map 7.1).

Meanwhile, in the latter stages of the war, Soviet forces liberated much of Eastern and central Europe from Nazi German rule. By 1945, as the war's end approached, Poland, Czechoslovakia, Hungary, Romania, Bulgaria, and eastern Germany were under Soviet occupation. Determined to protect his western borders by creating a buffer zone of countries friendly to the USSR between it and Germany, and eager to bring these nations and their peoples into the Communist fold, Stalin used rigged elections and harsh, oppressive tactics to install Communist-controlled regimes in each of these places. Imposed from outside by the USSR and kept in place by Soviet forces and the threat of Soviet invasion, these "satellite" regimes represented a new form of colonial control. In theory they were independent, but in practice they were solidly under Soviet sway, components of what was often called either the Soviet Bloc or the Communist Bloc.

Spreading and instilling Communism, after all, was still central to the Soviet mission. Moscow was no longer called the Third Rome, but it was nonetheless the center of a global movement that promised to provide a form of salvation for the world's oppressed working masses and colonized peoples. And the Marxist-Leninist vision of a classless, socialist society based on equality, justice, and community had long since replaced the old tsarist ideology of Orthodoxy, Autocracy, and Nationality. But the Soviet Bloc was still in many ways a revival of the old Russian Empire, with a Soviet government that was autocratic and authoritarian, a regime that was made up mainly of Russians ruling over many non-Russians, and an ideology that justified expansionism as a necessity for saving humanity and spreading the true faith—in this case Soviet Communism.

After Stalin's death in 1953, his successors, despite their desire to distance themselves from the harshest features of his rule, continued his support for Russians and Russian rule within the Soviet realm. Nikita

---

*In 1939 the Soviets claimed eastern Poland, Latvia, Estonia, and later Lithuania through agreements with Nazi Germany, followed up by conquest (and later by reconquest from the Germans in 1944–1945). In 1939–1940 they added land from Finland through a "Winter War" against the Finns. In 1945, at the end of World War II, the Soviets took part of East Prussia from Germany (the other part went to Poland), they took the Carpathian region from Czechoslovakia, and they took southern Sakhalin Island and the Kuril Island chain from Japan. Poland was partially compensated with territory to its north and west that was taken from defeated Germany (map 7.1).

Map 7.1. European Boundary Changes and Soviet Satellites, 1945–1948

Khrushchev, who was head of the Soviet Communist Party from 1953
to 1964 and also Soviet premier from 1958 to 1964, promoted the study
of Russian language among non-Russian nationalities, fostered the mass
movement of ethnic Russians to non-Russian Soviet republics,[2] and made
sure that Russians held most key positions in the Communist Party, the
Soviet state, and the security police. Like Stalin, Khrushchev and his
comrades apparently saw Russians as more loyal to the USSR than the
non-Russian nationalities were, and more likely to identify with its interests—especially since Russians made up its ruling class and the Russian
republic encompassed three-quarters of its territory. Even Khrushchev's

transfer of the Crimean Peninsula from the RSFSR to Ukraine in 1954, depicted as a gift designed to honor Ukrainians and reinforce their loyalty, added substantially to the Ukrainian SSR's Russian population, since in the Crimea Russians outnumbered Ukrainians three to one.

ANTI-IMPERIAL EFFORTS AND THE SOVIET RESPONSE

Khrushchev and his cohort, while seeking to support the liberation of Asian and African nations, acted resolutely—and sometimes brutally—to maintain Soviet control over Eastern European nations. In 1955, partly in response to the expansion of the West's NATO alliance, the Soviet leaders created the Warsaw Pact, an alliance that included the USSR and its Eastern and central European satellites (map 7.2).* Ostensibly a defensive alliance, it also had an important but unstated purpose: to reinforce and justify continued Soviet dominance of Eastern Europe.

This unstated purpose became quite apparent in 1956, when protests in Poland and Hungary helped bring to power reformist Communist regimes. The new Polish leader, Władysław Gomułka, kept his country in the Warsaw Pact (named after Poland's capital, where it had been signed). But Hungary's new leader, Imre Nagy, pledged to withdraw from that alliance and hold free multiparty elections, thereby alarming and angering the USSR. In early November, while denouncing France and Britain for their "imperialist" role in the simultaneous Suez Crisis (see chapter 4), the Soviets sent troops and tanks to brutally crush the "Hungarian revolt" and then installed a harsh new regime that would be subservient to them and stay in their Warsaw Pact alliance.

In 1968 a reform regime in Czechoslovakia met a similar fate. Even though the Czechoslovak reformers had pledged to stay in the alliance, the USSR—supported by other Warsaw Pact regimes that feared the reform movement might spread to their countries and undermine their power—again sent in troops and tanks to end the reforms and eventually removed the reformers.

These "revolts" were directed not against Communism per se—indeed, in both cases, the reform leaders were Communists—but rather against Russian rule. As such they can be seen as independence movements, similar to those that sought self-rule for Asians and Africans during those same decades. Hungarian rebels in 1956 formed "Petőfi circles," named

---

*In 1952 NATO added Greece and Turkey, a nation that bordered the USSR itself, and on May 5, 1955, West Germany was also added. Eleven days later the Soviets formed the Warsaw Pact, allying themselves with Poland, Czechoslovakia, East Germany, Hungary, Romania, Bulgaria, and Albania. The alliance lasted until 1991, but Albania, which in the 1960s sided with China against the USSR, withdrew in 1968.

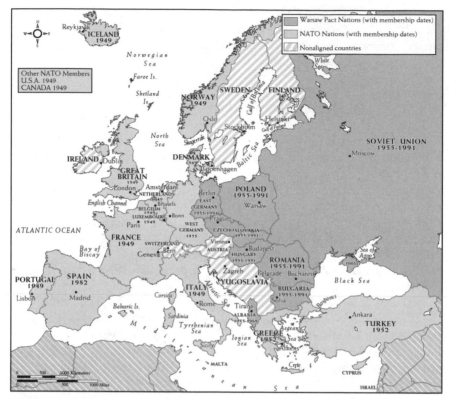

Map 7.2.   Divided Europe: NATO versus Warsaw Pact, 1955–1991

for their great nineteenth-century nationalist poet, and defiantly sang his "national song"—a patriotic hymn in which they vowed no longer to be slaves to foreign rule—as they rallied around the statues of past national heroes. The reforms in Czechoslovakia, although less radical and nationalistic, sought to incorporate Western-style freedoms in a unique form of Czechoslovak "socialism with a human face"—achieving a modicum of independence while nominally staying in the Soviet sphere.

But in both cases the move toward independence posed a threat to the Soviet Empire. Fearful that most Eastern European peoples—and most non-Russians in the USSR—would prefer to have their own independent national states rather than to keep living under Soviet Russian rule, the Soviets saw a need to crush these movements before the national independence virus could spread. Otherwise, if it did, the whole Soviet Bloc, and perhaps the entire USSR, might unravel. So, much as Western Europe's imperial powers had earlier done, they sought to use repressive force to keep their subject peoples in line, and thus to hold their vast multinational empire together. Although Hungary and Czechoslovakia allegedly were Soviet allies, in practice they were treated much like colonies that had dared to act independently of their mother country.

In the fall of 1968, in an effort to justify their invasion of Czechoslovakia, the Soviets put forth what came to be called the Brezhnev Doctrine—an assertion of both policy and principle that provided a new pretext for Soviet imperial control. In a speech in November in Poland, Leonid Brezhnev, who had replaced Nikita Khrushchev as Soviet Communist Party boss in 1964, declared that the USSR could and should act forcefully to protect the "security of the socialist commonwealth as a whole" against "internal and external forces hostile to socialism."[3]

Although wrapped in the mantle of "socialist solidarity," the Brezhnev Doctrine was in effect both an expression and an instrument of Soviet imperialism. By "socialist commonwealth" it really meant the Soviet Bloc, and the "forces hostile to socialism" proved to be the nationalist aspirations of peoples longing for independence from Soviet Russian rule. The moderate Communists who introduced reforms in Hungary and Czechoslovakia were not so much a threat to socialism as to Soviet control. And in the face of widespread opposition and national unrest, such control could be maintained only by force and the ever-present threat of force, which served as the glue that held the whole Soviet Russian empire together.

The threat of force proved temporarily effective for the Soviets in Poland, where a failing economy with rising prices, combined with religious and nationalist fervor, led to widespread unrest in the 1970s. In 1978, in the midst of this unrest, Karol Wojtyła, a Roman Catholic cardinal from Poland, was elected pope and thus leader of the international church to which most Poles belonged. His election, and his return trip to Poland the next year as Pope John Paul II, galvanized the country's religious and nationalist zeal, deepening resentment of its domination by atheistic communistic Russians.[*] Then in 1980 a shipyard strike in the Polish port of Gdansk resulted in the formation of an independent labor union called Solidarity, led by a laid-off electrician and Polish nationalist named Lech Wałęsa. It proceeded to organize strikes and patriotic demonstrations nationwide, growing ever bolder and more popular over the next year. But in 1981, fearful that the unrest was getting out of hand and concerned that it could spread across Eastern Europe, the Soviets staged military exercises near the Polish border, raising the specter of an armed invasion of yet another satellite country. This tacit threat of force apparently did the trick: at the end of that year General Wojciech Jaruzelski, a new Polish

---

*It should be noted that, while the Soviet leaders were atheistic Communists, many of the USSR's people were Russian Orthodox Christians. This religion, however, was little better than atheism in the eyes of militantly Roman Catholic Poles.

Communist leader, declared martial law and outlawed Solidarity, arresting its leaders and driving it underground. Poland thus stayed within the Soviet Bloc, at least for the time being.

Meanwhile, however, not even the massive application of force could forestall a Soviet debacle in Afghanistan, where a 1978 coup had brought to power a Communist regime and thus created a new Soviet client on the USSR's southern border. But the new Afghan regime soon came under control of an extremist faction, headed by Hafizullah Amin, that tried to impose radical atheistic communism on the devoutly Muslim and fiercely independent Afghans, triggering widespread rebellion. Late in 1979, in a brutal bid to save the situation, Soviet forces invaded Afghanistan en masse, deposing and killing Amin and replacing him with a moderate pro-Soviet Marxist named Babrak Karmal. Instead of stanching the Afghan revolt, these actions further inflamed it as diverse Afghan rebels, united by their allegiance to Islam and by the mass influx of a hundred thousand Soviet soldiers into their country, fought an effective guerrilla war against the foreign "infidel" invaders. Later, increasingly armed and aided by the Americans, British, and Chinese, as well as by other Muslim countries, they would manage to humble the Soviet superpower, setting the stage for the end of the Soviet Empire.

THE GORBACHEV TRANSFORMATION

Brezhnev's death in 1982 did little to change the situation, as both of the next two Soviet leaders grew ill and died within a year or so of taking office. But in 1985, when the youthful and vigorous Mikhail Gorbachev took over as head of the Soviet Communist Party, a new generation of leaders started to seek new solutions to the Soviet empire's pressing problems.

Many of these problems were economic. Despite its status as a superpower, and to some extent owing to the huge financial burdens of maintaining both its military might and a wide array of client states dependent on Soviet support, the USSR was in deep economic trouble. Its economy was hobbled by declining growth rates, obsolete equipment, outmoded infrastructure, shoddy products, chronic shortages, inadequate agricultural output, substandard housing, poor living standards, and rampant corruption and cronyism, complicated by incessant alcohol consumption and worker absenteeism.

Gorbachev sought to confront these challenges through what he called **perestroika** (restructuring), seasoning Soviet socialism with some common capitalist practices and selectively adopting policies that seemed to work well in the West. Among other things, he increased autonomy and profit incentives for farmers and factory managers, experimented with privately owned businesses and a limited market economy, and granted people more freedom to frankly assess and critique Soviet policies and procedures, while restricting access to alcohol and encouraging foreign enterprises to invest in the USSR. His programs were at first quite popular, but they also raised people's expectations, which led to broad disillusionment when the Soviet economy failed to improve.*

But economic woes alone could not account for the Soviets' sorry situation. Like earlier large multinational realms, the Soviet Bloc was filled with non-Russians who resented Russian rule and who longed for liberation from it, hoping somehow to achieve independence as sovereign nations of their own. Saddled with satellites and client states that drained its resources and disliked its dominance, and filled with non-Russians who nurtured their own nationalistic aspirations, the USSR had managed to maintain its domination mainly through force and the fear of force. But force had a very high price tag, especially given the vast expenses of the Soviet military and the sad state of the Soviet economy.† And even force had its limitations, as the ongoing anguish in Afghanistan seemed clearly to confirm.

Much as Clement Attlee's government in Britain had been determined to cut back on costly overseas imperial commitments in the wake of World War II,‡ Gorbachev was resolved to reduce the costs of maintaining the USSR's vast military forces and its network of satellite and client states. He thus began to take a series of steps based on what he called "new thinking" in world affairs.[4] First, in a bid to reduce his realm's vast military expenses and to curb its costly arms race with the United States, he sought accommodations with Western leaders through arms and force reduction agreements. Second, after first at-

---

*After modest growth in the mid-1980s, the Soviet economy declined, in part because of global declines in the price of oil, which was one of the country's most important export products. By 1989–1991 there were widespread shortages and strikes. See Michael J. Ellman and Vladimir Kontorovich, eds., *The Disintegration of the Soviet Economic System* (London: Routledge, Chapman and Hall, 1998), 86–103, 193–214; Donald Filtzer, *Soviet Workers and the Collapse of Perestroika* (Cambridge, UK: Cambridge University Press, 1994), 94–108.

†By the mid-1980s, according to expert analysis, the USSR was spending about 27 percent of its gross domestic product (GDP) on its military forces, while its economy stagnated. American military spending, by comparison, was about 7 percent of its (much higher) GDP in the 1980s. See Mark Kramer, "The Collapse of the Soviet Union (Part 2): Introduction," special issue, *Journal of Cold War Studies* 5 (2003): 34; Odd Arne Westad, *The Global Cold War* (Cambridge, UK: Cambridge University Press, 2007), 336; and "US Defense Spending History," *United States Government Spending* (blog), http://www.usgovernmentspending.com/defense_spending.

‡Elected in July 1945, Attlee's government had moved to cut back on overseas expenses and commitments so that it could focus on improving the lives of the British people. Its efforts led, among other things, to reduction of British military forces and to British withdrawal from India (chapter 3). Gorbachev likewise sought to cut back on military and client state commitments so he could focus on improving the Soviet economy and living standards.

tempting to resolve the Afghan conflict by sending in more troops, he changed his approach and started seeking a negotiated settlement that would enable the Soviet Union to withdraw its forces. And third, he began to relax his country's grip on its Eastern European satellites, reducing its military presence there, and he pledged not to intervene by force in their affairs, suggesting that they should be free to pursue their own paths to socialism.

In a series of meetings with Western leaders, and especially with US President Ronald Reagan, Gorbachev offered to negotiate dramatic reductions in nuclear weaponry, in part to reduce global tensions and the threat of nuclear war and in part to cut back on the enormous costs of maintaining a massive arsenal of missiles, warheads, submarines, and bombers. His proposals, which included first working toward a 50 percent cutback in the nuclear arms of both sides, and then planning to eliminate *all* nuclear weapons in three stages by the year 2000, met with a mixed response from Ronald Reagan. On one hand, the president was eager to end the balance of terror that purportedly prevented nuclear war through **mutual assured destruction**—aptly abbreviated **MAD**—the belief that neither side would dare to start a conflict that could obliterate them both. On the other hand, he was wedded to his dream of a **Strategic Defense Initiative (SDI)**, a plan he put forth in 1983 to develop an elaborate space-based system that could intercept and destroy incoming enemy nuclear missiles, which Gorbachev's proposals pointedly precluded.* In the end, the two men were able to agree on a 1987 treaty to eliminate intermediate-range nuclear missiles, but progress on reducing long-range nuclear weapons had to wait until after Reagan was replaced in 1989 by George H. W. Bush, a pragmatic president less wedded to SDI.

With regard to Afghanistan, Gorbachev felt that he needed to extricate his country from the conflict there, which he saw as needlessly draining its resources and sacrificing its young men. His initial instinct to end the war quickly by sending in more troops resulted only in increased casualties, with no resolution in sight. So in 1986 he began to seek a negotiated settlement, removing Babrak Karmal, the ineffectual and much-despised Afghan leader that the Soviets had installed in 1979, and calling for a "national reconciliation" that would presumably include anti-Soviet Afghan rebels in a new coalition government. Unfortunately for Gorbachev, the Americans soon undermined this effort by furnishing the rebels with sophisticated "Stinger" antiaircraft missiles, enabling them to shoot down

---

*Gorbachev feared that a workable SDI, by protecting the United States from Soviet nuclear missile attack, would leave the Americans free to attack the USSR without fear of retaliation. Although Reagan offered to share SDI technology with the Soviets, Gorbachev remained skeptical and insisted that SDI research must be stopped, or at least confined to the laboratory, as part of any agreement to eliminate long-range nuclear weaponry.

Soviet planes and helicopters and reducing any incentive they might have to bargain with the Soviet side.

Finally, in February 1988, with no such bargain in sight, the Soviet leader made a stunning announcement. The USSR, he said, was willing to withdraw its forces over a ten-month period, beginning that May, provided that an agreement could be reached that would bar outside interference.[5] Such an agreement at first proved elusive, as the Americans insisted on the right to keep aiding the Afghan rebels, but the US side finally did agree to gradually reduce its aid "symmetrical" with Soviet withdrawal. So the Soviet evacuation of Afghanistan proceeded, finishing in February 1989.

The USSR's pullout from Afghanistan had momentous implications. The relatively primitive rebels, fueled by religious fervor, inspired by nationalist resentment of foreign rule, and armed with weapons supplied by the other superpower, had managed to fight the once mighty Soviet forces to a standstill. A one-time Soviet client state and satellite had gained its independence, showing other such places that determined resistance could bring freedom from imperial rule, as Asians and Africans had earlier shown in their struggles to free themselves from Western domination. And Gorbachev was showing that he seemed to be serious about ending Soviet forceful interference in affairs of neighboring nations.

The Soviet leader himself underscored his seriousness. In an extraordinary address at the United Nations in New York in December 1988, even before the Soviet withdrawal from Afghanistan was complete, he avowed that great powers must renounce the use of force in dealing with other nations, called for freedom of choice for all peoples, and pledged sizable reductions in Soviet forces, including those that were stationed in Eastern Europe.[6] Did this mean that the USSR was disavowing the Brezhnev Doctrine? And, if so, what were the implications for the people in the Soviet satellites?

THE LIBERATION OF EASTERN EUROPE

By and large, the people in the Soviet satellites had little use for Soviet dominance, or even for Soviet socialism, a system imposed on them by Stalin's subordinates in the wake of World War II. In the four decades since then, they had chafed under Soviet imperial subjugation, while Asians and Africans had worked to gain freedom from Western imperial rule. Hungarians, Czechs and Slovaks, and Poles had fought at times for greater independence, only to be forced back into line.

By 1989, however, Gorbachev's "new thinking" was giving new hope to Eastern Europeans. His evacuation of Soviet troops from Afghanistan, his withdrawal of funding for Third World leftist regimes, his implicit renunciation of the Brezhnev Doctrine,* and his reduction of Soviet force levels in the Warsaw Pact nations all seemed to suggest that he might well be serious about forsaking forceful foreign interventions. If so, then perhaps the way was open for substantive change.

Poland and Hungary were the first countries to test the changing situation. In both places, the ruling Communists, aware of the people's thirst for independence and resentment of Russian rule, realized that their regimes rested mainly on Soviet support and sensed that their survival could well be in jeopardy if Gorbachev's talk about stopping such support was serious.

In Poland, a series of worker strikes in 1988 promoted political as well as economic goals, demanding that Poles be given greater freedom and that the banned Solidarity union be legalized. By the year's end General Jaruzelski, the man who had banned it and declared martial law in 1981, had come to realize that the outlawed union had far more support than his regime did among the Polish people. Seeing himself as a nationalist and Polish patriot, he helped to convince his Communist comrades of the need to hold talks with the union leaders, resulting in "roundtable" discussions in early 1989. These talks in turn led to an April agreement that legalized Solidarity and scheduled free parliamentary elections for June 4 of that year. The result was a resounding triumph for the union, which won all but one of the contested seats, on the same day as authorities in China used deadly force to end pro-democracy student demonstrations in Beijing.† Instead of acting to support the defeated Polish Communists, Gorbachev, who had himself only recently returned to Moscow from China, pressed the Poles to accept a coalition government, with Jaruzelski as president and Solidarity's Tadeusz Mazowiecki as prime minister. Perhaps the Soviet leader really meant what he had said about nonintervention.

Hungary likewise pressed for greater national freedom in 1989. Assured that Gorbachev would not intervene, its new reform-minded Communist leaders allowed nationalist demonstrations on Hungary's National Day (March 15), passed constitutional reforms that guaranteed

---

*According to one of his key advisors, shortly after Gorbachev took office in 1985, he informed Eastern European Communist leaders that they were on their own and that he would not interfere in their affairs, even at their request. See *Masterpieces of History: The Peaceful End of the Cold War in Europe, 1989*, edited by Svetlana Savranskaya, Thomas S. Blanton, and V. M. Zubok (Budapest: Central European University Press, 2010), 121–22.

†In the spring of 1989, thousands of protesters held mass demonstrations in Beijing's huge Tiananmen Square, calling for more freedom and an end to government corruption and oppression. But on June 3 and 4, on orders from China's Communist leaders, loyal army units armed with tanks and automatic weapons forcibly cleared the square, killing hundreds of people.

basic freedoms, and scheduled free elections for the following year. And momentously, with Gorbachev's acquiescence,[7] they opened up their border with Austria in May, dismantling the barbwire fences that kept people from crossing to the West—thereby opening a gaping hole in the "iron curtain" that separated East from West. Poland and Hungary were going their own way* and were doing so with Gorbachev's blessing.

Hungary's border opening proved portentous. For more than four decades, travel from Eastern to Western Europe had been effectively restricted by laws enacted in the Soviet satellites and enforced by a boundary of border guards and fences. Most notorious was the **Berlin Wall**, a twenty-seven-mile urban barricade built in 1961 to prevent East Germans from escaping through East Berlin to the city's western sectors, occupied since World War II by British, French, and US forces. In the summer of 1989, thousands of East Germans, eager to experience West Germany's greater freedom and prosperity, traveled to Hungary hoping to head westward through the opened border with Austria (map 7.2). Initially the Hungarian regime refused to let them go, but in September it relented and allowed the East Germans to complete their westward trip. Then, when the East German government sought to stem the flow by banning travel to Hungary, thousands of others seeking to escape went instead to Czechoslovakia, where they crowded into the West German embassy in the city of Prague until they were finally allowed to go to West Germany in special trains in early October.

Other East Germans, instead of leaving, agitated to free their homeland fully from both Soviet domination and Communist rule. In September a patriotic group that called itself "New Forum" started holding antigovernment protests in the city of Leipzig. By October these protests had grown into massive demonstrations, and the regime was weighing the use of massive force to crush them. But early in the month Gorbachev arrived to help celebrate the fortieth anniversary of the founding of the widely despised East German regime. Greeted by large, enthusiastic crowds who called for him to help them gain their freedom, he urged the regime to reform itself while it still had time, warning its leaders that "life itself will punish us if we are late."[8]

Time was quickly running out on the East German Communists. Opting to avoid mass bloodshed, they allowed the demonstrations to go on, as the number of people taking part in them surpassed a hundred thousand. Egon Krenz, a new Communist leader, went to Moscow on No-

---

*Later that year, Soviet spokesman Gennadi Gerasimov, referring to a signature song by a famous American singer, suggested that the Brezhnev Doctrine had been replaced by the "Frank Sinatra doctrine." "He has a song, 'I Did It My Way,'" Gerasimov explained. "So every country decides on its own which road to take." *Los Ángeles Times*, October 25, 1989, http://articles.latimes.com/1989-10-25/news/mn-745_1_warsaw-pact.

vember 1 to meet with Gorbachev, who urged him to enact reforms that would make his country more open. But even when Krenz returned home and called for free elections, the mass protests and ongoing exodus to the West continued. Finally on November 9, gambling that people would be less likely to protest, and also less likely to leave permanently for the West, if they knew they could legally go back and forth, the Communists decided to reduce restrictions on such travel.[9] In a press conference that same day, not fully informed of the details of the decision, a spokesperson mistakenly stated that the Berlin Wall border crossings were to be opened at once.

That evening, as the news quickly spread, excited Berliners assembled at the border crossings, overwhelming the confused border guards, who finally let them go through. Before long they were dancing on the wall and then dismantling it brick by brick. The most unsightly symbol of Soviet suppression was soon gone.

The events in East Germany, culminating in the Berlin Wall's fall, sent shock waves across Eastern Europe. In Bulgaria, the Communists, having successfully suppressed protests in October, now saw that the momentum had shifted and that the Soviet leader supported the shift. Suddenly sacking their longtime dictator on November 10, they swiftly announced a series of reforms, with free elections scheduled for the following June. In Czechoslovakia, where the Communists had crushed patriotic demonstrations in Prague on October 28, new protests on November 17 also met with violent force, as riot police administered beatings in an effort to disperse the crowd. This time, however, the protesters refused to be cowed and the demonstrations continued to grow, so that within a few days Prague's Wenceslaus Square was filled with half a million people chanting for freedom and singing patriotic songs. By early December, seeing that they had lost control, most of the country's Communist leaders quit, and by the year's end a new government had formed, with dissident playwright Václav Havel as president and Alexander Dubček (who had sponsored the ill-fated 1968 reforms) as chairman of the National Assembly.

Czechoslovakia's "Velvet Revolution," achieved with minimal violence, coincided with a bloody one in Communist Romania, where longtime strongman Nicolae Ceaușescu sought to sustain himself in power by ruthlessly resorting to force. His security police used wanton violence in crushing mid-December demonstrations against ethnic and religious repression. But on December 22 the army defied his orders and refused to shoot at protesting crowds who were storming government offices. Ceaușescu and his wife tried to flee, but they were captured, quickly tried, and executed three days later.

The 1989 revolutions were followed the next year by national elections in each former Soviet satellite. Most notable were the ones in East

Germany in March 1990, which brought sweeping victory for candidates favoring German reunification. Gorbachev at first demurred, but in summer of that year, after West Germany agreed to pay East German debts to the USSR and to grant it vast financial credits, he agreed not to block German unity, which then took effect on October 3, 1990. The East German state simply ceased to exist as the West German government took over the whole country.

Elections elsewhere in Eastern Europe by then had brought to power national leaders not beholden to Moscow. And on July 1, 1991, the Warsaw Pact—an odd alliance that had used its forces only to keep its own members in line—was officially disbanded.

Thus ended Soviet domination of Eastern and central Europe. Like Asians and Africans before them, Eastern Europeans had gained national liberation, perceiving that the Soviets no longer would use force to sustain repressive and unpopular regimes. And like Western European leaders before him, Gorbachev had concluded that the costs of maintaining imperial rule were simply not worth the price. For decades both superpowers had been preaching national self-determination while practicing imperialism; now the leader of one superpower momentously decided to really practice what he preached. And his decision not to intervene enabled Eastern Europe's transformation.

THE DISINTEGRATION OF THE SOVIET REALM

Gorbachev's decision also had immense implications for the USSR, where many nationalities longed for national independence and freedom from Soviet Russian rule. His reforms had given the Soviet peoples more freedom in hopes that they would use it collectively to help resolve the USSR's many problems. But the reforms also raised economic expectations that they proved unable to fulfill and—combined with his decision not to intervene to save the Soviet satellite regimes—they emboldened diverse peoples to defy his rule and seek national independence. In the end, national and ethnic loyalties far outweighed any sense of allegiance to the Soviet state.

First to push for greater autonomy were the Baltic republics of Estonia, Latvia, and Lithuania, whose peoples for the most part had never accepted their annexation by the USSR during World War II.* As early as 1988, while the Soviet Union and the Soviet Bloc still seemed solid, Lithuanians and Estonians staged large nationalistic demonstrations, centered

---

*The United States and a number of other Western nations also refused to formally recognize the Soviet annexation of the Baltic republics.

on the singing of patriotic songs, while Latvians formed independence movements that likewise held patriotic demonstrations. In November of that year, Estonia's legislative leaders issued a "sovereignty declaration," asserting that their laws superseded those of the USSR, and Lithuania restored its former national flag and national anthem, dating from its earlier independence.

In 1989, as the wind of change was sweeping across Eastern Europe, much as it had swept across Africa three decades earlier (chapter 5), the quest for national autonomy spread among the Soviet republics. Following Estonia's lead, Lithuania and Latvia both proclaimed sovereignty, declaring invalid their annexation by the USSR but not yet asserting their full independence. In Georgia, Soviet suppression of nationalistic demonstrations in April did not reduce the fervor for freedom but rather reinforced it by raising the level of anti-Soviet resentment, as reflected in widespread worker strikes and growing separatist sentiment. In Ukraine, a nationalistic organization called "Rukh" ("the Movement") emerged and increasingly began to agitate for Ukrainian independence.

In 1990, as anti-Soviet separatist sentiments spread across the USSR, all of the Soviet republics were engulfed. In March Lithuania declared its full independence, defying a plea from Gorbachev for restraint, and elected an anticommunist president before finally agreeing in May to hold off on enforcing its decision to leave the USSR. Estonia and Latvia, meanwhile, similarly asserted their intention to pursue full independence, as did the Armenian republic that summer. By the end of the year all the Soviet republics (map 7.3) had asserted some form of enhanced autonomy, including the massive Russian Soviet Federative Socialist Republic (RSFSR).

Russia's challenge to Soviet authority was engineered by Boris Yeltsin, a radical reformer who in 1987 had broken with Gorbachev because he saw the latter's reforms as too timid and too slow. Ousted from Communist Party leadership, he nonetheless managed to get elected chairman of the RSFSR parliament (Supreme Soviet) in May 1990, thus becoming the main leader of the mammoth Russian republic. Courageous, confrontational, and flamboyant, he had emerged as a popular hero, while Gorbachev's popularity had plummeted. Under Yeltsin, overwhelmingly elected by Russians the next year to the new post of Russian president, the RSFSR declared itself sovereign and asserted that its laws took precedence over those of the Soviet Union.

The rise of Russian separatism posed a far more serious threat to the USSR than the national independence movements in other Soviet Republics. As troublesome as the latter efforts were, the Soviet Union could no doubt survive without the Baltic states, as it had before World War II, and perhaps even without the Armenians and Georgians. But the Soviet leadership had always presumed that the Russians, who dominated the USSR and identified it as their homeland, would work loyally to preserve the Soviet state. Their dominance, however, to some extent was threatened by Gorbachev's reforms, and their loyalty to him and the Soviet state was increasingly on the wane.* Without their support—and certainly without the RSFSR—the Soviet Union could not hope to survive.

The Soviet leaders sought tenaciously to keep the whole country together and to combat the national separatist movements that were tearing it apart. Early in January 1991, in an effort to crack down on draft dodgers and military deserters, they dispatched paratroopers to seven separatist republics. Later that month they sent troops, tanks, and special forces to Lithuania and Latvia, seizing control of media and security facilities in those troublesome republics. Gorbachev himself denied ordering these attacks, implying instead that they were directed by hard-liners in his government, but it was hard to see how they could have done so without his knowledge and tacit acquiescence.

Gorbachev's preference, nonetheless, was to compromise with the nationalists, not to crush them. Perhaps if the national republics had more autonomy and a greater sense of sovereignty, most of them would be willing to stay within the Soviet Union.† He thus proposed a new "Union Treaty," drafted in early 1991, which among other things would change the word "Socialist" to "Sovereign" in the USSR's title, making it the "Union of Soviet Sovereign Republics." Under the terms of this treaty, the Soviet government would keep control of finances, military forces, and various other resources (including transportation and communication), but each republic could run its own internal affairs, and each would be free to employ its own economic and social system. In a March 1991 referendum, by a 76 percent majority, Soviet voters overwhelmingly supported the preservation of the USSR as a "renewed federation of equal sovereign republics, in which the rights and freedoms of an individual of any nationality will be fully guaranteed."[10]

Although the referendum was marred by the fact that six of the fifteen Soviet republics did not participate,‡ Gorbachev considered it a victory and proceeded with his plans to implement the new union treaty. After final details were hammered out with the remaining nine republics, eight

---

*A new Congress of People's Deputies, created by Gorbachev to make the USSR government more representative of its peoples, was elected in 1989 with non-Russians in the majority. And on May 1, 1990, shortly before Yeltsin emerged as the RSFSR's main leader, Gorbachev was loudly jeered by protesters at May Day festivities in Moscow.

†This thinking was similar to that of the East German authorities in November of 1989, when they had eased travel restrictions to the West in hopes that, if their citizens could come and go as they wished, they would choose to stay.

‡The Estonian, Latvian, Lithuanian, Georgian, Armenian, and Moldavian SSRs boycotted the referendum.

of them ratified it that summer, with Ukraine opting to delay. The treaty's formal signing was set to take place on August 20, 1991.

But the signing of the treaty did not occur. Instead, hard-liners in Gorbachev's government, dismayed that the Soviet government would be giving up some of its powers, decided to take matters into their own hands. Detaining Gorbachev on August 18 at his summer home in the south, the next day they announced that he had been relieved of his duties "for health reasons." Forming an eight-man "emergency committee"—which included the vice president and the heads of the security forces—they declared a six-month state of emergency and directed that their decisions would be "mandatory for unswerving fulfillment by all agencies of power and administration, officials and citizens throughout the territory of the USSR."[11] They also ordered troops and tanks to move into Moscow and directed Soviet forces to blockade the Baltic republics. This was the onset of what came to be called the "August coup."

Almost from the start, however, the coup began to unravel. At a televised news conference on August 19, Vice President Gennadii Yanaev, the committee's ostensible leader, appeared to be both nervous and drunk as he introduced his comrades and warily described the measures they had taken. That same day, Russian President Yeltsin, in stark and courageous contrast, dramatically stood on a tank in front of the Russian parliament headquarters in Moscow, and read a statement calling on all Russians to resist the "anti-constitutional coup."[12] Then, as tens of thousands of Muscovites surrounded it in support, he holed up in that building for the next few days, receiving supportive calls from US President George H. W. Bush and boldly defying the coup. On August 20 the coup leaders decided to order an attack upon the surrounded building, but the military leaders, fearful of causing a massive bloodbath if they tried to attack through the crowd, delayed it and finally called it off the next morning. The attempted coup, derisively dubbed by disdainful Russians as the "vodka putsch,"* came to an inglorious end.

The Soviet Union, too, was nearing its end. Gorbachev was freed, and he resumed his role as Soviet leader, but momentum had shifted to Yeltsin's Russia and the non-Russian republics. As Yeltsin's government took over many Soviet functions, the other republics again asserted independence, while Gorbachev scrambled to keep it all together by promoting a new union treaty designed to give them even more autonomy. But nationalism and separatism prevailed. On December 1 the people of Ukraine

---

*A *putsch*, like a *coup*, is a sudden attempt to seize power. The term *vodka putsch* derives from the impression that the coup leaders, especially Yanaev, drank heavily during the coup to shore up their shaky nerves. After the coup failed, its leaders were arrested. One committed suicide; others, including Yanaev, were later released under amnesty from the post-Soviet Russian government.

voted for independence; a week later Yeltsin met with its president and also the leader of Belarus (formerly the Belorussian SSR) to create a loose federation called the **Commonwealth of Independent States**—effectively declaring that the Soviet Union was dead. On December 25, after all other republics but Georgia and the Baltic states had agreed to join the new "commonwealth," a disconsolate Gorbachev formally resigned as president of the USSR—a regime that had essentially ceased to exist. His brief resignation speech,[13] and the subsequent lowering of the Soviet flag that had long flown above the government complex, signaled the demise of one of history's most formidable empires, and its replacement by fifteen new national states (map 7.3).

CONNECTIONS AND CONCLUSIONS

The factors contributing to this demise included the USSR's economic crisis, the financial burden of its military forces and the Cold War nuclear arms race, the inefficiency and oppressiveness of the Soviet system, its failure to foster innovation, and widespread discontent with bureaucratic waste and corruption. But central to the split-up of the Soviet state were the nationalist aspirations of its diverse peoples. Gorbachev had gambled that by giving them more freedom he could gain their cooperation and support in solving the society's problems. Instead, freed by his "new thinking" from the fear of force that had held the vast empire together, the peoples opted to aim for independence from Soviet Russian rule.

Ironically, this independence was enabled by Russians themselves. At critical moments in 1989, Gorbachev, a Russian,* chose not to intervene to save the Soviet satellites, thus allowing Eastern European nations to determine their own destinies. At the crucial junctures of 1991, when faced with the possible restoration of repressive imperial rule, Yeltsin and his Russian government, supported by great masses of Russians, not only thwarted the hard-line August coup but also obstructed Gorbachev's efforts to sustain some semblance of a centralized state. As with the earlier endings of the Western European empires, the fight for freedom of the subject peoples was aided by the actions and acquiescence of the old "mother country."

The old "mother country" nonetheless survived in the form of the Russian Federation, a multinational realm with a number of "republics" and "autonomous regions" populated mainly by non-Russians. Even after the disintegration of the USSR, its surviving Russian metropole—still far

---

*Although Gorbachev was part Ukrainian by heritage, he was raised in Russia, considered himself a Russian, and failed to fully grasp the extent to which other nationalities in the USSR resented Russian domination.

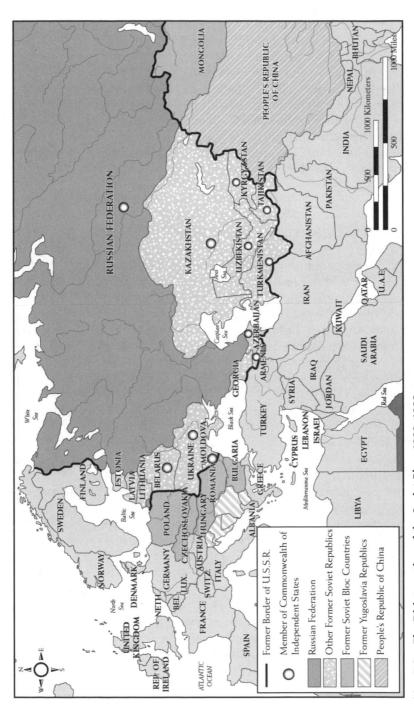

Map 7.3. The Disintegration of the Soviet Bloc, 1989–1992

and away the world's largest country—remained in many ways an imperial domain, heir to the tsars and successor to the Soviets, weakened but
by no means vanquished. And like many of the old European colonial
metropoles, it continued to assert and maintain a variety of economic and
cultural ties with some of its former "colonial" subjects. As in the West,
so too in the East: the end of an empire did not necessarily signify the end
of imperialist connections.

8

~∿

"Empires Wax and Wane"
Overview and Conclusions

"Empires wax and wane; states cleave asunder and coalesce."[1] Thus begins an English version of the *Romance of the Three Kingdoms*, a venerable and ageless Chinese classic. And indeed, for at least four thousand years strong powers have worked their will on the weak, badgering, intimidating, attacking, invading, and conquering others to promote their interests, enhance their power, increase their wealth, and often expand their domains. As the great Greek historian Thucydides once wrote, "The strong do what they have the power to do, and the weak accept what they have to accept."[2]

For thousands of years, empires were widely regarded as a normal, natural, and even beneficial feature of human societies—uniting diverse peoples and places; spreading ideas, knowledge, and techniques; imposing peace and stability; and often advancing commercial and cultural connections. The Egyptians, Persians, Chinese, Romans, Byzantines, Muslims, Mongols, Turks, Aztecs, Incas, Russians, and others all took pride in the great land empires they created. And the Portuguese, Spanish, Dutch, British, French, and Belgians tended to regard their overseas colonial empires as purveyors and conveyors of modern civilizing values. Empires signified power and prestige, progress and pride, central authority and regional diversity.

Then came the twentieth century. The norms and ideals of nationalism, nurtured in the nineteenth century, suggested that the optimal sociopolitical organization was not the multinational empire but the national state, uniting people of a single language, custom, culture, and tradition. Idealists and ideologues from V. I. Lenin to Woodrow Wilson asserted

that all peoples had a right to national self-determination—the entitle-
ment of each nationality to decide its own political status, and the right of
people to live in a country that honors and embodies their language, customs, and culture. The century's great world wars, fought mainly among
imperialist powers seeking to expand or protect their realms, seemed to
show that imperialism was harmful not only to its victims but also to its
practitioners.

The era of anticolonialism and Cold War, encompassing the four and a
half decades following World War II, saw the disintegration of Europe's
great colonial empires, aided by the "anti-imperialism" of both the United
States and the USSR. Imperialism, discredited as both an ideal and a
practice, was denounced by each of the Cold War superpowers even
as they pursued their own imperialistic aims. In their efforts to expand
their influence and advance their ideological visions, each provided aid
to emerging nations, thus creating client states that depended on their
aid and were hence expected to support their ideals and goals. And each
saw fit at times to intervene in such states, aiming thereby to advance its
own interests and prevent potential advances by the other side. But even
as they thus limited their client states' independence, both sides publicly
promoted the ideals of nationalism and national liberation, the quest for
which then helped to bring about both the Cold War's end and the Soviet
Empire's demise.

As we have argued, and as the preceding chapters have shown, the
Cold War and the struggle against imperialism were not simply parallel
developments that intersected at various times and places. They were, in
fact, so closely interconnected that they might better be understood as a
single interlocking global struggle among imperial powers and emerging
national states—a complex and convoluted struggle that helped to free
colonized peoples from formal colonial rule while simultaneously sub-
jecting them to less formal methods of imperial control. This struggle can
profitably be divided into four distinctive phases, as outlined in the overview below, which highlights and summarizes the main points presented
in the preceding chapters.

LIBERATION AND CONFLICT
IN THE EARLY POSTWAR ERA, 1945–1954

The first phase of the struggle, the early postwar era, was marked by
the onset of the Cold War and the age of decolonization, both of which
began in earnest in the wake of World War II. It is true, of course, that
anti-imperial sentiments and tensions between communism and capitalism existed before that conflict, and that ideals and developments after

that war were rooted in ideals and developments that predated it. But the prewar balance of forces and technologies had favored the capitalistic and imperialistic Western powers, and the relative weakness of both the colonial anti-imperialist movements and the new Soviet state made effective anti-Western resistance difficult. The Second World War helped to change this dynamic in several important ways:

- It shattered whatever remained of the myth of Western European superiority. In the early stages of the war, Nazi Germany quickly conquered three key imperial powers—the Netherlands, Belgium, and France—and then Japan, an *Asian* power, overran the Asian possessions of France, Britain, the United States, and the Netherlands. The Western powers thus suffered a series of devastating and humiliating defeats.
- Britain, France, Belgium, and the Netherlands, the leading colonial imperialists, were weakened by the war and rescued from defeat by the Soviet Union and the United States. These results paved the way not only for the emergence of the latter two countries—each having anti-imperialist roots and ideals—as superpowers that would both eclipse Europe and divide and dominate that continent during the Cold War decades, but also for the success of the anti-imperialist movements that would liberate Asians and Africans from European colonial rule during those very same decades.
- The appalling brutality of racist imperialism as practiced by the Axis Powers, and the Allied struggle against this racist imperialism, convinced many in the West that both racism and imperialism were inherently immoral, undermining popular support for any policies that smacked of either set of attitudes. Although each of the Cold War superpowers would practice a form of imperialism, both of them outwardly extolled the ideals of anti-imperialism and national self-determination, making it both morally and politically difficult for Western Europeans to maintain their colonial empires.

Inspired by these realities, and eager to exploit them, several key anti-imperialist Asians wasted no time in asserting independence as World War II wound down. On August 17, 1945—two days after Japan's Emperor Hirohito had agreed to surrender to the Allied Powers—in the Dutch East Indies the nationalist leader Sukarno issued a Proclamation of Indonesian Independence. On September 2, the day of the formal Japanese surrender, the revolutionary Marxist Ho Chi Minh declared independence for the Democratic Republic of Vietnam. That same day, in its surrender instructions to Japan, the United States ended Japanese imperial rule in Korea, but effectively divided it into Soviet and US occupation zones.* On September 20, Mohandas Gandhi and Jawaharlal Nehru, the main leaders of the Indian National Congress, demanded that the British withdraw from India.[3] And on October 10, in China, in a vain attempt to head off civil war, Chinese Communist and National leaders formally agreed to work peaceably together to build an independent China, much of which had recently been freed from Japanese imperial occupation.[4]

Each of these episodes brought conflict, and each of these conflicts would eventually generate Cold War connections. The Dutch, who were eager to restore their lucrative East Indies empire, branded Sukarno as a wartime traitor and sent armies to crush his liberation movement—until fierce guerrilla warfare by Sukarno's supporters, combined with US pressure on the Dutch to withdraw for fear that the war might be aiding the Communists, led the Netherlands to recognize Indonesian independence at the end of 1949. The French, who were likewise keen to reestablish their rule over Indochina, fought an unsuccessful eight-year war. It was financed in part by the United States, which decided to back its Cold War ally France because France was battling against the Communist Ho Chi Minh and his comrades. The Chinese Communists and Nationalists, unable and unwilling to coexist for long once the Japanese were gone, fought a brutal civil war (1946–1949) that was won by the Communists, who founded the People's Republic of China on the mainland, while the Nationalists fled to the island of Taiwan and survived there under US protection. The British did indeed withdraw from India in 1947, but their division of it into the Hindu-led Republic of India and the Islamic Republic of Pakistan triggered mass migrations of Muslims from the former and Hindus from the latter, marred by violent clashes between them that took perhaps a million lives, and left the two new nations as bitterly hostile neighbors who would eventually take aid from opposing Cold War camps. And postcolonial Korea also divided into two hostile states, leading to an inconclusive three-year war that began when the Communist North invaded the nationalist South in 1950, and then expanded when US-led UN forces aided South Korea and troops from Communist China poured in to help the North. Although millions of Asians gained independence from foreign imperial rule, their struggles and successes combined with Cold War conflicts brought neither peace nor stability to Asia in the wake of World War II.

In the Middle East, nationalist sentiments and Cold War concerns also led to crises and conflicts, complicated by the oil abundance of the Per-

---

*General Order No. 1, approved by President Harry Truman on August 17, 1945, and issued on September 2, directed Japanese commanders in Korea north of 38° north latitude to surrender to Soviet forces and ordered those south of that line to surrender to the US Army, thereby dividing Korea at the 38th parallel. See Office of the Supreme Commander for the Allied Powers, General Order No. 1 (2 September 1945), 2–3, http://www.mofa.go.jp/mofaj/files/000097066.pdf; and chapter 3 of this volume.

sian Gulf countries and by the emergence of a Jewish state in the midst of the Muslim Arab world. The first Cold War crisis occurred in oil-rich Iran in 1946, when the Soviets, having balked at removing their forces by the date on which they and the British had agreed to do so, instead sought to set up a client state in the north. Faced with pressure from the British (who had earlier withdrawn their forces), the Americans, and the Shah of Iran, the Soviets eventually withdrew and their client state was dismantled. But the Shah effectively became a US client, especially after the Americans in 1953 conspired with Iranian forces to oust Iran's elected anti-imperialist prime minister, Mohammad Mosaddeq, who in a bid to boost Iran's economic independence had dared to nationalize a British-owned oil company. American imperialism thus superseded that of the Soviets and the British in Iran.

The British fared no better in their Palestine mandate, where sympathy for Jews in the wake of the Holocaust put pressure on London to keep a long-standing promise to create a national homeland for the Jewish people (see chapter 4), much to the dismay of the region's Arabs. Unable to satisfy both the Jews and Arabs, in 1947 Britain turned the mandate over to the UN, which partitioned it into two states—one Arab and one Jewish—leading to formation of the State of Israel in 1948. Enraged and dismayed, six Arab countries at once attacked Israel, only to be soundly defeated, resulting in humiliation and bitter soul-searching throughout the Arab world. Although both the Americans and Soviets initially backed Israel, as Arab nationalists came to see the Jewish Zionist state as an extension of Western imperialism, they would seek and gain Soviet support against the US-aided Israelis, thus connecting the Cold War with Arab anti-imperialism in the Middle East.

In Africa, the struggle against imperialism took longer to get under way in earnest than it did in Asia. In October 1945, the Fifth Pan-African Congress, filled with fiery anticolonial speeches, featured several of the men who would later lead parts of Africa to independence. But the congress took place not in Africa but in England, and most of the participants— many of whom had not been in Africa for years—expected that it might take several decades for Africans to gain independence. Still, since many African nationalist leaders were attracted to Marxist ideals and socialist economic systems, their goals and movements had potential Cold War implications, which would later surface when they started making head-way in the mid-to-late 1950s.

In Europe, in the immediate postwar era, the anticolonial struggle had very different meanings in the East and West. In the East, the main countries—East Germany, Poland, Czechoslovakia, Hungary, Romania, and Bulgaria—found themselves subjected to a new form of colonialism, as postwar Soviet occupation resulted in the formation of Moscow-dominated

Communist satellite regimes. In the West, reluctantly and often unwillingly, the once great imperial powers—mainly the British, French, and Dutch—were beginning to free their overseas colonies, especially the ones in Asia, while coming under US protection as members of the new NATO anti-Soviet Cold War alliance.

THE KHRUSHCHEV ERA AND
THE WIND OF CHANGE, 1954–1964

In 1954 and 1955 several key developments marked the transition from the first to the second phase of the postwar anti-imperialist struggle. In July 1954 the Geneva Accords ended the First Indochina War, removing the French imperialists and dividing their former colony into the newly independent nations of North Vietnam, South Vietnam, Laos, and Cambodia. In November of that year in North Africa, inspired by the success of the Southeast Asians in gaining their freedom from France, Algerians began a fierce revolt that would eventually do the same for them in 1962. In April 1955 the twenty-nine-nation Asian-African Conference, hosted by Sukarno in Bandung, Indonesia, not only engendered a Non-Aligned Movement of new nations seeking neutrality in the Cold War but also energized African nationalists hoping to gain freedom from the Western imperialists, as Asians already had done. In May the new Soviet leader, Nikita Khrushchev, engineered the formation of the Warsaw Pact, a Cold War alliance that was billed as anti-imperialist but actually served as a convenient cover for Moscow's continued colonial control over its "allied" satellites in Eastern Europe. Then in June he welcomed a visit from India's Nehru, which was followed in October by a Khrushchev trip to India, signaling an enhanced Soviet effort to support new nations that had emerged from Western colonial rule—and later even to back "national liberation wars" against the Western imperialists.[5] Hence, while perpetuating Soviet imperialism in Eastern Europe, he overtly identified the USSR with the global anti-imperialist struggle, thereby further combining it with the Cold War.*

In 1956 the focus of both the Cold War and the struggle against imperialism shifted to the Middle East. There Gamal Abdel Nasser, a charismatic army officer who had risen to power in Egypt after helping to overthrow its monarchy in 1952, was preaching pan-Arabism—a nationalistic concept that sought to unite all Arabs as a single people—and working to end Britain's indirect but palpable imperialistic sway over Egypt and the

---

*A further example of this combination emerged that same year (1955) when Communist Czechoslovakia, a Soviet satellite and ally, began sending arms via Egypt to Algerians, for the latter's "national liberation war" against France.

Suez Canal. London was willing to negotiate with Nasser to curtail Britain's military presence along the canal, while Washington worked to woo him with US aid. But his decisions to transport Soviet Bloc weapons to Algerian rebels in 1955 and to recognize Communist China the next year led the Americans to end their assistance—prompting Nasser in turn to take Soviet aid and to nationalize the Suez Canal in July 1956. His dramatic moves brought the Cold War to the Middle East and shocked the British and French, who then conspired with Israel to start a war with Egypt so that they could use it as a pretext to retake control of the canal. When Israel attacked Egypt that fall, and Britain and France intervened to "restore order" (but really to reclaim the canal), their actions were condemned by both the Soviets (who at one point threatened to intervene with nuclear weapons against the Western imperialists) and the United States (which had not been informed of its allies' plans and eventually pressured them to accept a cease-fire and withdraw).

The Suez Crisis of 1956 had profound repercussions. Nasser emerged as a pan-Arab hero who had thwarted the Western imperialists and could now use both Soviet aid and lucrative canal tolls to finance his costly projects. Relations for a time were strained between Washington and its two main NATO allies, Britain and France, who suffered severe humiliation and feared (not without justification) that Washington's underlying purpose in opposing their Suez venture was the desire to replace them as the dominant imperial power in the Middle East. And the Suez debacle, having mortified and disgraced both the British and French, would serve as a death knell for what was left of their once great African empires, aiding the ambitions of the anticolonialists over the next eight years.

Unfortunately for the Soviets, events that same year in Eastern Europe undermined their attempts to exploit the West's Suez fiasco and project an anti-imperialist image. Demonstrations and riots in the summer and fall of 1956 signaled that, like Asians and Africans, the people of Poland and Hungary longed for national liberation. The brutal crushing of the Hungarian revolt by Soviet troops, coming in the midst of the Suez Crisis, showed the ruthlessly repressive nature of Soviet-style imperialism. And pan-Arab nationalist Nasser, although happy to take Soviet aid, proved a staunch anti-Marxist who repressed communists in Egypt and Syria, which were joined together under his leadership from 1958 to 1961 as the United Arab Republic.

Meanwhile the British, chastened and chagrined by their Suez debacle, began to further dismantle their empire in Africa. In 1957, following a decade of protests and preparation, Britain granted independence to its West African Gold Coast colony, which became the new nation of Ghana. Its leader, the redoubtable pan-Africanist Kwame Nkrumah, hosted two conferences in 1958 that assembled and inspired national liberation

Map 8.1.   Decolonization and Cold War Clashes in Africa and the Middle East, 1945–1990

leaders from all over Africa. That same year, as France moved to grant
its colonies autonomy as members of a new "French Community" with
ample French economic aid, colonial Guinea, led by Ahmed Sékou Touré,
refused the offer and opted instead for immediate independence. France's
spiteful retaliation, marked by its rapid removal of French assets and
abrupt end of French aid, unsettled other French colonies, most of which
sought and gained both independence and continued French aid by the
end of 1960 (map 8.1). French influence in Africa remained, but France's
direct rule in Africa had largely come to an end.*

---

*Algeria, which the French had regarded not as a colony but as a part of France, gained
independence in 1962, and Djibouti, a small French colony in eastern Africa, did so in 1977.

The end of Britain's direct rule in Africa was not far behind. In early 1960, during a six-week tour of Africa, British Prime Minister Harold Macmillan made speeches in which he famously declared that "the wind of change is blowing through this continent" and that the growth of African nationalism could no longer be denied. In the next four years, most of Britain's remaining African colonies would formally gain independence.

But in Africa, as elsewhere, efforts to achieve full independence were complicated by both poverty and the Cold War. Aware that many new African leaders resented the Western imperialists, sympathized with socialist ideals, and badly needed economic assistance, Soviet leader Khrushchev saw this situation as a chance to woo them to the Soviet side. Both Ghana's Nkrumah and Guinea's Sékou Touré sought to play off the Soviets against the Americans and thus get aid from both, but in so doing they raised mutual suspicions that complicated their efforts. Khrushchev and the Soviets sent aid but were outbid by the wealthier Americans, and in the long run neither the superpowers nor the Africans gained much from these endeavors.

More consequential to the Cold War was the complex conflict in Congo. In 1960 the Belgians, spooked by anti-imperialist riots in their huge Congo colony and by British and French decisions to liberate their own African domains, opted quickly to liberate the Congo realm and hope for the best. But instead the new Congo nation got the worst, in part because the Belgians had left it woefully unprepared for self-governance, in part because regional and tribal loyalties trumped the need for national unity, in part because Congo's few able leaders could not work well together, and in part because Cold War rivalries badly aggravated Congolese conflicts. In the fifteen months that followed, the Congo leaders conflicted with each other; the resource-rich province of Katanga seceded; a complex four-way civil war broke out; the Soviets, Americans, and Belgians backed opposing sides; the gifted and volatile young prime minister Lumumba was murdered; and UN Secretary-General Dag Hammarskjöld was killed in a plane crash as he sought to end the strife. Katanga's secession, which might otherwise have been rectified in a few months, lasted until early 1963 because of the intersection of two toxic tendencies: Cold War rivalries and the conviction that Europeans were using the secession to reassert imperial control. Finally, in 1965, the Congo was reunified (and later renamed Zaire) by Mobutu, a brutal and corrupt US-backed dictator who ruled with an iron fist until 1997. Here, as elsewhere, America's anticommunist imperialism trumped its professed devotion to democracy and human rights.

In the meantime the Cold War and the anti-imperial struggle had spread to Latin America, where nations looked to free themselves, not from European colonial rule (most of which had ended in the 1800s), but from economic dominance and periodic political interference by the United States. In 1954 a US-backed coup had deposed the pro-communist Árbenz regime in Guatemala, thereby showing that Washington, like the Soviets in Eastern Europe, was resolved to have friendly governments run the countries in its "backyard." But this resolve was challenged again after 1959, when a revolution in Cuba brought to power Fidel Castro, a fierce Cuban nationalist with Marxist sympathies who deeply resented the many decades that his nation had been dominated by US economic and political imperialism. Sensing a chance both to strike a blow against American imperialism and to gain an ally on the US doorstep, Khrushchev and the Soviets wooed Castro into their camp with a 1960 trade pact and pledges of aid and support. When the US-backed Bay of Pigs invasion, an attempt to overthrow the Castro regime, was crushed by loyal Cuban forces in April 1961, Castro requested more Soviet assistance to defend his regime against any potential future invasion by the American imperialists.

But Khrushchev also had other problems in his own imperial backyard. In August 1961, in a bid to stop the exodus of people going from East to West Berlin to escape from Communist East Germany, the Soviets and East Germans began building the Berlin Wall across the city. For twenty-seven years it would serve as a symbol of Soviet imperial control, depicting the Soviet Bloc as a prison camp from which the escape routes were blocked by the wall and by miles of barbed wire fences. And to make matters worse for the Soviets, although the wall did curb the human outflow, the British, French, and Americans still controlled West Berlin.

By 1962 Khrushchev was thus faced with three major challenges. How could he protect the Castro regime against a possible US invasion? How could he get the Western powers out of West Berlin? And how could he narrow the gap in long-range nuclear missiles, in numbers of which his country lagged far behind the much wealthier Americans?* His answer was creative but extremely risky: he would secretly ship some of his midrange missiles to Cuba, from which they would be close enough to hit the American homeland, posing a threat that would surely deter a potential US attack. Once the missiles were in place he planned to reveal their presence and offer to remove some or all of them if the Western powers would vacate West Berlin. From his perspective, this was a clever gamble intended to solve three problems at once, but from a Western perspective it was an audacious example of

---

*In the early 1960s, although the Soviets had dozens of midrange nuclear missiles capable of hitting Western Europe, they had only about a half dozen long-range intercontinental ballistic missiles (ICBMs) capable of hitting the United States from the USSR. The Americans, by contrast, had fifty-four functional ICBMs and were building one thousand new ones.

blatant Soviet imperialism—an effort to extend Soviet imperial control over both Cuba and West Berlin.

Khrushchev's gamble almost proved catastrophic. The Americans, who detected the Soviet missiles in Cuba before they were fully installed, demanded that the Soviets remove them and imposed a naval quarantine to keep further missile components from reaching Cuba. The resulting Cuban Missile Crisis, arising out of the Cold War clash between the imperialist concerns of the superpowers, took them (and the world) to the brink of nuclear war for several very frightening days in October 1962. But Khrushchev eventually (and prudently) backed down, agreeing to remove his missiles from Cuba in return for a US pledge not to invade the island.*

The Cuban crisis and its resolution had profound and enduring implications. It contributed to the growing split between the Soviets and the Chinese Communists, who were furious with Khrushchev for yielding to the American imperialists and who openly broke with the USSR in 1963 and 1964. It undermined Khrushchev's position and played a key role in his ouster from power in 1964. It led his successor, Leonid Brezhnev, to pursue a massive naval and nuclear buildup in a bid to match US might, thus enhancing the USSR's status as a global imperial power, but also accelerating the arms race and further straining Soviet resources. It left the Western imperialists in control of West Berlin, as a small but significant and visible challenge to Soviet imperial dominance in Eastern Europe. And it helped the Castro regime in Cuba survive, throughout the Cold War and beyond, as a small but significant and visible challenge to US imperial dominance in the Western hemisphere.

By 1964, then, the second phase of the Cold War and the anti-imperialist struggle was coming to an end. The wind of change had swept through Africa, and almost all former British, French, and Belgian colonies had gained their independence. Khrushchev had been swept away, removed and replaced by his own former comrades who were frustrated by his foibles and failures, including the rather meager results of his efforts to gain Third World clients. The Non-Aligned Movement had been founded but to some extent had foundered;† the Suez Canal had been seized by the Egyptians; the Hungarian revolt had been crushed; the Berlin Wall had been built; the Soviets and the Chinese Communists had split; and the world had survived the Cuban Crisis.

---

*As related in chapter 6, the United States also privately promised to remove its outdated missiles from Turkey. See Philip Nash, *The Other Missiles of October* (Chapel Hill, NC, 1997).

†Most of the key leaders of the Non-Aligned Movement—Indonesia's Sukarno, India's Nehru, Egypt's Nasser, and Ghana's Nkrumah—wound up taking aid from the Soviets and/or Americans, and thus were to some extent beholden to their benefactors. True nonalignment proved difficult for poor countries during the Cold War.

CONFLICTS AND CRISES,
DIVISION AND DÉTENTE, 1964–1979

The third phase of the Cold War and anticolonial era brought bloody conflicts and complex crises in Asia, the Middle East, and Africa. It also witnessed deep divisions within the Communist world, and a brief era of wary détente between East and West.

In 1964 and for much of the decade that followed, the focus of the Cold War and the struggle against imperialism shifted mainly to Asia. Most prominent there was the war in Southeast Asia, known to Americans as the Vietnam War and later as the Second Indochina War. But the mid-to-late 1960s also witnessed the ouster of Sukarno and his replacement by the US-backed dictator Suharto in Indonesia, the massive internal upheavals of the Great Proletarian Cultural Revolution in China, and a limited but deadly border war between the Soviets and Chinese. In the 1970s, even as the agonies of Asia continued, the superpowers managed to strike deals to reduce tensions and bring about a measure of détente, but their efforts to maintain it were undermined by crisis in the Middle East and brutal wars in Africa.

In Vietnam, a smoldering civil war in the south between the US-backed regime and Communist Vietcong rebels became an international conflict in 1964, when North Vietnam sent troops south to aid the rebels and Washington responded by sending armed forces to assist the regime. By 1965 it was an all-out war, with Americans fighting in the South and bombing the North, while the Soviets and Communist Chinese sent aid to help the Vietnamese Communists. From the Marxist-Leninist perspective, this was a classic war of national liberation, with the Vietnamese fighting to free the south from the vestiges of Western domination, and with the United States having taken France's place as the imperial power. From a US perspective, however, this was a war to protect South Vietnam from a worse form of imperial tyranny: a vast network of Communist dictatorships that were to some extent satellites or client states of the USSR. The building of the Berlin Wall in 1961, the crushing of the reform movement in Czechoslovakia in 1968, and the subsequent promulgation of the Brezhnev Doctrine all lent credence to this Western view of Communist imperial oppression.

By then, however, divisions in the Communist world had become obvious to all. Despite an early bid by Brezhnev and the Soviets to repair relations with China, their dealings continued to deteriorate, especially after 1966, when Chinese leader Mao Zedong launched his Great Proletarian Cultural Revolution. That radical internal mass movement, which included condemnation of the Soviet system accompanied by student assaults on the Soviet embassy in Beijing, helped to set the stage for bloody border clashes between the two Communist powers in 1969. It also set the stage for US efforts to exploit this growing rift, including President Richard Nixon's celebrated trip to China in 1972, and for Deng Xiaoping's incisive UN speech in 1974, deftly depicting both the Soviets and the Americans as hegemonic imperialists.

On the Cold War front, these developments and others helped to pave the way for a brief era of détente between the superpowers in the 1970s. But détente involved mainly arms control agreements and scientific-cultural exchanges; it did not extend to Third World conflicts and national liberation wars. The Vietnam War, expanded by President Lyndon Johnson in the 1960s, continued under Nixon, who took office in 1969 and widened the war to Cambodia the next year. Only in 1973 did he manage to cut a deal with the Communists to extricate US forces, but even then the war between North and South Vietnam soon resumed, resulting in a Communist victory in 1975. As in so many colonial conflicts, the local anti-imperialist insurgencies succeeded, not so much by winning big battlefield victories, but rather by enduring and outlasting the foreign imperial power, whose efforts were undermined by war-weariness and antiwar sentiments at home.

Détente was also tested by crisis in the Middle East (map 8.2). In 1967, fearing an imminent Arab attack, Israel had launched a devastating offensive, decisively defeating Egypt and its allies in the Six-Day War. This triumph left Israel in occupation of various Arab lands—including Gaza, the Golan Heights, the West Bank of the Jordan River, and the Sinai Peninsula—which to Arabs was a clear case of Israeli Zionist imperialism. In October 1973, in a bid to reverse this humiliation, Egypt and its allies attacked the Israelis on the Jewish holy day of Yom Kippur (and in the Muslim holy month of Ramadan), catching them off guard and making some early gains before Israel rebounded with massive American aid. The Soviets then called for a cease-fire but also threatened to intervene to prevent an Egyptian defeat, sparking a short but severe Cold War crisis when the US responded by placing its military and nuclear forces on global alert. Within a few days the crisis eased as a truce was arranged to end the fighting in the October War.

These events had some serious ramifications. First, they showed that détente, although it eased the arms race, could not necessarily keep the superpowers from being sucked into a conflict between their clients. Second, they sparked a global oil embargo, imposed by oil-exporting Arab countries against the United States and other nations that had supported the "Israeli imperialists," creating severe hardships in these places in the winter of 1973–1974. Third, they left the West Bank and Gaza, peopled mainly by Palestinian Arabs, under Israeli control—thus enhancing both Israel's imperialist image and Arab support for the PLO (Palestine Liberation

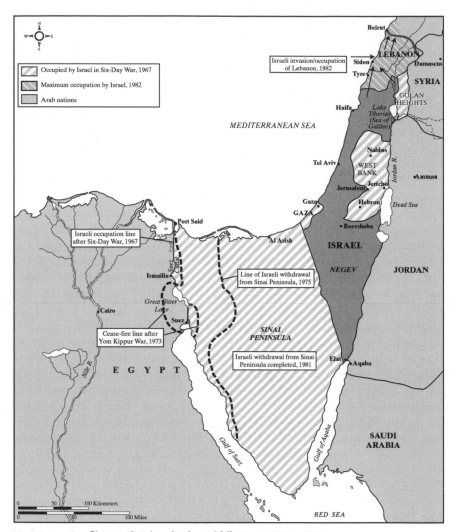

Map 8.2.   Conflicts and Crises in the Middle East, 1960s–1980s

Organization), a militant anti-Zionist "national liberation movement" that resorted at times to terrorist attacks. Fourth, they gave Egyptian President Anwar el-Sadat, buoyed by his country's early successes in the October War, the standing he needed to break through the impasse and work toward a peace treaty with Israel that was finalized in 1979.*

---

*Under the terms of this treaty, Egypt regained the Sinai Peninsula, with Israeli's withdrawal completed in 1981. But Middle East peace continued to prove elusive, as Sadat was

Détente also failed to stop crises and conflicts elsewhere in the Third World. In 1973 Chile's democratically elected Marxist government was ousted by a military coup, after US efforts had helped to undermine its economy and subvert its leader, Salvador Allende. This was a victory of sorts for US economic imperialism, but the brutal dictatorship that followed in Chile belied any sense of American commitment to democracy and human rights. In 1975 Communists won victories not just in Vietnam but also in Laos and Cambodia. But the ensuing genocide in Communist Cambodia, followed by Communist Vietnam's invasion of Cambodia in 1978 and then by Communist China's brief armed intrusion into Vietnam later that year, highlighted the deep divisions within the Communist camp. In 1975 the liberation of Portugal's colonies in Africa, ending the oldest and last of Europe's African empires, led to Communist governments and lengthy civil wars in Mozambique and Angola. Their Marxist regimes became Soviet client states (backed in Angola by troops from Cuba), effectively replacing one form of imperialism with another.

By 1979, then, almost all of Europe's old Asian and African colonies had formally gained at least nominal independence. Having conquered colonial imperialism, however, they frequently found themselves buffeted by Cold War conflicts and subjected to other sorts of imperialist imposition. The struggle against imperialism had won numerous notable victories, but in the Cold War context it rarely brought real freedom, stability, or prosperity to the peoples of the liberated nations.

THE END OF THE COLD WAR AND
THE SOVIET EMPIRE, 1979–1991

The fourth and final phase of the Cold War and the struggle against imperialism began with developments in 1979 and 1980 that, in the short run at least, brought about the demise of détente and the Cold War's return with full fury. These included the Islamic Revolution in Iran, the Soviet invasion of Afghanistan, the renewed US arms buildup ordered in response by President Jimmy Carter, and the 1980 election of Ronald Reagan as his successor. Few could have foreseen that these events would be followed by others in the next decade that would lead to the end of the Cold War and the disintegration of the Soviet Union.

Iran's Islamic Revolution was similar in some respects to other anti-imperialist efforts, but it also differed in a few fundamental ways. Since 1953, Iran had effectively been a US client state, and its Shah had been a

---

murdered that year by Egyptians who deemed the treaty traitorous, and Israel invaded Lebanon the next year to drive out the PLO.

key supporter of the West. Like liberation leaders elsewhere, Ayatollah Khomeini, who took power in early 1979 following the Shah's departure, was anti-Western and anti-imperialist, but unlike them he was also deeply religious, ultraconservative, antisecular, and antimaterialist. Like a number of other such leaders, he practiced nonalignment, but unlike them he did not seek aid from either the Americans or Soviets, and instead disparaged them both as the "Great Satan" and the "Lesser Satan."

His revolt nonetheless had important Cold War consequences. It deprived the Americans of the electronic listening posts they had stationed in Iran to monitor Soviet missile tests, which in turn led to US failure to ratify an arms-control treaty with the USSR that was a centerpiece of détente.* It led to a toxic eight-year war (1980–1988) between Iran and neighboring Iraq, the latter having started the war in an effort to exploit the perceived weakness of Iran's new regime. And it heightened Moscow's fears that Iran's revolutionary Islamist views could spread to Soviet central Asia, where most of the people were Muslims, and thus undermine the Soviet empire itself. Such considerations in turn contributed to Moscow's disastrous decision to invade Afghanistan, a Muslim country on the USSR's border, where a Marxist Soviet client regime was facing an Islamic rebellion.

The Soviet invasion of Afghanistan in December 1979 dealt a death blow to what remained of détente and helped to renew the Cold War with full force. President Carter, fearful that the Soviets were using this invasion to put their forces within striking distance of the Persian Gulf and thus potentially disrupt the West's main source of oil, reacted fervidly and forcefully. He threatened to use force to protect the Persian Gulf, increased defense spending and began a US arms buildup, imposed sanctions on sales of technology and grain to the USSR, and even organized a multination boycott of the 1980 Moscow Olympic Summer Games. But many Americans saw his actions as too little too late, and in the fall of 1980 he lost his presidential reelection bid to Ronald W. Reagan.

Reagan's presidency at first welcomed the renewal of the Cold War and the arms race. A strident anticommunist with deep distrust for the Soviets, he accelerated the US arms buildup, partly to further expand the American arsenal and partly in hopes that a renewed arms race would undermine the already weak Soviet economy. Providing his own distinctive brand of "anti-imperialism," he depicted the USSR as an "evil empire," and had the CIA supply arms and resources to anticommunist "freedom

---

*In 1979, after years of difficult negotiations, the United States and USSR agreed to a new Strategic Arms Limitation Treaty, widely known as SALT II. See "The SALT II Agreement, 1979," in Edward H. Judge and John W. Langdon, eds., *The Cold War through Documents: A Global History*, 3rd ed. (Lanham, MD: Rowman & Littlefield, 2018), 277–79. The loss of Iranian listening posts, however, led key US senators to balk at ratification, for fear the United States could no longer monitor Soviet compliance with the terms of the treaty. Following the Soviet invasion of Afghanistan, President Carter asked the Senate to postpone further consideration of the unratified treaty.

fighters" in places such as Afghanistan, Angola, and Nicaragua. From his perspective, the Cold War was a righteous global struggle against *Soviet imperialism*—a "struggle between right and wrong, good and evil."[6]

His perspective was shared by many people in the Soviet Bloc, who saw their nations and themselves as victims of Soviet imperialism. But some, like the Hungarians in 1956 and the Czechoslovakians in 1968, had seen their dreams of liberation dashed by brutal Soviet force, and others were kept in line by the fear of such force, the use of which was entailed by the Brezhnev Doctrine. In 1980 and 1981, the Poles tried massive strikes and patriotic protests, but Poland's Communist regime, fearful that these protests would provoke a Soviet invasion, imposed martial law and banned public protests at the end of 1981. Europe's old colonial empires were gone, but the Soviet empire remained intact, with dozens of different nationalities living under what was often perceived as a form of colonial control.

Things began to change, however, after Mikhail Gorbachev became the Soviet leader in 1985. Eager to improve the Soviet economy, he took steps to combat alcoholism and corruption, and he introduced limited market incentives, thus emulating capitalistic practice. Convinced, moreover, that the economy was crippled by the huge costs of maintaining and defending the vast Soviet empire, he worked to reduce these expenses by negotiating with the Americans in a bid to end the arms race, and also by cutting back on support for Soviet satellites and client states. In 1988–1989 he even withdrew the Soviet forces from Afghanistan, ending a war that had drained his country's resources and cost it thousands of lives. In sum, he opted to try to cut costs by curtailing Cold War competition and softening Soviet imperialism.

Unfortunately for Gorbachev, his efforts had mixed results. His economic reforms raised people's hopes but failed to improve their lives, leading to widespread dissatisfaction by the late 1980s. His efforts to reduce Cold War armaments and tensions met with a positive response from Ronald Reagan, but their hopes for an agreement on deep cuts in strategic nuclear weapons were hindered by Reagan's desire to develop a space-based missile defense system, which Gorbachev strongly opposed. And his cutbacks on support for satellite regimes, along with his withdrawal from Afghanistan, gave hope to subject peoples in the Soviet Bloc while also removing the fear of Soviet force that held that bloc together.

Freed from that fear, in 1989 the peoples of Eastern Europe began to push for independence—and their Communist rulers, who could no longer count on Soviet support, began to meet some of their demands. Poland held free elections, and Hungary opened its border with the West, thus providing a circuitous escape route to the West for many East Germans that summer and fall. When other East Germans began to hold mass protest demonstrations that fall, the regime eventually decided to ease restrictions on travel to the West, leading to the fall of the Berlin Wall on November 9. By the year's end all of Eastern Europe's Soviet satellite countries had staged successful revolutions, effectively ending imperial rule in what had been the Soviet Bloc.

Over the next eighteen months, as Germany reunified and the Warsaw Pact dissolved, the Cold War came to an end. But imperial rule still existed in the USSR, whose numerous nationalities, emboldened by Gorbachev's reforms and by events in Eastern Europe, were also organizing protests and seeking national liberation. By 1991 all fifteen of the national republics that made up the USSR had proclaimed some sort of autonomy, and several had even declared full independence. Working to hold the realm together, Gorbachev drafted a new "Union Treaty," designed to give the republics greater autonomy, but in August Soviet hardliners staged a coup to block it. They detained Gorbachev and declared a state of emergency, but Boris Yeltsin, president of the Russian republic, called on Russians to resist the coup, and the armed forces opted not to follow the coup leaders' orders to attack the crowds of people heeding Yeltsin's call. The coup collapsed and Gorbachev was freed, but Yeltsin and the leaders of some other republics, resisting his bid to preserve the USSR, formed a loose Commonwealth of Independent states to replace the Soviet realm. By December 25, when Gorbachev finally resigned, the once formidable Soviet realm had dissolved into fifteen independent republics (map 8.3). Another great empire had fallen to the forces of nationalism and national liberation.

THE SURVIVAL AND PERSISTENCE OF IMPERIALISM

The collapse of the Soviet state marked not only the end of a Communist superpower but also the disintegration of one of history's largest and mightiest land empires. Its demise, like the unraveling of the Dutch, British, French, Belgian, and Portuguese colonial empires in the decades after World War II, signified the triumph of the forces of national liberation and national self-determination. Empires, at least in the formal and official sense, were discredited and dismantled, replaced by nations as the preferred form of social, cultural, and political organization and association.

By the early twenty-first century, then, nationalism seemed to have triumphed. Numerous subject peoples the world over had sought and gained at least nominal independence, as the United Nations expanded from fifty member nations in 1945 to 193 in 2011.* Nations looked to be the engines of the present and future; empires appeared to be relics of the past.

---

*In 2012 the United Nations General Assembly passed a resolution designating Palestine as a "non-member observer state." The Palestinian National Authority had also previously submitted to the Security Council an application for full UN membership, which, if ever approved, would make Palestine the 194th member nation.

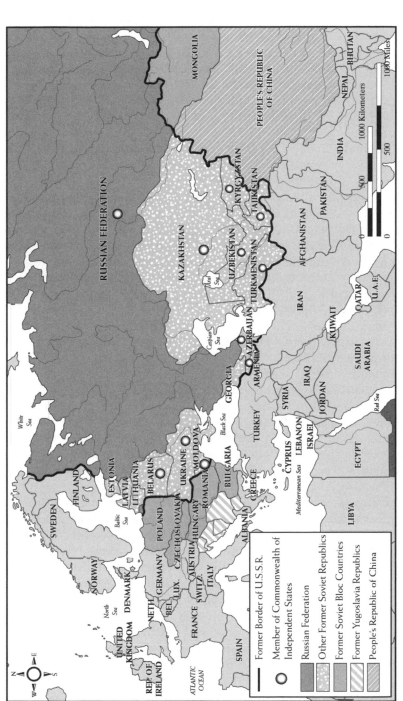

Map 8.3. The Disintegration of the Soviet Bloc, 1989–1992

Imperialism nonetheless survived and even proved resilient and persistent, despite the fact that it was denied and denounced by its main
practitioners. The old European colonial powers continued to employ
what was sometimes called neocolonialism, imposing and maintaining
close cultural and economic ties with some of their former colonies while
also expanding their own military and economic coalitions (NATO and
the European Union) into what had only recently been the Soviet imperial sphere.

The United States, as the sole remaining superpower, persisted in its
own distinctive brand of imperialism. Born as a series of colonies that
united and won independence from their colonial rulers, the Americans
had expanded westward across North America, decimating and subjugating its indigenous inhabitants, to create an immense land empire
dominated by people of European heritage. They had also extended
economic dominance over much of Latin America and even acquired
some relatively modest overseas colonial possessions. In the post–Cold
War era, the United States then continued its imperialist proclivities,
spearheading the NATO expansion and using its immense resources
to work its will upon lesser powers through aid, intervention, and
economic clout, seeking to advance its own enduring vision of a world
full of capitalistic democratic nations that both supported and reflected
American interests and values.

Communist China, despite its persistent denunciations of US and Soviet imperialism, likewise maintained and expanded its own land empire,
subjugating and suppressing various national and religious minorities,
including the mostly-Muslim Uyghur Turks and Tibetan Buddhists.
Emerging as an economic powerhouse in the wake of the Cold War,
China became increasingly imperialistic (and even capitalistic), enlarging
its political and economic influence in Africa and Asia, and extending its
dominance and sway over much of the South China Sea.

Even Russia, with its Soviet empire gone, remained a multinational
realm that repressed subject nationalities, including especially the mostly
Muslim Chechens, who fought two wars in an unsuccessful effort to gain
independence. Responding to the eastward expansion of NATO and the
European Union, the Russians also sought to restore and maintain their
domination over other former Soviet republics, intervening forcibly in
Georgia in 2008, seizing Crimea from Ukraine in 2014, and then supporting pro-Russian separatist rebels in eastern Ukraine.

Each of these actors earnestly denied that it had imperial ambitions,
and none of them openly sought to create (or resurrect) a colonial empire.
With few formal colonies remaining of their own, and with official ideals
that celebrated nationalism and national self-determination, they could
readily reject the "imperialist" label and justify their actions as designed

mainly to prevent atrocities, enforce stability, enhance commerce, defend democracy, or protect weaker friends and neighbors. And indeed it is arguable that such behaviors might better be labeled "hegemonism" than "imperialism," as they led not to the imposition and expansion of formal imperial rule but rather to the exercise of informal and unofficial hegemony over other peoples and powers. But if we define imperialism, as we did in chapter 2, as the exercise of hegemony—that is, economic, cultural, and political dominance—over other societies, the distinction becomes largely semantic. In the post–Cold War and postcolonial world, imperialism continued to exist in practice though not in name, and was sometimes even portrayed by its practitioners as a form of anti-imperialism, much as the Cold War era superpowers had earlier depicted their imperialist behaviors.

CONNECTIONS AND CONCLUSIONS

The Cold War and the struggle against imperialism were exceedingly complex confrontations that unfolded over the course of the four and a half decades following World War II. During those decades, these two intertwined global developments dominated decisions and events in most regions of the world, influencing policies and practices of nations large and small, strong and weak, rich and poor. Millions of people suffered and millions of lives were lost in complicated conflicts fueled by the hopes and dreams, passions and ideals, fears and ambitions of the peoples, movements, nations, and leaders involved. Each set of circumstances was distinctive, each nation had its own unique interests, and many decisions were based on information that was ambiguous, imprecise, or incomplete. With the benefit of hindsight, nevertheless, we can make some key connections and arrive at some overall conclusions:

- As we have argued and shown throughout this book, the Cold War and the struggle against imperialism were inextricably interconnected. To be sure, some aspects of the Cold War (such as the nuclear arms race) were not directly linked with anticolonialism, and some anticolonial efforts (such as those in Belize*) were not closely connected with the Cold War. But in most respects the postwar era's two dominant developments were tied together so tightly that neither can be fully understood without the other. From the outset, for example, the Soviets identified capitalism with imperialism and

---

*With no apparent Cold War connections, the nation of Belize (formerly British Honduras) in Central America gained independence from Britain in 1981.

communism with anti-imperialism—an identification cemented by the resolve of Khrushchev and his successors to support wars of national liberation and nations emerging from colonial rule. The Americans, in response, despite their inherent and oft expressed aversion to colonialism, tended to oppose many leftist anticolonial leaders whom they perceived as Communists, and to view many national liberation struggles mainly through a Cold War prism. And the leaders of these liberation struggles and new nations emerging from them, often badly in need of support and assistance, tended to either identify with one or the other Cold War camp, or else to try to get aid from both by playing them against each other. Whatever the case, more often than not, their movements and nations typically wound up as clients of either the Soviet Union or the United States, frequently espousing (or at least paying lip service to) the ideals of the superpower that supported them. Freed from one form of imperialism, they thus often found themselves subjected to another.

- In most successful anti-imperialist struggles, the impetus for independence came not only from colonial rebels who were fighting for national liberation but also from the people and their leaders in the mother countries, many of whom over time had grown weary of the costs and burdens of supporting a colonial empire. Indeed, Gandhi's strategy of noncooperation with Britain's rule in India was designed in part to make continued rule of India more costly and burdensome to the British than it would be worth—a consideration central to Britain's decision to grant India independence in 1947. Similarly, the decisions by Britain and France in the 1950s and early 1960s and by Portugal in the 1970s to free their African colonies were influenced by outlooks in the metropoles, where the people and at least some of their leaders had tired of colonial costs—and sometimes even morally sympathized with the anti-imperialist liberation efforts of the colonial peoples. Similarly, the US withdrawal from Vietnam and the Soviet withdrawal from Afghanistan resulted from a comparable phenomenon in which the foreign superpower's forces were outlasted by the local anti-imperialist insurgents, who persisted (with aid from the other superpower) until their external foe concluded that the costs of continuing the conflict were too burdensome to bear. And finally, the disintegration of the Soviet empire in 1989–1991 was prompted not only by nationalistic movements among its non-Russian subjects but also by Gorbachev, who made efforts to cut the costs of supporting Soviet satellites, and by Yeltsin and his fellow Russians, who opted to no longer support the continued existence of the USSR.

- The United States and the Soviet Union, the superpowers of the Cold War era, despite their historic and idealistic opposition to colonial imperialism, each practiced its own form of imperialism. Each maintained a far-flung network of naval, air, and military bases, enabling it potentially to project its power, support its allies and clients, and intimidate its foes. Each perceived itself as having a global mission, similar in some ways to the civilizing missions of the old colonial powers, but even more extensive and global in their grasp. But despite the Soviet commitment to Marxist socialism, and despite the American commitment to capitalist democracy, each supported and assisted clients and allies who did not share its expressed ideals and values.

- The support and promotion of anticolonial nationalism and national liberation by the superpowers may have helped each of them at times to gain friends and clients in the Third World, but it also carried serious risks for both. For the Americans, the obvious gap between their ideals and practices—especially their support for brutal dictatorships and authoritarian regimes that claimed to be pro-American and anticommunist—undermined the credibility of US efforts to promote such ideals as liberal democracy, human rights, and national self-determination. To many Third World observers, it seemed that the Americans talked a good game but did not always practice what they preached. This disparity between principles and practice was even more evident with regard to the USSR—and even more dangerous to that state, which despite its ideals in many ways clearly functioned as a multinational empire, with dozens of different nations and nationality groups under Soviet imperial rule. Their aims and efforts to gain independence, like the earlier aims and efforts of the liberation movements in the old European colonies, eventually bore fruit and helped to bring about the collapse of the USSR. In promoting anti-imperialism and national self-determination, the Soviets hence inadvertently helped to pave the way for the end of the Soviet Empire.
- The end of the Soviet Empire, and the earlier demise of Europe's old colonial empires, did not spell the end of imperialism. Despite the downfall of the Dutch, French, British, Belgian, Portuguese, and Soviet Russian empires, and the emergence of numerous new nations made up of peoples who were formerly under their rule, imperialism survived and persisted in various informal and noncolonial forms. Even after colonialism was defeated and discredited, and even after the Cold War had come to an end, the Europeans, Americans, Chinese, and Russians continued to act in ways that could reasonably be considered imperialistic, despite their professed official opposition to imperialism. The sun may have set on the old colonial empires, but imperialism lived on, denied by its practitioners, denounced by one and all, yet still quite prevalent in the post–Cold War and postcolonial world.

Notes

CHAPTER 1:
INTRODUCTION: THE STRUGGLE AGAINST
IMPERIALISM AND ITS COLD WAR CONNECTIONS

1. There are many fine traditional treatments of the Cold War era, including our own companion volumes: Edward H. Judge and John W. Langdon, *A Hard and Bitter Peace: A Global History of the Cold War*, 3rd ed. (Lanham, MD: Rowman & Littlefield, 2018); and Edward H. Judge and John W. Langdon, eds., *The Cold War through Documents: A Global History*, 3rd ed. (Lanham, MD: Rowman & Littlefield, 2018). For others see "Suggestions for Further Reading" at the end of this book.

CHAPTER 2:
EMPIRES, IDEOLOGIES, AND NATIONS:
IMPERIALISM, ANTI-IMPERIALISM, AND THE COLD WAR

1. Ho Chi Minh, "Declaration of Independence of the Democratic Republic of Vietnam" (Hanoi, September 2, 1945), http://historymatters.gmu.edu/d/5139/.
2. Ho Chi Minh, "Declaration of Independence."
3. Ho Chi Minh, "Declaration of Independence."
4. For a comprehensive overview of Europe's colonial empires and their history, see David B. Abernethy, *The Dynamics of Global Dominance: European Overseas Empires, 1415–1980* (New Haven, CT: Yale University Press, 2000). For interesting discussions of empire and imperialism see Dominic Lieven, *Empire: The Russian Empire and Its Rivals* (New Haven, CT: Yale University Press, 2001) and Trevor R. Getz and Heather Streets Salter, *Empires and Colonies in the Modern World: A Global Perspective* (New York: Oxford University Press, 2015).

5. "The Declaration of Independence: In Congress, July 4, 1776, The Unanimous Declaration of the Thirteen United States of America," http://www.archives.gov/exhibits/charters/declaration_transcript.html.

6. "The Declaration of the Rights of Man, Approved by the National Assembly of France, August 26, 1789," http://avalon.law.yale.edu/18th_century/rightsof.asp.

7. For a detailed and comprehensive study of these issues and interactions see Odd Arne Westad, *The Global Cold War: Third World Interventions and the Making of Our Times* (New York: Cambridge University Press, 2005). For a briefer but still useful study, see David S. Painter, *The Cold War: An International History* (London: Routledge, 1999).

8. Winston Churchill, "The Sinews of Peace ('Iron Curtain Speech')," Fulton, Missouri, March 5, 1946, http://www.winstonchurchill.org/resources/speeches/235-1946-1963-elder-statesman/120-the-sinews-of-peace.

9. Harry S Truman, "The Truman Doctrine," Speech delivered before a joint session of Congress, March 12, 1947, http://www.americanrhetoric.com/speeches/harrystrumantrumandoctrine.html.

10. Andrei Zhdanov, "Report on the International Situation to the Cominform," September 22, 1947, http://slantchev.ucsd.edu/courses/ps142j/documents/zhdanov-response-to-x.html.

11. Zhdanov, "Report on the International Situation."

12. See, for example, "Khrushchev on Peaceful Coexistence," in Edward H. Judge and John W. Langdon, eds., *The Cold War through Documents: A Global History*, 3rd ed. (Lanham, MD: Rowman & Littlefield, 2018), 117–19.

13. "The Brezhnev Doctrine, 1968," in Judge and Langdon, eds., *The Cold War through Documents*, 219–21.

14. For a thorough discussion of the appeal of Soviet socialism to national liberation movements in the Third World, see S. Neil MacFarlane, *Superpower Rivalry and Third World Radicalism: The Idea of National Liberation* (Baltimore: Johns Hopkins University Press, 1985).

CHAPTER 3:
"LONG LIVE THE VICTORY OF PEOPLE'S WAR":
ANTI-IMPERIALISM AND THE COLD WAR IN ASIA

The chapter title is drawn from Lin Biao, *Long Live the Victory of People's War!* (Beijing: Foreign Languages Press, 1965), https://www.marxists.org/reference/archive/lin-biao/1965/09/peoples_war/.

1. From Mao Zedong's order to form the Chinese People's Volunteers, October 8, 1950, cited in Chen Jian, *China's Road to the Korean War* (New York: Columbia University Press, 1994), 186.

2. Robert J. McMahon, *Colonialism and Cold War* (Ithaca, NY: Cornell University Press, 1981), 28.

3. For a discussion of the importance of these colonies and their resources to European recovery and US prosperity, see Robert E. Wood, "From the Marshall

Plan to the Third World," in *Origins of the Cold War: An International History*, ed. Melvyn P. Leffler and David S. Painter (New York: Routledge, 2005), 239–49.

4. See "Excerpts from Speech by Indonesian President Sukarno at the Opening of the Asian-African Conference in Bandung, 18 April 1955," in Edward H. Judge and John W. Langdon, eds., *The Cold War through Documents: A Global History*, 3rd ed. (Lanham, MD: Rowman & Littlefield, 2018), 109–11.

5. Rex Mortimer, *Indonesian Communism under Sukarno: Ideology and Politics, 1959–1965* (Singapore: Equinox Publishing, 2006), 268, citing Tjin-Kie Tan, *Sukarno's Guided Indonesia* (Brisbane: Jacaranda Press, 1967), 39–40.

6. See "The Gulf of Tonkin Resolution, 10 August 1964," in Judge and Langdon, eds., *The Cold War through Documents*, 203.

7. Lin Biao, *Long Live the Victory of People's War!* (Beijing: Foreign Languages Press, 1965), https://www.marxists.org/reference/archive/lin-biao/1965/09/peoples_war/.

8. For discussion of these issues, see Gary J. Bass, *The Blood Telegram: Nixon, Kissinger, and a Forgotten Genocide* (New York: Alfred A. Knopf, 2013).

9. See "Excerpts from Speech by India's Prime Minister Nehru to the Bandung Conference Political Committee, April 1955," in Judge and Langdon, eds., *The Cold War through Documents*, 111–12.

10. "Main Speech by Premier Zhou Enlai, Head of the Delegation of the People's Republic of China, Distributed at the Plenary Session of the Asian-African Conference, April 19,1955," translation from *China and the Asian-African Conference (Documents)* (Peking: Foreign Languages Press, 1955), 9–20, History and Public Policy Program Digital Archive, http://digitalarchive.wilsoncenter.org/document/121623.

11. The Editorial Department of *Hongqi*, *Long Live Leninism*, 3rd ed. (Peking: Foreign Languages Press, 1960), 1–55. The article originally appeared in *Hongqi* ("Red Flag"), a magazine published by the Chinese Communist Party, no. 8 (April 16, 1960), https://www.marxists.org/history/international/comintern/sino-soviet-split/cpc/leninism.htm.

12. "Excerpts from Zhou Enlai's Speech at the Romanian Embassy, 23 August 1968," in Judge and Langdon, eds., *The Cold War through Documents*, 217–18.

13. "The Brezhnev Doctrine, 1968," in Judge and Langdon, eds., *The Cold War through Documents*, 219–21.

14. "Highlights of Speech by Chinese Vice-Premier Deng Xiaoping to the U.N. General Assembly, 10 April 1974," in Judge and Langdon, eds., *The Cold War through Documents*, 252–54.

CHAPTER 4:
"WE ARE TODAY FREE AND INDEPENDENT":
ANTI-IMPERIALISM AND THE
COLD WAR IN THE MIDDLE EAST

The chapter title was drawn from Gamal Abdel Nasser, speech nationalizing the Suez Canal, Alexandria, Egypt, July 26, 1956.

1. Ronald Hyam, *Britain's Declining Empire* (Cambridge: Cambridge University Press, 2006), 231.

2. Dwight D. Eisenhower, message to Congress, January 5, 1957, in *Public Papers of the President: Dwight D. Eisenhower, 1957* (Washington, DC: US Government Printing Office, 1958), 10.

3. Amin Saikal, *The Rise and Fall of the Shah* (Princeton, NJ: Princeton University Press, 1980), 78.

CHAPTER 5:
"SCRAM FROM AFRICA!":
ANTI-IMPERIALISM AND THE COLD WAR IN AFRICA

The chapter title is drawn from Tom Mboya, Speech at the All-African Peoples' Conference, Accra, Ghana, December 1958.

1. Kwame Nkrumah, *I Speak of Freedom* (The Hague, 1973), 48.

2. *Time*, December 22, 1958.

3. On this point see Philip Muehlenbeck, *Betting on the Africans: John F. Kennedy's Courting of African Nationalism* (Oxford: Oxford University Press, 2012).

4. Harold Macmillan, Address to the South African Parliament, February 3, 1960, http://www.famous-speeches-and-speech-topics.info/.

5. Ian Douglas Smith, *Unilateral Declaration of the Independence of Rhodesia*, November 11, 1965, http://www.rhodesia.com/docs/other/udi.htm.

CHAPTER 6:
"SO FAR FROM GOD . . . SO CLOSE TO
THE UNITED STATES": ANTI-IMPERIALISM
AND THE COLD WAR IN LATIN AMERICA

The chapter title is drawn from Porfirio Díaz, President of Mexico, magazine interview, December 1908.

1. Aleksandr Fursenko and Timothy Naftali, *"One Hell of a Gamble"* (New York: Norton, 1998).

2. Richard R. Fagen, "The United States and Chile: Roots and Branches," *Foreign Affairs* 53, no. 2 (January 1975): 305.

CHAPTER 7:
"EVERY COUNTRY DECIDES WHICH ROAD TO TAKE":
THE END OF THE SOVIET RUSSIAN EMPIRE

The chapter title is drawn from "'Sinatra Doctrine' at Work in Warsaw Pact, Soviet Says," *Los Angeles Times*, October 25, 1989, http://articles.latimes.com/1989-10-25/news/mn-745_1_warsaw-pact.

1. See Filofei, "Filofei's Concept of the 'Third Rome,'" in Basil Dmytryshyn, ed. and trans., *Medieval Russia, A Source Book: 850–1700, Fourth Edition* (Fort Worth, TX: Harcourt Brace Jovanovich College Publishers, 2000), 259–61, http://wps.pearsoncustom.com/wps/media/objects/2426/2484749/chap_assets/documents/doc9_5.html.

2. By 1989, Russians made up 38 percent of the population in Kazakhstan (a large central Asian SSR), 34 percent in Latvia, 30 percent in Estonia, and 22 percent in Ukraine. See Robert J. Kaiser, *The Geography of Nationalism in Russia and the USSR* (Princeton, NJ: Princeton University Press, 1994), 174, table 4.3.

3. Brezhnev's remarks to the Polish Party Congress, November 12, 1968, *The Current Digest of the Soviet Press*, 20, no. 46 (December 4, 1968): 3–5. See also "The Brezhnev Doctrine, 1968," in Edward H. Judge and John W. Langdon, eds., *The Cold War through Documents: A Global History*, 3rd ed. (Lanham, MD: Rowman & Littlefield, 2018), 219–21.

4. See Mikhail S. Gorbachev, "New Political Thinking," in *Perestroika: New Thinking for Our Country and the World* (New York: HarperCollins, 1987), 139–44.

5. See "Gorbachev's Statement on Soviet Withdrawal from Afghanistan, 8 February 1988," in Judge and Langdon, eds., *The Cold War through Documents*, 336–37.

6. See "Excerpts from Gorbachev's Speech to the United Nations, 7 December 1988," in Judge and Langdon, eds., *The Cold War through Documents*, 339–42.

7. "Record of Conversation between Mikhail Gorbachev and Miklos Nemeth, March 3, 1989," Archive of the Gorbachev Foundation, Fond 2, Opis 1, in *Masterpieces of History*, edited by Svetlana Savranskaya et al., 412–13.

8. "Record of Conversation between Mikhail Gorbachev and Members of the CC SED Politburo," in Svetlana Savranskaya and Thomas Blanton, eds., *National Security Archive Electronic Briefing Book No. 290*, Document 6, https://nsarchive2.gwu.edu/NSAEBB/NSAEBB290/doc06.pdf.

9. See "Statement Allowing East Germans to Travel Abroad or Emigrate, 9 November 1989," in Judge and Langdon, eds., *The Cold War through Documents*, 347–48.

10. Commission on Security and Cooperation in Europe, *Referendum in the Soviet Union: A Compendium of Reports on the March 17, 1991 Referendum on the Future of the USSR* (Washington, DC: Commission on Security and Cooperation in Europe, 1991), 3.

11. See "Announcement on Gorbachev's Removal and Formation of Emergency Committee, 19 August 1991," in Judge and Langdon, eds., *The Cold War through Documents*, 360.

12. See "Yeltsin's Call to Resist the Coup Attempt, 19 August 1991," in Judge and Langdon, eds., *The Cold War through Documents*, 361.

13. See "Highlights of Gorbachev's Resignation Speech, 25 December 1991," in Judge and Langdon, eds., *The Cold War through Documents*, 364–65.

CHAPTER 8:
"EMPIRES WAX AND WANE":
OVERVIEW AND CONCLUSIONS

The chapter title is drawn from Lo Kuan-Chung (Luo Guanzhong), *Romance of the Three Kingdoms*, trans. C. H. Brewitt-Taylor (Rutland, VT, and Tokyo: Charles E. Tuttle Company, 1959), I:2.

1. Lo Kuan-Chung (Luo Guanzhong), *Romance of the Three Kingdoms*, I:2.

2. Thucydides, "The Melian Dialogue," in his *History of the Peloponnesian War*, as cited in Alexander Kemos, "The Influence of Thucydides in the Modern World," HR-Net (Hellenic Resources Network), http://www.hri.org/por/thucydides.html.

3. John S. Bowman, ed., *Columbia Chronologies of Asian History and Culture* (New York: Columbia University Press, 2000), 311.

4. See Chen Jian, *Mao's China and the Cold War* (Chapel Hill: University of North Carolina Press, 2001), 28–29.

5. See "Khrushchev on Wars of National Liberation, January 1961," in Edward H. Judge and John W. Langdon, eds., *The Cold War through Documents: A Global History*, 3rd ed. (Lanham, MD: Rowman & Littlefield, 2018), 164–66.

6. "Excerpt from Reagan's 'Evil Empire' Speech, 8 March 1983," in Judge and Langdon, eds., *The Cold War through Documents*, 300–301.

Glossary

Alliance for Progress A ten-point program launched by the Kennedy Administration in 1961 and designed to transform Latin America through political and social reform, economic development, and the alleviation of poverty, illiteracy, and disease.

anticolonialism Opposition to the formation or continuance of colonial empires, and support for the liberation of colonies from imperial control.

anti-imperialism Opposition to the exercise of any form of economic, cultural, and/or political dominance of a centralized state power over other societies.

Baghdad Pact A British-sponsored coalition with Muslim nations (Iran, Iraq, Pakistan, and Turkey) formed in 1955 to combat **communism** in the Middle East. Its name was changed to **CENTO** (Central Treaty Organization) in 1959, when Iraq (ruled from Baghdad) withdrew. The United States supported this alliance but did not join it. Unlike **NATO**, it had no structure for collective defense.

Bandung Conference Officially called the Asian-African Conference, this was a 1955 meeting in Bandung, Indonesia, of prominent leaders of emerging nations. Its goals were to combat **colonialism**, to promote economic and cultural cooperation, and to chart a course independent of the **Cold War** camps.

Berlin Blockade An eleven-month Soviet effort in 1948–1949 to prevent food and supplies from reaching West Berlin, which was occupied by British, French, and US forces, by cutting off overland access to that city through Soviet-occupied East Germany. The Americans and British supplied West Berlin by airlift until the blockade was lifted in 1949.

Berlin Wall   A twenty-seven-mile urban barricade that divided Berlin from 1961 to 1989, built to prevent people from escaping from Communist East Berlin to the city's western sectors, occupied during the **Cold War** by British, French, and US forces.

Bolsheviks   The revolutionary **Marxists**, led by V. I. Lenin, that seized power in Russia in 1917. Later known as the Russian Communist Party (and eventually as the Communist Party of the Soviet Union), they created and led the Soviet state.

bourgeoisie   A class of relatively affluent urban dwellers, often also referred to as the "urban middle class." In Marxist terms, the bourgeoisie is the economic class that owns capital wealth and controls the means of production.

Brezhnev Doctrine   A claim advanced by Soviet leader Leonid Brezhnev and others after the 1968 Soviet invasion of Communist Czechoslovakia that the USSR had the right and duty to intervene in other communist countries when doing so was necessary to protect the overall interests of world socialism.

British Commonwealth   See **Commonwealth of Nations**.

capitalism   An economic system based on free market competition and private or corporate ownership and control of commerce and production.

CENTO (Central Treaty Organization)   The new name given to the former **Baghdad Pact** alliance (Britain, Iran, Iraq, Pakistan, and Turkey) in 1959 when Iraq (ruled from Baghdad) withdrew.

Cold War   An intense international conflict between the communist East, led by the Soviet Union, and the capitalist West, led by the United States, waged by all means short of direct all-out combat, and lasting from the mid-to-late 1940s through the 1980s.

colonial empire   A term historically used to describe a diverse group of dependent societies, or **colonies**, controlled by a centralized state power, sometimes called the **metropole**, or "mother country."

colonialism (**colonial imperialism**)   The policy or practice by a centralized state power of creating and controlling **colonies**. See also **colonial empire**.

colonies   Dependent societies controlled by a centralized state power. See **colonial empire**.

Commonwealth of Independent States   A loose confederation of former Soviet republics, created in December 1991 as the USSR was disintegrating.

Commonwealth of Nations   An association of countries (initially called the **British Commonwealth**) that includes Great Britain and many of its former colonies. Intended to maintain cooperative connections among them, it is symbolically headed by the British monarch.

communism (communists) A revolutionary form of **socialism** in which in theory all wealth is collectively owned by the people in an equal and classless society, but in practice typically involves control by a single authoritarian party. Also referred to as **Marxism** or **Marxism-Leninism**.

containment of Communism A US policy designed to stop the spread of Soviet Communism by aiding countries that were resisting communist pressures, threats, or insurrections. Embodied in the Truman Doctrine, it became a central tenet of US Cold War foreign policy.

decolonization The process by which colonies gain their political independence from the colonial power (or "mother country") and/or the relinquishing by the colonial power of formal political control over its colonies.

détente The easing of global tensions and reduction of direct hostility, especially as pursued by the United States and the Soviet Union during the 1970s.

dominion The exercise of power and/or authority. A dominion can also be a self-governing nation, typically a former colony that has attained political independence but maintains close ties and allegiance to its former mother country.

domino theory A concern, based on a "falling domino" comment by US President Eisenhower in 1954, that Communism's triumph in South Vietnam could cause a chain reaction ("domino effect") that would bring the whole region under Communist control.

Eisenhower Doctrine A 1957 US congressional resolution authorizing military intervention to defend any nation in the Middle East "requesting such aid, against overt armed aggression from any nation controlled by International Communism."

Fifth Pan-African Congress A major 1945 meeting of African nationalist leaders in Manchester, England.

FLN *Front de la Libération Nationale,* or National Liberation Front, the underground organization that fought French forces in Algeria between 1954 and 1962.

golpe de estado The Spanish translation of the French term coup d'état.

hegemony The economic, cultural, and/or political dominance by one society over another. Imperialist powers are said to exercise hegemony over others.

ideologies Comprehensive secular systems of thought intended to explain and transform modern societies in accordance with certain political, socioeconomic, and/or cultural ideals.

imperialism The policy or practice by a centralized state power of extending and exercising economic, cultural, and/or political dominance over other societies. A power that establishes colonies is said to practice **colonialism** or **colonial imperialism**; a power that exercises dominance over other societies without making them formal colonies is said to practice **informal imperialism**.

Industrial Revolution The historic transition from an agrarian economy (in which most people lived in rural villages and produced their own food and goods through manual labor) to an urban system of mechanized production (in which people lived in cities and used machines in factories to make goods to be sold in a commercial economy).

informal imperialism The policy or practice by a centralized state power of exercising dominance over other societies without making them formal colonies.

Iran-Contra Scandal A US political scandal that erupted in 1986 when it was learned that the US government had been selling weapons to Iran and using the revenue to fund the anti-Sandinista Contra rebellion in Nicaragua.

iron curtain A term devised by Winston Churchill to refer to the heavily fortified borderline between the countries of the **Soviet Bloc** and the capitalist democracies of Western Europe.

liberalism An ideology based on the principle of liberty, typically involving representative governance, protection of human rights, and free market economics. In the West the term has also come to involve support for political and social reforms to benefit the common people.

M-26-7 Fidel Castro's 26th of July revolutionary movement in Cuba, which took power January 1, 1959.

Majlis The Iranian parliament.

Marshall Plan A US "European Recovery Program" that extended vast economic aid to war-torn European nations, fortifying them to resist **communism** by reviving capitalist prosperity.

Marxism (Marxists) Communist ideology as initially devised and developed by Karl Marx.

Marxism-Leninism Communist ideology as devised by Karl Marx and enhanced by V. I. Lenin to include, among other things, the identification of imperialism as an advanced stage of **capitalism**, thereby combining the anti-imperialist struggles of non-Western peoples with the anticapitalist struggles of Western industrial workers into a global anticapitalist, anti-imperialist crusade. It was the form of **communism** espoused by the Soviet Union and its allies.

MEDO Middle East Defense Organization, a British-sponsored association designed to oppose a Soviet invasion of the Middle East.

metropole The central homeland and dominating power of a **colonial empire**; also called the "mother country."

mutual assured destruction (MAD) The belief that the possession of massive nuclear strike capability by both Cold War superpowers would prevent a nuclear war between them because neither side would dare to start a suicidal conflict that could obliterate them both.

nationalism A fervent devotion to one's own ethnic group (nationality) and to its embodiment in a unified, strong, and independent country (national state).

national self-determination The right of each nationality to freely decide its own political status, typically in the form of a unified and independent national state that honors and embodies their language, customs, and culture.

NATO A military alliance formed in 1949 by the United States, Canada, and a number of European democracies to provide for collective defense of their homelands and interests. During the **Cold War**, it relied on US military (and nuclear) might to deter a Soviet attack.

neocolonialism The continuance or reassertion of economic, cultural, and/or political dominance of an imperialist power over other societies, typically its former colonies.

Non-Aligned Movement A group of nations that sought to practice neutrality and avoid direct affiliation with any of the major power blocs. Inspired by the Asian-African Conference in 1955 in Bandung, Indonesia, it was formally founded in 1961 in Belgrade, Yugoslavia.

peaceful coexistence The concept, advanced by Soviet leader Khrushchev and others, that since nuclear weapons could destroy both sides in an all-out war, communists and capitalists must find ways to live together and compete without direct conflict between the superpowers.

perestroika A series of programs put forth by Soviet leader Gorbachev for "restructuring" the Soviet socialist economy by introducing limited market-type reforms and other policies that seemed to work well in the West.

persona non grata A diplomatic term meaning "an unwelcome person."

PLO Palestine Liberation Organization, an umbrella group of Palestinian guerrilla and lobbying agencies established by Egyptian President Nasser in 1964 as a way of keeping the Palestinian cause before the world.

proletariat A class of landless laborers living in cities and working in industry for wages, also often referred to as the "urban working class."

Río Treaty Officially called the Inter-American Treaty of Reciprocal Assistance, this collective security pact, signed in 1947, formalized the anticommunist protections embodied in the 1945 Act of Chapultepec.

Sandinistas The left-wing Nicaraguan guerrilla movement that took power in 1979, after ousting dictator Anastasio Somoza.

SAVAK The intelligence and security organization created by the Shah of Iran in 1953.

SEATO (Southeast Asia Treaty Organization) A US-sponsored alliance designed to counter communism's spread in Southeast Asia. Unlike **NATO**, it had no structure for collective defense; its members were required only to consult one another in case one or more was attacked by an outside force.

socialism A system that aims at equal distribution of wealth and collective cooperation for the welfare of all, often with community or state control of production and commerce.

soviets Councils formed among Russian working classes during the Russian Revolution. This term was later used to refer to the leaders and peoples of the Soviet Union (USSR).

Soviet Bloc A term applied to the USSR and the satellite communist countries under its sway, typically referring to the nations belonging to the **Warsaw Pact** alliance.

Strategic Defense Initiative (SDI) A plan put forth by US President Reagan in 1983 to develop an elaborate space-based system that could intercept and destroy incoming enemy nuclear missiles.

struggle against imperialism A complex series of movements, endeavors, campaigns, and conflicts by which oppressed peoples and colonized nations sought to gain freedom from imperial subjugation and other forms of foreign domination.

Third Rome A claim originating in the fifteenth and sixteenth centuries that Moscow was the successor to Rome and Constantinople as the center of the true Christian faith, and that its rulers were thus successors to the Roman and Byzantine emperors as leaders and defenders of that faith.

Third World A term widely used during the **Cold War** to refer collectively to nations and peoples in Asia, the Middle East, Africa, and Latin America that did not belong directly to either of the two main Cold War camps.

Truman Doctrine A 1947 pledge by US President Truman "to support free peoples who are resisting attempted subjugation by armed minorities or outside pressures," effectively promising US assistance to countries threatened by **communism**. It came to support and signify the US Cold War policy of "containment of communism."

UAR The United Arab Republic of Egypt and Syria, formed on February 1, 1958, and disbanded in September 1961.

ulema In Islamic countries, the body of prominent scholars and teachers who possess teaching authority and interpret the sharia, the holy law of Islam.

United Nations An international organization founded in 1945 to keep the peace, prevent aggression, and promote cooperation in solving world problems among its member nations, which eventually came to include most countries of the world. It has a General Assembly (UNGA) with delegates from all member nations, and a Security Council (UNSC) with five permanent members—Britain, China, France, the United States, and Russia (initially the USSR)—and a number of rotating temporary members, elected by the General Assembly.

Vietminh (League for the Independence of Vietnam) A coalition of anti-imperialist parties and movements committed to independence for Vietnam. It was led by Ho Chi Minh and the Indochinese Communist Party (later the Lao Dong, or Vietnamese Workers' Party).

Warsaw Pact A military alliance formed in 1955 by the USSR and the communist countries of Eastern Europe. Officially intended to provide for their collective defense, it also helped to maintain Soviet power in Eastern Europe during the Cold War era.

Suggestions for Further Reading

Although numerous works have been published that deal with either the Cold War or the struggle against imperialism, there are relatively few that seek to provide a comprehensive global treatment of both. Among them are the books by Odd Arne Westad (*The Global Cold War: Third World Interventions and the Making of Our Times*), S. Neil MacFarlane (*Superpower Rivalry and Third World Radicalism: The Idea of National Liberation*), David S. Painter (*The Cold War: An International History*), Henry Heller (*The Cold War and the New Imperialism: A Global History*), and Edward H. Judge and John W. Langdon (*A Hard and Bitter Peace: A Global History of the Cold War*) that are listed below under General Works and Sources. Unlike the current volume, however, these books tend to approach the era mainly from a Cold War perspective, with the struggle against imperialism incorporated into that perspective.

GENERAL WORKS AND SOURCES

Abernethy, David B. *The Dynamics of Global Dominance: European Overseas Empires, 1415–1980*. New Haven, CT, 2000.

Ansprenger, Franz. *The Dissolution of the Colonial Empires*. New York, 1981.

Bush, Barbara. *Imperialism and Postcolonialism*. Harrow, UK, 2006.

Chamberlain, Muriel E. *Decolonization: The Fall of the European Empires*. Oxford, 1999.

Chamberlain, Muriel E. *The Longman Companion to European Decolonisation*. New York, 1998, 2013.

The Cold War: Global Perspectives on East-West Tensions, 1945–1991, from the Archives of the Central Intelligence Agency. Readex.

"Cold War International History Project." Wilson Center, http://www.wil soncenter.org/program/cold-war-international-history-project. Washington, DC, 1991–2018.

Getz, Trevor R., and Heather Streets-Salter. *Empires and Colonies in the Modern World: A Global Perspective.* New York, 2016.

Gilbert, Mark. *Cold War Europe: The Politics of a Contested Continent.* Lanham, MD, 2014.

Hahn, Peter, and Mary Ann Heiss, eds. *Empire and Revolution: The US and the Third World since 1945.* Columbus, OH, 2001.

Heller, Henry. *The Cold War and the New Imperialism: A Global History, 1945–2005.* New York, 2006.

Holland, R. F. *European Decolonization, 1918–1981: An Introductory Survey.* New York, 1985.

Jansen, Jan C., and Jürgen Osterhammel. *Decolonization: A Short History.* Princeton, NJ, 2017.

Judge, Edward H., and John W. Langdon, eds. *The Cold War through Documents: A Global History.* 3rd ed. Lanham, MD, 2018.

Judge, Edward H., and John W. Langdon. *A Hard and Bitter Peace: A Global History of the Cold War.* 3rd ed. Lanham, MD, 2018.

Leffler, Melvyn P., and David S. Painter, eds. *Origins of the Cold War: An International History.* New York, 2005.

Leffler, Melvyn P., and Odd Arne Westad, eds. *The Cambridge History of the Cold War.* 3 vols. Cambridge, UK, 2010.

MacFarlane, S. Neil. *Superpower Rivalry and Third World Radicalism: The Idea of National Liberation.* Baltimore, 1985.

National Security Archive Electronic Briefing Books. http://www.gwu.edu/~ns archiv/NSAEBB/. Washington, DC, 1985–2018.

Northrop, Douglas. *An Imperial World: Empires and Colonies since 1750.* Upper Saddle River, NJ, 2013.

Painter, David S. *The Cold War: An International History.* London, 1999.

Rothermund, Dietmar. *The Routledge Companion to European Decolonization.* New York, 2006.

Springhall, John. *Decolonization since 1945: The Collapse of European Overseas Empires.* New York, 2001.

Westad, Odd Arne. *The Global Cold War: Third World Interventions and the Making of Our Times.* Cambridge, UK, 2005.

ASIA

Aldrich, Richard, Gary Rawnsley, and Ming-Yeh T. Rawnsley, eds. *The Clandestine Cold War in Asia, 1945–1965.* London, 2000.

Ali, S. Mahmud. *Cold War in the High Himalayas: The USA, China, and South Asia in the 1950s.* New York, 1999.

Ang Cheng Guan. *Ending the Vietnam War: The Vietnamese Communists' Perspective.* London, 2004.

Ang Cheng Guan. *The Vietnam War from the Other Side: The Vietnamese Communists' Perspective*. London, 2002.

Brackman, Arnold. *The Communist Collapse in Indonesia*. New York, 1969.

Buhite, Russell D. *Soviet-American Relations in Asia, 1945–1954*. Norman, OK, 1989.

Catton, Philip E. *Diem's Final Failure: Prelude to America's War in Vietnam*. Lawrence, KS, 2002.

Chang, Gordon. *Friends and Enemies: The United States, China, and the Soviet Union, 1948–1972*. Stanford, CA, 1990.

Chen Jian. *China's Road to the Korean War: The Making of the Sino-American Confrontation*. New York, 1994.

Chen Jian. *Mao's China and the Cold War*. Chapel Hill, NC, 2001.

Christensen, Thomas J. *Worse than a Monolith: Alliance Politics and Problems of Coercive Diplomacy in Asia*. Princeton, NJ, 2011.

Christie, Clive J. *A Modern History of Southeast Asia: Decolonization, Nationalism and Separatism*. London, 1996.

Cohen, Stephen P. "Pakistan and the Cold War." In *Superpower Rivalry and Conflict: The Long Shadow of the Cold War on the Twenty-First Century*, edited by Chandra Chari, 74–97. London, 2010.

Colbert, Evelyn. *Southeast Asia in International Politics, 1941–1956*. Ithaca, NY, 1977.

Cumings, Bruce. *The Korean War: A History*. New York, 2010.

Cumings, Bruce. *The Origins of the Korean War*. 2 vols. Princeton, NJ, 1981, 1990.

Currey, Cecil B. *Victory at Any Cost: The Genius of Viet Nam's Gen. Vo Nguyen Giap*. New York, 1997.

Duiker, William J. *Ho Chi Minh*. New York, 2000.

Duiker, William J. *U.S. Containment Policy and the Conflict in Indochina*. Stanford, CA, 1994.

Duncan, Peter J. S. *The Soviet Union and India*. London, 1989.

Fall, Bernard B. *Anatomy of a Crisis: The Laotian Crisis of 1960–61*. New York, 1969.

Friend, Theodore. *Indonesian Destinies*. Cambridge, MA, 2003.

Gaiduk, Ilya V. *Confronting Vietnam: Soviet Policy toward the Indochina Conflict, 1954–1963*. Washington, DC, 2003.

Gaiduk, Ilya V. *The Soviet Union and the Vietnam War*. Chicago, 1996.

Ganguly, Sumit. *Conflict Unending: India-Pakistan Tensions since 1947*. New York, 2001.

Garver, John W. *Protracted Contest: Sino-Indian Rivalry in the Twentieth Century*. Seattle, 2001.

George, Alexander L., and William E. Simons, eds. *The Limits of Coercive Diplomacy*. Boulder, CO, 1994.

Gibbons, William C. *The U.S. Government and the Vietnam War*. 4 vols. Princeton, NJ, 1986–1994.

Gilks, Anne. *The Breakdown of the Sino-Vietnamese Alliance, 1970–1979*. Berkeley, CA, 1992.

Goncharov, Sergei N., John W. Lewis, and Xue Litai. *Uncertain Partners: Stalin, Mao, and the Korean War*. Stanford, 1993.

Goscha, Christopher E., and Christian F. Ostermann, eds. *Connecting Histories: Decolonization and the Cold War in Southeast Asia, 1945–1962*. Stanford, CA, 2009.

Hering, Bob. *Soekarno: Founding Father of Indonesia*. Leiden, 2002.

Herring, George C. *America's Longest War: The United States and Vietnam*. New York, 1996.

Hoffmann, Steven. *India and the China Crisis*. Berkeley, CA, 1990.

Hunt, Michael. *The Genesis of Chinese Communist Foreign Policy*. New York, 1996.

Jackson, Richard L. *The Non-Aligned, the UN, and the Superpowers*. New York, 1983.

Jacobs, Seth. *Cold War Mandarin: Ngo Dinh Diem and the Origins of America's War in Vietnam, 1950–1963*. Lanham, MD, 2006.

Jacobs, Seth. *The Universe Unraveling: American Foreign Policy in Cold War Laos*. Ithaca, NY, 2012.

Jager, Sheila Miyoshi. *Brothers at War: The Unending Conflict in Korea*. New York, 2013.

Jones, Matthew. *Conflict and Confrontation in Southeast Asia, 1961–1965*. Cambridge, UK, 2002.

Kahin, George. *The Asian-African Conference: Bandung, Indonesia, April, 1955*. Ithaca, NY, 1956.

Keith, Ronald. *The Diplomacy of Zhou Enlai*. London, 1989.

Kux, Dennis. *India and the United States: Estranged Democracies, 1941–1991*. Washington, DC, 1993.

Kux, Dennis. *The United States and Pakistan, 1947–2000*. Washington, DC, 2001.

Lawrence, Mark Atwood, and Fredrik Logevall, eds. *The First Vietnam War: Colonial Conflict and Cold War Crisis*. Cambridge, MA, 2007.

Legge, John D. *Sukarno: A Political Biography*. Singapore, 2003. First published 1972.

Li Xiaobing. *China's Battle for Korea*. Bloomington, IN, 2014.

Logevall, Fredrik. *Embers of War: The Fall of an Empire and the Making of America's Vietnam*. New York, 2012.

McMahon, Robert. *The Cold War on the Periphery: The United States, India, and Pakistan*. New York, 1994.

McMahon, Robert. *Colonialism and the Cold War: The United States and the Struggle for Indonesian Independence, 1945–49*. Ithaca, NY, 1981.

McMahon, Robert. *The Limits of Empire: The United States and Southeast Asia since World War II*. New York, 1999.

McMahon, Robert, ed. *Major Problems in the History of the Vietnam War*. Boston, 2008.

Miller, Alice Lyman. *Becoming Asia: Change and Continuity in Asian International Relations since World War II*. Stanford, CA, 2011.

Millett, Allan R. *The War for Korea, 1950–1951*. Lawrence, KS, 2010.

Mortimer, Rex. *Indonesian Communism under Sukarno: Ideology and Politics, 1959–1965*. Singapore, 2006. First published 1974.

Porter, Gareth. *Perils of Dominance: Imbalance of Power and the Road to War in Vietnam*. Berkeley, CA, 2005.

Prados, John. *Vietnam: The History of an Unwinnable War*. Lawrence, KS, 2009.

Qiang Zhai. *China and the Vietnam Wars, 1950–1975*. Chapel Hill, NC, 2000.

Qiang Zhai. *The Dragon, the Lion, and the Eagle: Chinese-British-American Relations, 1949–1958*. Kent, OH, 1994.

Roosa, John. *Pretext for Mass Murder: The September 30th Movement and Suharto's Coup d'Etat in Indonesia*. Madison, WI, 2006.

Rotter, Andrew J. *Comrades at Odds: The United States and India, 1947–1964*. Ithaca, NY, 2000.

Schaller, Michael. *The American Occupation of Japan: The Origins of the Cold War in Asia*. Oxford and New York, 1985.

Shao Kuo-Kang. *Zhou Enlai and the Foundations of Chinese Foreign Policy*. Basingstoke, UK, 1996.

Shen Zhihua. *Mao, Stalin and the Korean War*. London, 2012.

Shen Zhihua, and Xia Yafeng. *Mao and the Sino-Soviet Partnership, 1945–1959*. Lanham, MD, 2015.

Simpson, Bradley R. *Economists with Guns: Authoritarian Development and US-Indonesian Relations, 1960–1968*. Stanford, CA, 2008.

Statler, Kathryn. *Replacing France: Origins of American Intervention in Vietnam*. Lexington, KY, 2007.

Stueck, William. *The Korean War: An International History*. Princeton, NJ, 1995.

Stueck, William. *Rethinking the Korean War: A New Diplomatic and Strategic History*. Princeton, NJ, 2002.

Taylor, Alastair M. *Indonesian Independence and the United Nations*. Westport, CT, 1975.

Westad, Odd Arne, ed. *Brothers in Arms: The Rise and Fall of the Sino-Soviet Alliance, 1945–1963*. Stanford, CA, 1998.

Westad, Odd Arne. *Cold War and Revolution: Soviet-American Rivalry and the Origins of the Chinese Civil War, 1944–1946*. New York, 1993.

Westad, Odd Arne. *Decisive Encounters: The Chinese Civil War, 1946–1950*. Stanford, CA, 2003.

Willetts, Peter. *The Non-Aligned Movement: The Origins of a Third World Alliance*. London, 1983.

Wolpert, Stanley. *India and Pakistan*. Berkeley, CA, 2011.

Wolpert, Stanley. *Shameful Flight: The Last Years of the British Empire in India*. Oxford, UK, 2009.

Zhang Shuguang. *Mao's Military Romanticism: China and the Korean War*. Lawrence KS, 1995.

Zheng Yangwen, Hong Liu, and Michael Szonyi, eds. *The Cold War in Asia: The Battle for Hearts and Minds*. Leiden, 2010.

THE MIDDLE EAST

Ashton, Nigel John. *The Cold War in the Middle East: Regional Conflict and the Superpowers, 1967–73*. London, 2007.

Ashton, Nigel John. *Eisenhower, Macmillan, and the Problem of Nasser*. New York, 1996.

Ashton, Nigel John. *Kennedy, Macmillan, and the Cold War*. New York, 2002.

Barrett, Roby C. *The Greater Middle East and the Cold War*. London, 2010.

Bayandor, Darioush. *Iran and the CIA: The Fall of Mosaddeq Revisited*. Basingstoke, UK, 2010.

Connelly, Matthew. *A Diplomatic Revolution*. New York, 2002.

Evans, Martin. *Algeria: France's Undeclared War*. Oxford, 2012.

Fawcett, Louise L'Estrange. *Iran and the Cold War: The Azerbaijan Crisis of 1946*. Cambridge, UK, 1992.

Freiberger, Steven. *Dawn over Suez*. Chicago, 1992.

Gasiorowski, Mark, and Malcolm Byrne, eds. *Mohammad Mosaddeq and the 1953 Coup in Iran*. Syracuse, NY, 2004.

Hahn, Peter. *The United States, Great Britain, and Egypt, 1945–1956*. London, 1991.

Horne, Alistair. *A Savage War of Peace*. London, 1978.

Keddie, Nikki R. *Roots of Revolution*. New Haven, CT, 1981.

Kinzer, Stephen. *All the Shah's Men*. Hoboken, NJ, 2003.

Kunz, Diane. *The Economic Diplomacy of the Suez Crisis*. London, 1991.

Kyle, Keith. *Suez*. London, 1991.

Louis, Wm. Roger. *The British Empire in the Middle East, 1945–1951*. Oxford, 1984.

Louis, Wm. Roger, and Roger Owen, eds. *A Revolutionary Year: The Middle East in 1958*. London, 2002.

Lucas, W. Scott. *Divided We Stand: Britain, the United States, and the Suez Crisis*. London, 1991.

Nutting, Anthony. *Nasser*. London, 1972.

Ro'i, Yaacov, and Boris Morozov, eds. *The Soviet Union and the June 1967 Six Day War*. Stanford, CA, 2008.

Saikal, Amin. *The Rise and Fall of the Shah*. Princeton, NJ, 1980.

Sayigh, Yezid, and Avi Shlaim, eds. *The Cold War and the Middle East*. Oxford, 1997.

Takeyh, Ray. *The Origins of the Eisenhower Doctrine*. Oxford, 2000.

Yaqub, Salim. *Containing Arab Nationalism: The Eisenhower Doctrine and the Middle East*. Chapel Hill, NC, 2004.

AFRICA

Attwood, William. *The Reds and the Blacks: A Personal Adventure*. New York, 1967.

Birmingham, David. *The Decolonization of Africa*. London, 1995.

Borstelmann, Thomas. *The Cold War and the Color Line*. Cambridge, MA, 2001.

Clayton, Anthony. *The Wars of French Decolonization*. London, 1994.

Darwin, John. *Britain and Decolonisation*. London, 1988.

Devlin, Lawrence. *Chief of Station, Congo*. New York, 2007.

Fursenko, Aleksandr, and Timothy Naftali. *Khrushchev's Cold War*. New York, 2006.

Gerard, Emmanuel, and Bruce Kuklick. *Death in the Congo*. Cambridge, MA, 2015.

Gifford, Prosser, and Wm. Roger Louis, eds. *Decolonization and African Independence: The Transfers of Power, 1960–1980*. New Haven, CT, 1988.

Gifford, Prosser, and Wm. Roger Louis, eds. *The Transfer of Power in Africa: Decolonization, 1940–1960*. New Haven, CT, 1982.

Gleijeses, Piero. *Conflicting Missions: Havana, Washington, and Africa, 1959–1976*. Chapel Hill, NC, 2002.

Guimarães, Fernando. *The Origins of the Angolan Civil War*. New York, 1988.

Hoskyns, Catherine. *The Congo since Independence*. Oxford, 1965.

Kalb, Madeleine. *The Congo Cables*. New York, 1982.

Legvold, Robert. *Soviet Policy in West Africa*. Cambridge, MA, 1970.

MacQueen, Norrie. *The Decolonization of Portuguese Africa*. London, 1997.

Mahoney, Richard D. *JFK: Ordeal in Africa*. Oxford, 1983.

Marcum, John A. *The Angolan Revolution*. 2 vols. Cambridge, MA, 1969 and 1978.

Marcum, John A. *Portugal and Africa: The Politics of Indifference*. New York, 1972.

Mazov, Sergey. *A Distant Front in the Cold War*. Washington, DC, 2010.

Meredith, Martin. *The First Dance of Freedom*. New York, 1984.

Minter, William. *Apartheid's Contras*. Johannesburg, 1994.

Muehlenbeck, Philip. *Betting on the Africans*. Oxford, 2012.

Nkrumah, Kwame. *I Speak of Freedom*. The Hague, 1973.

Noer, Thomas. *Cold War and Black Liberation*. Columbia, MO, 1985.

Schmidt, Elizabeth. *Cold War and Decolonization in Guinea, 1946–1958*. Columbus, OH, 2007.

Spínola, António de. *Portugal and the Future*. London, 1974.

Statler, Kathryn C., and Andrew L. Johns, eds. *The Eisenhower Administration, the Third World, and the Globalization of the Cold War*. Lanham, MD, 2006.

Thompson, W. Scott. *Ghana's Foreign Policy, 1957–1966*. Princeton, 1969.

Urquhart, Brian. *Hammarskjöld*. New York, 1973.

Weissman, Steven. *American Foreign Policy in the Congo, 1961–1964*. Ithaca, NY, 1974.

Yordanov, Radoslav. *The Soviet Union and the Horn of Africa during the Cold War*. Lanham, MD, 2016.

LATIN AMERICA

Allison, Graham T. *Essence of Decision*. 2nd ed. Reading, PA, 1999.

Blasier, Cole. *The Giant's Rival*. Pittsburgh, PA, 1987.

Bonsal, Philip. *Cuba, Castro, and the United States*. Pittsburgh, PA, 1971.

Brugioni, Dino A. *Eyeball to Eyeball*. New York, 1991.

Cullather, Nick. *Secret History: The CIA's Account of Its Operations in Guatemala, 1952–1954*. Stanford, CA, 1999.

Domínguez, Jorge. *To Make a World Safe for Revolution: Cuba's Foreign Policy*. Cambridge, MA, 1989.

Fursenko, Aleksandr, and Timothy Naftali. *"One Hell of a Gamble": Khrushchev, Kennedy, and Castro, 1958–1964*. New York, 1998.

Gleijeses, Piero. *The Dominican Crisis*. Baltimore, 1978.

Gleijeses, Piero. *Shattered Hope*. Baltimore, 1991.

Gott, Richard. *Cuba: A New History*. New York, 2004.

Immerman, Richard H. *The CIA in Guatemala*. Austin, TX, 1982.

Jones, Howard. *The Bay of Pigs*. New York, 2008.

LaFeber, Walter. *Inevitable Revolutions: The United States in Central America*. 2nd ed. New York, 1993.

LeoGrande, William. *Our Own Backyard: The United States in Central America, 1977–1992*. New York, 1998.

Lowenthal, Abraham. *The Dominican Intervention*. New York, 1972.

May, Ernest R., and Philip D. Zelikow, eds. *The Kennedy Tapes*. Cambridge, MA, 1997.

Miller, Nicola. *Soviet Relations with Latin America, 1959–1987*. Cambridge, UK, 1989.

Nash, Philip. *The Other Missiles of October*. Chapel Hill, NC, 1997.

Rabe, Stephen C. *Eisenhower and Latin America: The Foreign Policy of Anti-Communism*. Chapel Hill, NC, 1988.

Rabe, Stephen C. *The Killing Zone*. 2nd ed. New York, 2016.

Rabe, Stephen C. *The Most Dangerous Area in the World*. Chapel Hill, NC, 1999.

Schlesinger, Stephen, and Stephen Kinzer. *Bitter Fruit: The Story of the American Coup in Guatemala*. Cambridge, MA, 2005.

Sigmund, Paul. *The Overthrow of Allende and the Politics of Chile*. Pittsburgh, PA, 1977.

Smith, Peter H. *Talons of the Eagle: Dynamics of U.S.-Latin American Relations*. New York, 2000.

Szulc, Tad. *Fidel: A Critical Portrait*. New York, 1987.

Thomas, Hugh. *Cuba: The Pursuit of Freedom*. New York, 1971.

Wyden, Peter. *Bay of Pigs*. New York, 1980.

RUSSIA AND EASTERN EUROPE

Beissinger, Mark R. *Nationalist Mobilization and the Collapse of the Soviet State*. Cambridge, UK, 2002.

Bekes, Csaba, Malcolm Byrne, and Janos Rainer, eds., *The 1956 Hungarian Revolution: A History in Documents*. Budapest, 2003.

Bischof, Günter, Stefan Karner, and Peter Ruggenthaler, eds. *The Prague Spring and the Warsaw Pact Invasion of Czechoslovakia in 1968*. Lanham, MD, 2009.

Blanton, Thomas S., and V. M. Zubok, eds. *Masterpieces of History: The Peaceful End of the Cold War in Europe, 1989*. Budapest, 2010.

Brown, Archie. *Seven Years That Changed the World: Perestroika in Perspective*. New York, 2007.

Brudny, Yitshak. *Reinventing Russia: Russian Nationalism and the Soviet State, 1953–1991*. Cambridge, MA, 1998.

Carrère d'Encausse, Hélène. *The End of the Soviet Empire: The Triumph of the Nations*. New York, 1993.

Carrère d'Encausse, Hélène. *The Great Challenge: Nationalities and the Bolshevik State 1917–1930*. New York, 1992.

Chernyaev, Anatoly. *My Six Years with Gorbachev*. College Park, PA, 2000.

Cordovez, Diego, and Selig Harrison. *Out of Afghanistan: The Inside Story of the Soviet Withdrawal*. Oxford, 1995.

Cox, Michael, ed. *Rethinking the Soviet Collapse*. London, 1998.

Dunlop, John B. *The Rise of Russia and the Fall of the Soviet Empire*. Princeton, NJ, 1993.

Ellman, Michael J., and Vladimir Kontorovich, eds. *The Disintegration of the Soviet Economic System*. London, 1998.

Filtzer, Donald. *Soviet Workers and the Collapse of Perestroika*. Cambridge, UK, 1994.

Gati, Charles. *Failed Illusions: Moscow, Washington, Budapest, and the 1956 Hungarian Revolt*. Stanford, CA, 2006.

Golan, Galia. *Reform Rule in Czechoslovakia: The Dubček Era, 1968–1969*. Cambridge, UK, 2008.

Gorbachev, Mikhail. *The August Coup: The Truth and the Lessons*. New York, 1991.

Gorbachev, Mikhail. *Memoirs*. New York, 1995.

Haslam, Jonathan. *Russia's Cold War*. New Haven, CT, 2011.

Herrmann, Richard, and Richard Ned Lebow, eds. *Ending the Cold War*. New York, 2004.

Hosking, Geoffrey. *Rulers and Victims: The Russians in the Soviet Union*. Cambridge, MA, 2006.

Hosking, Geoffrey, and Robert Service, eds. *Russian Nationalism, Past and Present*. New York, 1998.

Hough, Jerry. *Democratization and Revolution in the USSR, 1985-91*. Washington, DC, 1997.

Jones, Stephen F. "The Non-Russian Nationalities." In *Society and Politics in the Russian Revolution*, edited by Robert Service, 35–63. London, 1992.

Kaiser, Robert J. *The Geography of Nationalism in Russia and the USSR*. Princeton, NJ, 1994.

Kotkin, Stephen. *Armageddon Averted: The Soviet Collapse 1970–2000*. Oxford, 2008.

Kotz, David, and Fred Weir. *Revolution from Above: The Demise of the Soviet System*. London, 1997.

Kramer, Mark. *Crisis in Czechoslovakia, 1968: The Prague Spring and the Soviet Invasion*. Oxford, 2001.

Kramer, Mark, and Vit Smetana, eds. *Imposing, Maintaining, and Tearing Open the Iron Curtain: The Cold War and East-Central Europe, 1945–1989*. Lanham, MD, 2013.

Lévesque, Jacques. *The Enigma of 1989: The USSR and the Liberation of Eastern Europe*. Berkeley and Los Angeles, 1997.

Lieven, Dominic. *Empire: The Russian Empire and Its Rivals*. New Haven, CT, 2001.

Martin, Terry. *The Affirmative Action Empire: Nations and Nationalism in the Soviet Union, 1923–1939*. Ithaca, NY, 2001.

Mastny, Vojtech, and Malcolm Byrne. *A Cardboard Castle? An Inside History of the Warsaw Pact, 1955–1991*. Budapest, 2005.

Mastny, Vojtech, and Zhu Liqun, eds. *The Legacy of the Cold War*. Lanham, MD, 2013.

Matlock, Jack. *Autopsy on an Empire: The American Ambassador's Account of the Collapse of the Soviet Union*. New York, 1995.

Melvin, Neil. *Russians Beyond Russia: The Politics of National Identity*. London, 1995.

Mendelson, Sarah E. *Changing Course: Ideas, Politics, and the Soviet Withdrawal from Afghanistan*. Princeton, NJ, 1998.

Nahaylo, Bohdan, and Victor Swoboda. *Soviet Disunion: A History of the Nationalities Problem in the USSR*. New York, 1991.

Naimark, Norman, and Leonid Gibianskii, eds. *The Establishment of Communist Regimes in Eastern Europe, 1944–1949*. Boulder, CO, 1997.

Odom, William E. *The Collapse of the Soviet Military*. New Haven, CT, 1998.

Ouimet, Matthew J. *The Rise and Fall of the Brezhnev Doctrine in Soviet Foreign Policy*. Chapel Hill, NC, 2003.

Pipes, Richard. *The Formation of the Soviet Union: Communism and Nationalism, 1917–1923*. Cambridge, MA, 1954.

Ruggenthaler, Peter. *The Concept of Neutrality in Stalin's Foreign Policy, 1945–1953*. Lanham, MD, 2015.

Smith, Jeremy. *The Bolsheviks and the National Question 1917–23*. London, 1999.

Suny, Ronald G. *The Revenge of the Past: Nationalism, Revolution, and the Collapse of the Soviet Union*. Stanford, CA, 1993.

Valenta, Jiri. *Soviet Intervention in Czechoslovakia in 1968*. Baltimore, 1991.

Yeltsin, Boris. *The Struggle for Russia*. New York, 1994.

Yeltsin, Boris. *The View from the Kremlin*. London, 1994.

Zubok, Vladislav. *A Failed Empire: The Soviet Union in the Cold War from Stalin to Gorbachev*. Chapel Hill, NC, 2007.

Index

Note: Page references for maps are italicized.

ABAKO. *See Alliance des Bakongo*

Abdullah I bin al-Hussein (King of Jordan), 75

Acheson, Dean Gooderham (United States secretary of state), 43n*, 52

Act of Chapultepec, 121

Adoula, Cyrille (prime minister of Congo), 115–116

Adowa, battle of, 16

Afghanistan War (1979–1989). *See* Soviet-Afghan War (1979–1989)

AFM. *See* Armed Forces Movement

African Independence Party of Guinea and Cape Verde (PAIGC), 118

African National Congress, 16

Alessandri Rodríguez, Jorge (president of Chile), 136

Algerian War (1954–1962), 80–82, 102, 178, 179

All-African Peoples' Conference, 104, 117

Allende Gossens, Salvador (president of Chile), 135–139

Alliance des Bakongo (ABAKO), 112

Alliance for Progress, 128, 131

Allied Powers: and anti-imperialism, 26, 43, 52, 54–55, 175; and World War II, 23–24, 26, 37, 38, 43

American Revolution (1775–1783), 2, 8, 12

Amin, Hafizullah (president of Afghanistan), 158

Anaconda Copper Mining Company, 135

Anglo-Iranian Oil Company, 72

Anglo-Jordanian Treaty, 84

apartheid, 109

Arab American Oil Company (ARAMCO), 72

Arab League, 52, 92

Arafat, Yasser (leader of PLO), 92

Árbenz Guzmán, Jacobo (president of Guatemala), 124–127, 139, 143, 182

Arden-Clarke, Charles (British governor of Gold Coast), 103

Arévalo, Juan José (president of Guatemala), 123–124

Arias Sánchez, Óscar (president of Costa Rica), 142

Armed Forces Movement (AFM), 119

Association of Free Officers, 77

Aswan High Dam, 80, 82–83

Attlee, Clement (prime minister of the United Kingdom), 62, 159

August coup (1991), 168, 169, 190

Aung San (premier of Burma), 39

Aung San Suu Kyi (state counsellor of
    Myanmar), 39n*
Axis Powers, 22, 23, 175

Baghdad Pact, 63, 79, 82, 86–87, 203,
    204. *See also* CENTO
Balfour declaration, 74
Banda, Hastings Kamuzu, MD
    (president of Malawi): at All-
    African Peoples' Conference, 104;
    becomes president of Malawai, 110;
    at Fifth Pan-African Congress, 100;
    returns to Nyasaland, 109
Bandung Conference (1955), 53, 102,
    203; and Non-Aligned Movement,
    53, 64, 178, 207; and Zhou Enlai,
    66, 80
Barrientos Ortuño, René (president of
    Bolivia), 135
Batista y Zaldivar, Fulgencio
    (president of Cuba), 126
Battle of Algiers, 81
Bay of Pigs invasion (1961), 128, 182
Begin, Menachem Wolfovich (prime
    minister of Israel), 93
Ben-Gurion, David (prime minister of
    Israel), 82, 84
Berlin Blockade (1948–1949), 27–28, 38,
    52, 56, 203–204
Berlin Conference (1884–1885), 14
Berlin Crisis (1961), 127, 128
Berlin partition, 24, *28*
Berlin Wall, *28*, 182–183, 184, 204; fall
    of the, 163–164, 189
Betancourt Bello, Rómulo Ernesto
    (president of Venezuela), 132–133
Bevin, Ernest (foreign minister of
    United Kingdom), 74–75
Bolsheviks, 147, 151, 204
Bonaparte. *See* Napoleon Bonaparte
Boroujerdi, Grand Ayatollah Seyyed
    Hossein, 73
Bosch Gaviño, Juan Emilio (president
    of Dominican Republic), 131–133,
    135, 143
Boxer Rebellion, 15
Brazzaville Conference, 99–100, 104

Brezhnev, Leonid Ilyich (general
    secretary of the Communist Party
    of the Soviet Union and president),
    36, 65, 106, 108, 135, 138, 140, 158,
    204; and Black Volta dam, 106, 108;
    and Brezhnev Doctrine, 32, 157,
    204; and Communist China, 67, 184;
    and the United States, 35, 183
Brezhnev Doctrine, 32, 67, 157, 184,
    189, 204; Gorbachev and the, 36,
    161–162, 163n*
British Commonwealth. *See*
    Commonwealth of Nations
British East India Company, 7, 13, 62
Bulganin, Nikolai Alexandrovich
    (Soviet minister of defense and
    premier); and Suez Crisis, 85–86
Bush, George Herbert Walker
    (president of United States), 142,
    160, 168

Cabral, Amílcar Lopes da Costa, 104,
    118
Caetano, Marcelo José das Neves
    Alves (prime minister of Portugal),
    119
CAF. *See* Central African Federation
Carter, James Earl (president of the
    United States), 187, 188; and Egypt-
    Israel Peace Treaty, 93; and Iran, 96;
    and Nicaragua, 139–141
Castillo Armas, Carlos (president of
    Guatemala), 125
Castro Ruz, Fidel Alejandro (president
    of Cuba), 31, 35, 106, 115, 125–130,
    133, 135, 141, 143, 182, 183, 206
Castro Ruz, Raúl Modesto (president
    of Cuba), 126–127, 143
Catherine II (Empress of Russia;
    Catherine the Great), 149
Ceaușescu, Nicolae (general secretary
    of the Romanian Communist
    Party), 164
CENTO (Central Treaty Organization),
    63, 203, 204. *See also* Baghdad Pact
Central African Federation (CAF),
    109–110

Central Intelligence Agency (CIA),
53n†, 72–73, 124, 128–129, 136–137,
188
Chamorro Cardenal, Pedro Joaquín, 140
Chamoun, Camille (president of
Lebanon), 88
Chiang Kai-shek. *See* Jiang Jieshi
Chinese Civil War (1946–1949), 40–42,
41, 51, 176
Chitelco (Chilean Telephone
Company), 136
Churchill, Winston Leonard Spencer
(prime minister of the United
Kingdom), 26, 62, 206
CIA. *See* Central Intelligence Agency
Commonwealth of Independent States,
169, *170*, 190, *191*, 204
Commonwealth of Nations (British
Commonwealth), 63, 110, 204–205
CONAKAT. *See* Confédération des
associations tribales du Katanga
*Confédération des associations tribales du
Katanga* (CONAKAT), 112
"Contra" rebels, 141
Convention People's Party, 102
Cristiani Burkard, Alfredo Félix
(president of El Salvador), 143
Cuban Missile Crisis, 32, 34, 108, 129–
131, 140, 183
Cultural Revolution. *See* Great
Proletarian Cultural Revolution
Czechoslovakia reform movement
(1968), 32, 156, 157; Soviet crushing
of, 67, 69, 155, 157, 184, 189, 204

Darwin, Charles Robert, 15
Declaration of Lima, 121, 123
de Gaulle, General Charles (president
of France), 23; and African
independence, 104–105; and
Algerian War, 81; and Brazzaville
Conference, 99–100, 104
Deng Xiaoping, 68, 185
Devlin, Lawrence, 114
Devlin, Patrick, 109
Diem, Ngo Dinh (president of South
Vietnam), 58

Dien Bien Phu, battle of, 56, *57*
Dubček, Alexander (first secretary
of the Communist Party of
Czechoslovakia), 164
Dulles, Allen Welsh, 72
Dulles, John Foster (United States
secretary of state), 30; and 1953
oil dispute with Iran, 72; and 1958
Middle East crisis, 88; and Britain's
withdrawal from Egypt, 78–79; and
Suez Crisis, 83–84
Dutch East India Company, 7, 13, 46

Eden, Anthony (foreign minister
and prime minister of the United
Kingdom), 78; and Suez crisis,
83–85
Eisenhower, Dwight D. (president
of United States), 30, 58n*, 205;
and 1953 oil dispute with Iran,
72; and Congo Crisis, 113; and
Fidel Castro, 127; and fifteenth
anniversary of UN, 106; and
intervention in Guatemala, 124;
and Shah of Iran, 94; and Suez
Crisis, 83–86; and Upper Volta
dam, 106
Eisenhower Doctrine, 86–88
English East India Company. *See*
British East India Company
European Union, 192

Faisal II (King of Iraq), 87–88
Farabundo Marti National Liberation
Front (FMLN), 140–141, 143
Farouk I bin Fuad (King of Egypt), 77
Fifth Pan-African Congress (1945), 100,
177, 205
First Indochina War, 29, 50, 54–56,
57, 60n*, 176; French defeat and
withdrawal, 56, 58, 69, 80, 178
First World War. *See* World War I
FLN. *See* Front de Libération Nationale
FMLN. *See* Farabundo Marti National
Liberation Front
FNLA. *See* National Front for the
Liberation of Angola

Fourteen Points, Woodrow Wilson's, 19–20
Frei Montalva, Eduardo Nicanor (president of Chile), 136
FRELIMO. *See* Mozambican Liberation Front
French Community, 54, 104, 147
Front de Libération Nationale (FLN), 80–81
FSLN. *See* Sandinista National Liberation Front

Gandhi, Indira Priyadarshini (prime minister of India), 64, 65
Gandhi, Mohandas Karamchand, 21, 29, 62–63, 64, 176, 194
Gandhi, Rajiv Ratna (prime minister of India), 65
Geneva Accords (1954), 58, 66, 178
Geneva conference (1954), 56–58, 66
Geneva summit conference (1955), 30
Giap, Vo Nguyen, 56
Gomułka, Władysław (first secretary of the Polish Workers' Party), 155
Good Neighbor Policy, 122–123
Gorbachev, Mikhail Sergeyevich (general secretary of the Communist Party of the Soviet Union and president): and efforts to end Cold War, 36, 159–160, 189; and liberation of Eastern Europe, 36, 161–65, 189–190, 194; reforms of, 36, 158–159, 189, 207; and Soviet-Afghan War, 36, 160–161; and USSR's disintegration, 36, 165–169, 190, 194
Gordon, Abraham Lincoln, 131
Goulart, João Belchior Marques (president of Brazil), 130–131, 135
Great Leap Forward, 60, 66, 67n*
Great Proletarian Cultural Revolution, 59, 60, 67, 184
Great War. *See* World War I
Gromyko, Andrei Andreyevich (Soviet ambassador to UN, to US, and foreign minister), 75

Guevara, Ernest "Che," 125–127, 130, 133–135
Gulf of Tonkin incident, 57, 59
Guomindang (National People's Party), 40

Hammarskjöld, Dag Hjalmar Agne Carl (secretary general of United Nations), 181; and Congo Crisis, 113–116; killed in plane crash, 115–116; and Suez Crisis, 82, 84
Hatta, Muhammad (prime minister of Indonesia), 48, 49, 51
Havel, Václav (president of the Czech Republic), 164
Helsinki Accords, 35
Hezbollah, 141
Herter, Christian Archibald (United States secretary of state), 106, 113
Hirohito (Emperor of Japan), 37, 175
Hitler, Adolf (chancellor of Germany), 21–23, 26, 67
Hoare, Thomas Michael "Mad Mike," 116
Hobson, John Atkinson, 17
Ho Chi Minh (first secretary of the Workers' Party of Vietnam), 5–6, 20, 58, 60, 175; and First Indochina War, 29, 54–56, 66, 176
Ho Chi Minh Trail, 57, 59, 60
Huggins, Godfrey Martin (prime minister of Southern Rhodesia), 108–109
"Huk" revolt (Philippines), 39
Hungarian revolt (1956), 32, 85, 86, 155–156, 157, 179
Hussein I bin Talal (King of Jordan), 82, 87–88, 92

Indian National Congress, 16, 21, 62, 176
Indochina Wars, 33, 54–61. *See also* First Indochina War; Vietnam War
Inter-American Treaty of Reciprocal Assistance (Río Treaty), 121–122
International Monetary Fund (IMF), 85

International Telephone and Telegraph Corporation (ITT), 135–136
Iran-Contra scandal, 142
Irgun Zvai Leumi, 75
"iron curtain," 26, 27, 30, 142, 163, 206
Ivan III (Ivan the Great), 148
Ivan IV (Ivan the Terrible), 148

Jaruzelski, Wojciech (prime minister of Poland), 157–158, 162
Jiang Jieshi (Chiang Kai-shek), 40
Jinnah, Muhammad Ali (governor general of Pakistan), 62–63
John Paul II (Pope; Karol Wojtyła), 157
Johnson, Lyndon Baines (president of United States), 108; and Alliance for Progress, 128; and coup in Brazil, 131; and Dominican intervention, 131–132, 144; and Portuguese colonial wars, 118; and Security Council Resolution 242, 91; and Vietnam War, 59–60, 185

Karmal, Babrak (president of Afghanistan), 158, 160
Kasa Vubu, Joseph (president of Congo), 112–114, 116–117; as leader of ABAKO, 112
Kasai, province of Congo, 112, 115
Katanga, province of Congo, 112–116
Kaunda, Kenneth David Buchizwa (president of Zambia), 104
Keith, Minor Cooper, 122
Kennecott Copper Corporation, 135
Kennedy, John Fitzgerald (president of United States), 32, 58, 203; and Cuba, 128–129; denounced for Lumumba's murder, 106, 108; and Israeli atomic bomb project, 90; and Portuguese colonial wars, 117–118; and Upper Volta dam, 106
Kenyatta, Jomo (prime minister and president of Kenya), 100–101
Khmer Rouge, 60–61
Khomeini, Ayatollah Ruhollah, 95–97, 188

Khrushchev, Nikita Sergeyevich (first secretary of Communist Party of Soviet Union, premier), 30, 64–65, 102, 154–155, 182, 183; and 1958 Middle East Crisis, 88; and Communist China, 31, 32, 66, 67, 183; and Cuba, 31, 32, 34–35, 128–129, 144, 182–183; and Eastern Europe, 30, 32, 85, 155, 178; and fifteenth anniversary of UN, 106; and India, 31, 32, 65, 67, 178; and national liberation movements, 30–31, 65, 67, 178, 181, 194; and "peaceful coexistence," 30, 32, 64–65, 66, 207; removed from office, 135; and Suez Crisis, 85; and telegram from Congolese government, 113; and UN in Congo Crisis, 114–115
Kim Il-Sung (president of North Korea), 43–44, 45
Kim Jong-Il (president of North Korea), 45
Kim Jong-Un (president of North Korea), 45
King David Hotel, 75
Kipling, Rudyard, 15, 83
Kirkpatrick, Jeane Duane, 141
Kissinger, Henry Alfred (US national security advisor and secretary of state), 55n†, 64, 93, 119, 137, 139
Kivu, province of Congo, 115
Korean War (1950–1953), 29, 42–45, 44, 46, 56, 58, 176
Kosygin, Alexei Nikolayevich (premier of USSR), 89–90
Krenz, Egon (general secretary of the Socialist Unity Party of the German Democratic Republic), 163–164
Kwilu, province of Congo, 115

Lajes Field, 117–118
Lansky, Meyer, 126
League of Nations, 20, 74
League of Nations mandates, 20, 21, 33, 74–75, 177
Le Duc Tho, 55n†

Lenin, Vladimir Ilyich (chairman of
the Council of People's Commissars
of the Soviet Union), 22, 147, 152;
and anti-imperialism, 2, 17, 19,
147, 151, 173–174, 206; and Russian
Revolution, 19, 147, 151, 204
Leopold II (King of Belgium), 14
Linggadjati Agreement (1946), 50
Luciano, Charles "Lucky," 126
Lumumba, Patrice Émery (prime
minister of Congo), 112–115; at
All-African Peoples' Conference,
104, 117; as leader of MNC, 112;
murdered, 115; People's Friendship
University named for, 115

M-26-7 (26th of July Movement), 126,
128, 140, 143
MacArthur, Douglas, 49n*
Macmillan, Maurice Harold (prime
minister of United Kingdom),
88, 181; and African tour, 110;
and CAF, 109–110; and "wind of
change" speech, 110, 112
MAD. *See* mutual assured destruction
Magsaysay, Ramon del Fierro
(president of Philippines), 39
Majlis, 72
Mao Zedong (chairman of the
Communist Party of China), 40,
44, 56, 60, 66, 68; and Chinese Civil
War, 41–42, 51; and USSR, 66–67,
184–185
Marshall Plan (European Recovery
Program), 27, 38, 56, 206; and Dutch
exit from Indonesia, 50, 51–52
Marx, Karl, 2, 11, 89, 206
Mazowiecki, Tadeusz (prime minister
of Poland), 162
Mboya, Thomas Joseph Odhiambo
"Tom," 104
Mendés-France, Pierre (premier of
France), 56
MNC. *See Mouvement National
Congolais*
MEDO. *See* Middle East Defense
Organization

Meir, Golda (foreign minister and
prime minister of Israel): and Israeli
War for Independence, 75
Middle East Defense Organization
(MEDO), 78
Mikoyan, Anastas Ivanovich, 127
MIR. *See* Movement of the
Revolutionary Left
Mobutu, Joseph-Desiré (president of
Congo), 114, 116, 119, 181
Monckton, Walter Turner (minister of
defence of United Kingdom), 83–84
Mondlane, Eduardo Chivambo, 118
Monroe Doctrine, 121
Mossad (Israeli security service), 94
Mossadeq, Mohammad (prime
minister of Iran), 72–73, 96–97, 125,
177
Mountbatten, Louis Francis Albert
Victor Nicholas (Mountbatten of
Burma), 84
Mouvement National Congolais (MNC),
112
Movement of the Revolutionary Left
(MIR), 138
Mozambican Liberation Front
(FRELIMO), 118–119
MPLA. *See* Popular Movement for
Liberation of Angola
Mugabe, Robert Gabriel (president of
Zimbabwe), 111
Muslim League, 62
Mussolini, Benito, 21, 26,
mutual assured destruction (MAD),
160, 207

Naguib, Mohammed (president of
Egypt), 77
Napoleon Bonaparte, 9
Nasser, Gamal Abdel (president of
Egypt), 53n*, 178–179, 183n†, 207;
and 1958 Middle East crisis, 88; at
All-African Peoples' Conference,
104; and Czech weapons, 80, 127;
and fifteenth anniversary of UN,
106; and June 1967 War, 89–90;
and ouster of King Farouk I, 77;

and pan-Arabism, 78–79, 97; and
PLO, 92; and Suez Crisis, 82–86;
supplies arms to FLN, 80; and
UAR, 88–89
National Front for the Liberation of
Angola (FNLA), 119–120. *See also*
Union of Angolan Peoples
National Party of South Africa, 109
National Union for the Total
Independence of Angola (UNITA),
118–120
NATO (North Atlantic Treaty
Organization), 6, *31*, 34, 54, *156*,
179, 207; and anticolonialism, 34,
52, 54, 178; and Congo Crisis, 113;
creation of (1949), 6, 27–28, 38, 52,
56; expansion of, 192; and Warsaw
Pact, *31*, 155, *156*
Nazis (German National Socialists),
21–24, 26, 47, 54, 153, 175
Nazi-Soviet Pact (1939), 22
Nehru, Jawaharlal (prime minister of
India), 53n*, 64–65, 176, 178, 183n†;
at Bandung Conference, 102; and
fifteenth anniversary of UN, 106
Neto, António Agostinho (president of
Angola), 118
New Forum, 163
Ngo Dinh Diem. *See* Diem, Ngo Dinh
Nicholas I (Emperor of Russia), 149
Nicholas II (Emperor of Russia), 150
Nixon, Richard Milhous (vice
president and president of United
States), 35, 60, 64, 68, 185; and
Allende, 137, 139, 142; and Fidel
Castro, 127–128; and Ghana
independence day celebration, 105;
and Portuguese colonial wars, 118;
and support for Israel, 91
Nkomo, Joshua Mqabuko Nyongolo,
104
Nkrumah, Kwame (prime minister of
Gold Coast, president of Ghana),
53, 102–103, 117, 179, 181, 183n†; at
All-African Peoples' Conference,
104; at Fifth Pan-African Congress,
100; and Lumumba's murder, 106;

removed from office, 107; and
Upper Volta dam, 106
Non-Aligned Movement, 53, 64, 178,
183, 207
North Atlantic Treaty Organization.
See NATO
Nutting, Harold Anthony, 78, 84

October War (1973), 185, 186, *186*
Operation PBSUCCESS, 124
Operation STRAGGLE, 87
Opium Wars, 13, 15

Padmore, George, 100–101
Pahlavi, Mohammed Reza (Shah of
Iran), 72–73, 94–96, 177, 187–188, 208
Pahlavi, Reza Shah (Shah of Iran), 71
PAIGC. *See* African Independence
Party of Guinea and Cape Verde
Palestine Liberation Organization
(PLO), 92, 185–186, 207
pan-Africanism, 104
pan-Arabism, 34, 78–79, 178–179
Park Chung-hee (president of South
Korea), 45
Park Geun-Hye (president of South
Korea), 45n†
Paris Peace Accords (1973), 60
Paris Peace Conference (1919), 19–20
Paris Peace Talks (1969–1973), 55n†, 60
Paris summit conference (1960), 30, 128
Partai Komunis Indonesia (PKI), 47, 53
Partai Nasional Indonesia (PNI), 47–48
perestroika, 158–159, 207
Peter I (Emperor of Russia; Peter the
Great), 149
Petőfi circles, 155–156
Pham Van Dong (prime minister of
North Vietnam), 58
PKI. *See* Partai Komunis Indonesia
Platt Amendment, 122
PLO. *See* Palestine Liberation
Organization
PNI. *See* Partai Nasional Indonesia
Pol Pot (general secretary of the
Communist Party of Kampuchea),
60

Popular Movement for Liberation of
    Angola (MPLA), 118–120, 130
Prats González, Carlos, 138
Project ALPHA, 82
Project OMEGA, 82

Quadros, Jânio da Silva (president of
    Brazil), 130–131
Qavam, Ahmed (prime minister of
    Iran), 71–72

Reagan, Ronald Wilson (president of
    United States), 35, 141–142, 187,
    188, 208; and Gorbachev, 36, 160,
    189
Reid Cabral, Joseph Donald (president
    of Dominican Republic), 132
Renville Agreement (1948), 51
Revolution in Liberty, 136
Rhee, Syngman (president of South
    Korea), 43, 45
Rhodesian Front (RF), 110
Río Treaty. *See* Inter-American Treaty
    of Reciprocal Assistance
Roberto, Holden Álvaro (Angolan
    revolutionary): at All-African
    Peoples' Conference, 104; as leader
    of UPA, 117
Roosevelt, Franklin Delano (president
    of United States), 122; and Good
    Neighbor Policy, 122–123
Roosevelt, Kermit, Jr., 73
Roosevelt Corollary to the Monroe
    Doctrine, 122
Rukh ("the Movement"), 166
Russian Civil War (1918–1920), 151
Russian Revolution (1917), 19, 147,
    150–151, 204, 208
Russo-Japanese War (1904–1905), 17

el-Sadat, Muhammad Anwar
    (president of Egypt), 92–94, 186
Sainteny, Jean, 55
Salazar, António de Oliveira (prime
    minister of Portugal), 117–118
Sandinista National Liberation Front
    (FSLN), 140–143

SAVAK (Iranian security service), 94
Savimbi, Jonas Malheiro, 118
SDI. *See* Strategic Defense Initiative
SEATO (Southeast Asia Treaty
    Organization), 63, 208
Second Indochina War. *See* Vietnam
    War
Second World War. *See* World War II
Sékou Touré, Ahmed (president
    of Guinea), 180, 181; and
    independence, 105; and Konkouré
    dam, 107–108; and Lumumba's
    murder, 108; and nonalignment,
    107–108
Senghor, Léopold Sédar (president of
    Senegal), 100
Sepoy Rebellion, 15
Seven Years War (1756–1763), 8, 13
Shah of Iran. *See under* Pahlavi
Six-Day War (1967), 91, 185, *186*
Slovo, Joe (general secretary of
    South African Communist Party),
    110
Smith, Ian Douglas (prime minister of
    Rhodesia), 110–111
Solidarity (Polish labor union), 157–
    158, 162
Somoza Debayle, Anastasio (president
    of Nicaragua), 139–140
Southeast Asia Treaty Organization.
    See SEATO
Soviet-Afghan War (1979–1989), 35,
    158, 187, 188; Soviet withdrawal, 36,
    159–161, 189, 194; US aid to rebels,
    35, 64, 65, 158, 160–161
Spínola, António de, 119
Stalin, Joseph Vissarionovich (general
    secretary of the Communist Party of
    the Soviet Union), 22, 30, 67, 154; and
    1946 Iran crisis, 72; Khrushchev's
    denunciation of, 32, 66, 67; and
    Korean War, 43–44; and socialism
    in one country, 101; and Soviet
    imperialism, 22, 64, 151–153, 161
Stanleyville government, 115–116
Strategic Defense Initiative (SDI), 160,
    208

Suez Canal, 13, 21, 74, 77, 82–86, 178–179, 183
Suez Canal Company, 77, 83
Suez Crisis of 1956, 82–86, 102, 155, 179
Suharto (president of Indonesia), 33, 53, 54, 69, 184
Sukarno (president of Indonesia), 33, 184; at Bandung Conference, 53, 64, 102, 178; and fifteenth anniversary of UN, 106; and Indonesian independence movement, 47–52, 175, 176; as leader of independent Indonesia, 52–54, 69; and Non-Aligned Movement, 53, 69, 178, 183n†

Tet Offensive, 59–60
Third Rome, Moscow as, 148, 153, 208
Thucydides, 173
Tiananmen Square massacre (1989), 162
Tito, Josip Broz (president of Yugoslavia), 53n*
Tonkin Gulf incident. *See* Gulf of Tonkin incident
Trujillo Molina, Rafael Leónidas (president of Dominican Republic), 131
Truman Doctrine, 26, 30, 38, 205, 208
Truman, Harry S (president of United States), 26, 45, 74, 90, 176n*, 208
Tshombe, Moïse Kapenda (prime minister of Katanga and of Congo), 112–116; declares Katangese independence, 112; as leader of CONAKAT, 112
Tudeh Party, 73

U-2 incident (1960), 30, 128n*
Unilateral Declaration of Independence of Rhodesia, 111
Union of Angolan Peoples (UPA), 117. *See also* National Front for the Liberation of Angola
UNITA. *See* National Union for the Total Independence of Angola
United Arab Republic, 88–89
United Federal Party, 110

United Gold Coast Convention, 102
United Nations Organization (UN), 42, 161, 190, 209; and Congo Crisis, 113–116; fifteenth Anniversary in 1960, 106; Security Council Resolution 242, 90; Security Council Resolution 338, 93; vote to partition Palestine, 75
U Nu (prime minister of Burma), 39
UPA. *See* Union of Angolan Peoples
U Thant (secretary general of United Nations), 89, 116
Uvarov, Sergei, 149

Viet Cong, 59
Vietminh (League for the Independence of Vietnam), 29, 54–58, 60n*, 66, 209
Vietnam War (Second Indochina War), 33, *57*, 58–60, 68, 69, 184, 185; US withdrawal from, 33, 35, 55n†, 60, 68, 69, 185, 194
vodka putsch. *See* August coup (1991)
Vo Nguyen Giap. *See* Giap, Vo Nguyen

Wałęsa, Lech (president of Poland), 157
Warsaw Pact, 30, 155, 162, 165, 178, 208, 209; and NATO, *31*, 155n*, *156*; reduced and disbanded, 162, 165, 190
Welensky, Roland "Roy" (prime minister of Central African Federation), 109–111
West Berlin, 27, *28*, 32, 38
White Revolution, 94–95
Wilson, Thomas Woodrow (president of United States), 19–20, 173–174
Wilson, William, 122
Wojtyła, Karol. *See* John Paul II
World War I, 17–18, 50n*, 62, 153, 174; and imperialism, 2, 18–21; and Russian Revolution, 19, 147, 150–151
World War II, 22–23, 38–39, 152–153; and Asian anti-imperialism, 5, 23, 29, 38–39, 42, 46, 54–55, 61–62, 69, 174–176; and the Cold War, 1, 23–26, 29, 37–38, 145, 163, 174;

and the USSR, 21–22, 23–24, 147, 152–153, 161, 165, 166, 190; and the Western powers, 22–23, 29, 159, 174

Yanaev, Gennadii Ivanovich, 168
"Year of Africa," 106
Yeltsin, Boris Nikolayevich (president of the Russian Republic), 166, 167n*, 168–169, 190

Zahedi, Fazlollah (prime minister of Iran), 73
Zhou Enlai (foreign minister and prime minister of the People's Republic of China), 66–68, 80; and 1955 Czech arms deal, 80; and Bandung Conference, 80
Zionism, 75, 92
Zulu Wars, 15

About the Authors

Edward H. Judge and **John W. Langdon** are professors of history at Le Moyne College, where they team-teach courses in Cold War history and global history and have individually also taught courses in Russian, Asian, Latin American, and Modern European history. Ed earned his doctorate at the University of Michigan and spent a year in the USSR as an International Research and Exchanges Board (IREX) scholar. John earned his doctorate at Syracuse University's Maxwell School of Public Affairs, where he was a National Defense Fellow. Ed has taught at Le Moyne since 1978, was the college's Scholar of the Year in 1994, and was awarded the J. C. Georg Endowed Professorship in 1997. John has taught at Le Moyne since 1971, directed its Honors Program, and was awarded the O'Connell Distinguished Teaching Professorship in 1996. Each has been named the college's Teacher of the Year and has chaired its Department of History.

The authors have written or edited ten books—four in collaboration with each other, four as individuals, and two in collaboration with other scholars—most of them dealing with Cold War history and modern world history. They have a special interest in teaching and writing about the Cold War from a global perspective, and in researching and elucidating the connections and interactions between the Cold War and the various Third World anti-imperialist movements.

EXPLORING WORLD HISTORY

Series Editors
John McNeill, Georgetown University
Kenneth Pomeranz, University of Chicago
Jerry Bentley, founding editor

Plagues in World History
   by John Aberth
Crude Reality: Petroleum in World History, Updated Edition
   by Brian C. Black
The Age of Trade: The Manila Galleons and the Dawn of the Global Economy
   by Arturo Giraldez
The Struggle against Imperialism: Anticolonialism and the Cold War
   by Edward H. Judge and John W. Langdon
Smuggling: Contraband and Corruption in World History
   by Alan L. Karras
The First World War: A Concise Global History, Second Edition
   by William Kelleher Storey
Insatiable Appetite: The United States and the Ecological Degradation of the Tropical World, Concise Revised Edition
   by Richard P. Tucker